Organizational Resilience in Hospitality and Tourism

Although "VUCA" is not a new term, the features of the world it describes, a volatile, uncertain, complex, and ambiguous environment, have never been more valid. The VUCA world has become the new reality for business, specifically for hospitality and tourism organizations that are more vulnerable than any other sector due to the historically recognized turbulent environment in which they operate. In this book, the authors present unique factors that make hospitality and tourism organizations resilient in the VUCA world. With contacts at the center of their hospitality and tourism organizational resilience model, the organizational and psychological perspectives are also incorporated. This innovative volume tests the model of organizational resilience in hospitality and tourism organizations. The study identifies and validates organizational and individual factors that create a resilient organization in the hospitality and tourism sector. It will be of interest to researchers, academics, practitioners, and advanced students in the fields of organizational studies, strategic management, hospitality, and tourism management.

Malgorzata Rozkwitalska-Welenc is a professor in Economics, Management, and Quality Sciences and works at WSB Merito University in Gdansk, Poland.

Jacek Borzyszkowski is a doctor habilitated in Economics, Management, and Quality Sciences and works as an associate professor at WSB Merito University in Gdansk, Poland.

Beata A. Basinska is an associate professor of Work and Organizational Psychology in the Faculty of Management and Economics at Gdansk University of Technology, Poland.

Fevzi Okumus is the Central Florida Hotel and Lodging Association Preeminent Chair Professor within the Hospitality Services Department at the University of Central Florida's Rosen College of Hospitality Management, USA.

Osman M. Karatepe is a professor of Marketing in the Faculty of Tourism at Eastern Mediterranean University, North Cyprus, Türkiye.

Routledge Studies in Management, Organizations and Society

This series presents innovative work grounded in new realities, addressing issues crucial to an understanding of the contemporary world. This is the world of organized societies, where boundaries between formal and informal, public and private, local and global organizations have been displaced or have vanished, along with other nineteenth century dichotomies and oppositions. Management, apart from becoming a specialized profession for a growing number of people, is an everyday activity for most members of modern societies.

Similarly, at the level of enquiry, culture and technology, and literature and economics, can no longer be conceived as isolated intellectual fields; conventional canons and established mainstreams are contested. *Management, Organizations and Society* addresses these contemporary dynamics of transformation in a manner that transcends disciplinary boundaries, with books that will appeal to researchers, students and practitioners alike.

Recent titles in this series include:

The Ethics of Sustainability in Management
Storymaking in Organizations
Kenneth Mølbjerg Jørgensen

Relational Capital in Business
Innovation, Value and Competitiveness
Rafał Drewniak, Urszula Słupska, Zbigniew Drewniak, Iwona Posadzińska and Robert Karaszewski

Organizational Resilience in Hospitality and Tourism
Malgorzata Rozkwitalska-Welenc, Jacek Borzyszkowski, Beata A. Basinska, Fevzi Okumus and Osman M. Karatepe

Organizational Resilience in Hospitality and Tourism

Malgorzata Rozkwitalska-Welenc,
Jacek Borzyszkowski,
Beata A. Basinska, Fevzi Okumus and
Osman M. Karatepe

NEW YORK AND LONDON

First published 2024
by Routledge
605 Third Avenue, New York, NY 10158

and by Routledge
4 Park Square, Milton Park, Abingdon, Oxon, OX14 4RN

Routledge is an imprint of the Taylor & Francis Group, an informa business

© 2024 Malgorzata Rozkwitalska-Welenc, Jacek Borzyszkowski, Beata A. Basinska, Fevzi Okumus and Osman M. Karatepe

The right of Malgorzata Rozkwitalska-Welenc, Jacek Borzyszkowski, Beata A. Basinska, Fevzi Okumus and Osman M. Karatepe to be identified as authors of this work has been asserted in accordance with sections 77 and 78 of the Copyright, Designs and Patents Act 1988.

All rights reserved. No part of this book may be reprinted or reproduced or utilised in any form or by any electronic, mechanical, or other means, now known or hereafter invented, including photocopying and recording, or in any information storage or retrieval system, without permission in writing from the publishers.

Trademark notice: Product or corporate names may be trademarks or registered trademarks, and are used only for identification and explanation without intent to infringe.

ISBN: 978-1-032-27096-8 (hbk)
ISBN: 978-1-032-27100-2 (pbk)
ISBN: 978-1-003-29135-0 (ebk)

DOI: 10.4324/9781003291350

Typeset in Times New Roman
by Newgen Publishing UK

Contents

List of figures	*viii*
List of tables	*ix*
Acknowledgments	*xi*
Introduction	1

1 Organizational resilience, related constructs, and the VUCA
concept in organizational studies   8
  Organizational resilience 8
    Organizational resilience and related concepts 8
    Organizational resilience as a learning approach 14
    *Organizational resilience, related concepts, and cross-cultural
      differences 18*
  The VUCA concept 22
    The VUCA concept in organizational studies 22
    Current VUCA challenges, opportunities, and remedies 26

2 Organizational resilience and related concepts in hospitality
and tourism management studies   40
  *Hospitality and tourism organizational resilience versus hospitality
    and tourism crisis/disaster management 40*
  *Hospitality and tourism organizational resilience versus hospitality
    and tourism organizational sustainability 45*
  *Hospitality and tourism organizational resilience versus
    destination resilience 50*
  *Cross-cultural differences in hospitability and tourism and
    organizational resilience 54*

vi *Contents*

3   The conceptual model of organizational resilience in
    hospitality and tourism   72
    Models of organizational resilience 72
    Theoretical substantiation of the model 78
    Hypotheses, variables, and applied measures 81

4   Organizational resilience in Polish hospitality and tourism
    organizations   92
    The Polish hospitality and tourism sector – environmental
        analysis 92
    The structure of Polish hospitality and tourism organizations 98
    The assessment of organizational resilience in Polish
        organizations 105
        The Polish survey – sample characteristics and research
            procedure 105
        Measurement 106
        Descriptive statistics 109
        Analysis of the measurement model 109
        The summary of the Polish survey 117

5   Organizational resilience in hospitality and tourism
    organizations in Türkiye   125
    An overview of hospitality and tourism in Türkiye 125
        The Turkish hospitality and tourism sector environmental
            analysis 128
        The natural environment 131
        The political and legal environment 132
        The social environment 133
        The technological environment 135
    The research sample – Türkiye 136
        Sample and procedure 136
        Measurement 136
        Data analysis 137
    Results 138
        Measurement model assessment 138
        The assessment of organizational resilience in hotels in
            Türkiye 144

6   Organizational resilience in hospitality and tourism
    organizations in the United States   157
    The American hospitality and tourism sector environmental
        analysis 157

The political and legal environment 157
The economic environment 158
The social environment 160
The technological environment 162
The ecological environment 162
The structure of American hospitality and tourism
  organizations 163
  Accommodation and food services sectors 165
  Attractions and recreation sectors 167
The American research sample 167
  Sample characteristics and research procedure 167
  Measurement model 168
The assessment of organizational resilience in American
  organizations 171
  Conceptual and alternative structural models 171
  Structural conceptual modified model 173
  Structural alternative modified model 176
Summary of the American survey 177

7 Concluding remarks
182

Organizational resilience in hospitality and tourism
  organizations – a comparative analysis 182
Organizational resilience model for hospitality and tourism
  organizations – theoretical and practical contributions 185
The organizational resilience model – where does it lead us? 188

Index
193

Figures

0.1	Model of resilience in hotel and tourism organizations – a human capital-based view	2
3.1	Comprehensive conceptual model	81
3.2	The alternative comprehensive model	83
4.1	Structural equation model on the antecedents of organizational resilience with learning goal orientation as mediator	113
4.2	Structural equation model on the antecedents of employee resilience and organizational resilience and learning goal orientation as mediators	116
6.1	Structural equation model on the predictors of organizational resilience	174
6.2	Structural equation model on the predictors of employee resilience	176
7.1	The revised comprehensive conceptual model	189
7.2	The revised alternative comprehensive model	189

Tables

1.1	Hofstede's cultural dimensions and organizational/individual resilience	20
1.2	World trends and VUCA	27
1.3	Coping mechanisms and strategies for VUCA conditions	29
3.1	Models of organizational resilience	74
3.2	An overview of organizational resilience scales	76
4.1	Number of Polish hotel and tourism enterprises by PKD classification (data for 2021)	101
4.2	Basic data illustrating the hotel market in Poland between 2010 and 2020	103
4.3	Basic data showing the market for catering facilities in Poland from 2010 to 2020 (number of facilities)	104
4.4	Description of the Polish sample: socio-demographic, employment, and organizations (N = 500)	107
4.5	Study instruments: item number and validation	110
4.6	Means, standard deviations, and correlations of study variables	112
4.7	Results of bootstrapping in the direct and mediated models: unstandardized coefficients (B)	115
5.1	The number of arriving foreign tourists between 2013 and 2022 in Türkiye	127
5.2	The number of arriving German, British, Russian, Iranian, Bulgarian, and Georgian tourists between 2013 and 2022 in Türkiye	127
5.3	The total number of hotels, rooms, and beds (June 2023)	128
5.4	Tourism receipts between 2013 and 2022 in Türkiye	129
5.5	Participants' profile (n = 161)	137
5.6	Confirmatory composite analysis for the first- and second-order level (saturated model)	139
5.7	Assessment of the measurement model for first- and second-order reflective latent variables	140

x *List of tables*

5.8	Discriminant validity assessment	145
5.9	Summary statistics and correlations	146
5.10	Assessment of the comprehensive conceptual model	148
5.11	Test of the alternative comprehensive model	149
6.1	Description of the American sample	169
6.2	Means, standard deviations, and correlations of study variables	170
6.3	Measurement model validation	172
6.4	Bootstrapping results for mediated relationships (unstandardized coefficients)	175
6.5	Bootstrapping results for mediated relationships (unstandardized coefficients) – structural alternative modified model	177

Acknowledgments

The authors thank Dr. Elisa Rescalvo Martin (University of Granada) for the analysis of data in PLS-SEM, Dr. Mehmet Bahri Saydam (Eastern Mediterranean University), Dr. Hamed Rezapouraghdam (Eastern Mediterranean University), Research Assistant Victor Olorunsola (Eastern Mediterranean University) for the provision of relevant articles for Chapter 5, and Mr. Ali Cenk Yorulmaz (Owner of Doktorun Oteli in Ankara, Türkiye) for data collection in Türkiye.

The authors thank Dr. Gabriela Lelo de Larrea for her contribution in Chapter 6.

Introduction

Organizations live in a world where various challenges and opportunities determine their operations. Some have been present for years and will likely develop (e.g., climate change) or disappear in the future (e.g., the Fourth Industrial Revolution will be replaced by the fifth stage).[1] In contrast, others remain unclear and appear unexpectedly (e.g., future pandemics or armed conflicts), creating disruptions, crises, and hazards. Under such frequently novel, dramatic, and uncertain conditions, organizations need to recognize their weak signals to respond to them wisely, and organizational resilience is just such a wise response, especially in the case of hospitality and tourism (H&T) organizations, a particularly vulnerable sector.

Therefore, we have aimed to test the model of organizational resilience in H&T organizations. Our monograph identifies and validates organizational and individual factors that create a resilient organization in the H&T sector (Figure 0.1).

The relevance of the aim of the monograph has been stated in prior research. Organizational resilience is perceived as the core capability of a firm that helps it to outperform others (Jiang et al., 2019; Pathak & Joshi, 2020; Rodríguez-Sánchez et al., 2019) and is critical concerning the tourism sector (Chowdhury et al., 2019), which "is one of the most vulnerable one and the worst affected in case of any disaster" (Pathak & Joshi, 2020, p. 3). Prayag (2018) noticed that resilience building in the tourism industry is vital since the exceptional growth in the number of disasters and crises influencing the tourism industry worldwide can be observed. Likewise, Orth and Schuldis (2021) imply that tourism firms have to predict, deal with and recover from many disruptions, such as the last COVID-19 pandemic and other challenges caused by the current Fourth Industrial Revolution, political tensions, armed conflicts, natural disasters, and other forces, that contribute to the vulnerable, uncertain, complex, and ambiguous (VUCA) world, are becoming a new normality nowadays (Luthans & Broad, 2020). Such unprecedented changes, upheaval, and transformation can even accelerate shortly, revealing threatening and propitious business conditions (Levey & Levey, 2019). Organizational resilience determines whether tourism

DOI: 10.4324/9781003291350-1

2 Introduction

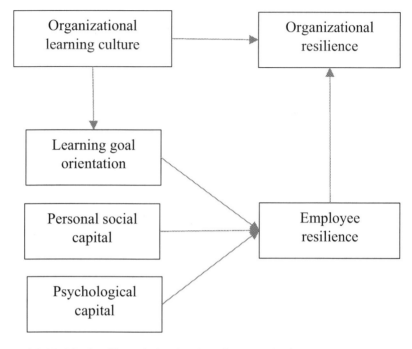

Figure 0.1 Model of resilience in hotel and tourism organizations – a human capital-based view.

businesses will overcome the severe challenges generated by the VUCA environment and thrive.

Some disruptions affecting the H&T sector may be considered consecutive disastrous events, which can be better addressed if a firm presents organizational resilience (Bhaskara & Filimonau, 2021). Similarly, Prayag (2018) claims that prior tourism research has put too much emphasis on crisis management. Consequently, "it is perhaps the opportune time to question the relationship between crisis and disaster management, and resilience" (p. 133). Also, Jiang et al. (2019) call for a shift toward resilience in tourism studies. Moreover, Ngoc Su et al. (2021) point out a need to study organizational resilience in H&T, as the phenomenon has not attracted significant attention.

Studies concerning factors that shape organizational resilience in H&T organizations remain underdeveloped (Chowdhury et al., 2019; Rodríguez-Sánchez et al., 2019). Nevertheless, various authors identify human capital amid the antecedents of organizational resilience (Bhaskara & Filimonau, 2021; Filimonau & De Coteau, 2020; Pathak & Joshi, 2020; Prayag et al., 2020). Therefore, our research has explored personal factors (i.e., personal resources such as personal social and psychological capital) that shape human capital and, as a result, organizational resilience. These factors have not yet been studied quantitatively or in combination with regard to organizational resilience (Bhaskara & Filimonau, 2021; Chowdhury et al., 2019; Pathak & Joshi, 2020). They can help individuals "to better anticipate and respond to adverse events" (Tasic et al., 2020, p. 3). Moreover, the concept prompts organizations to consider any disruption a learning opportunity (Bhaskara & Filimonau, 2021; Orth & Schuldis, 2021). Thus, we have analyzed how an organizational learning culture enforces individual learning orientation and further supports employee and organizational resilience (see Figure 0.1). We have conducted quantitative research since more qualitative studies have been carried out on the topic in organizational studies.

We have substantiated our research using two theories, namely the conservation of resources theory (Hobfoll et al., 2018) and the capital-based view in management theory (Lewin & Baetjer, 2011). Consequently, we have merged the approaches of two disciplines to explain organizational resilience in the H&T sector: organizational psychology and organizational studies, i.e., strategic management.

We have conducted our study in three emerging economies: Poland and Türkiye, and an advanced economy, the United States. Türkiye and the United States are among the most visited countries in the world, yet they have utterly diverse macro- and business landscapes. Although Poland is not a major tourism destination, before the pandemic, it had a significantly growing tourism sector (World Tourism Organization, 2021). We believe that comparing the results of studies from such different countries has allowed us to indicate the degree of generalizability of the proposed model and reveal discrepancies. It also fits into the cross-cultural discourse of organizational resilience research.

We have developed our discourse in seven chapters preceded by an Introduction.

Chapter 1 provides a comprehensive, thematic literature review regarding organizational resilience, related concepts, and VUCA in organizational studies. First, it refers to the birth of the concept of organizational resilience and its further development. It classifies various authors' approaches to organizational resilience and its components. Second, it contrasts organizational resilience with individual resilience, i.e., psychological and employee resilience. It discusses the importance of individual measures of resilience concerning organizational resilience. Third, the chapter implies that resilient organizations are learning organizations and discusses how learning, unlearning, and resilience are intertwined. It shows organizational learning capabilities' vital role in coping with tremendous crises. In addition, it claims that future research on the learning component in organizational resilience should be developed to offer more conclusive results. Fourth, the way people manage adversities is shaped by their cultures. Therefore, the subsequent part of the chapter emphasizes that

4 *Introduction*

organizational resilience depends on cultural context. Nevertheless, the literature has not adequately addressed the links between organizational resilience and national cultures, cross-cultural or within-country differences. The discourse expands on this path. The final section of Chapter 1 develops an understanding of the VUCA concept by discussing its roots, meaning, and how it has been approached in organizational studies. It also tries to identify current VUCA trends and suggests coping mechanisms and strategies for VUCA conditions.

Chapter 2 locates the concept of organizational resilience in tourism management studies. It begins with describing the alternative approach, i.e., tourism crisis/disaster management, and explains why the shift toward tourism organizational resilience is recommended. Further, it portrays another related concept, tourism organization sustainability, and implies similarities and differences between the two. It also shows how they complement each other. In the following subchapter, the authors present tourism organizational resilience within the broader idea of tourism destination resilience and point out that organizational resilience in the H&T sector influences destination resilience. Since this sector is labor-intensive and customer-centric, it is susceptible to cultural influences. Culture and cultural differences impact business success and the resilience of hospitality and tourism organizations. Hence, in the final part of Chapter 2, the authors attempt to identify previous research on organizational resilience and cultural factors in H&T. They conclude that the links between resilience and national/local culture are under-recognized, so it is recommended to study organizational resilience in hotel and tourism organizations in different countries to compare their results, as well as to verify the measurement properties of instruments in terms of their cultural load.

Chapter 3 contributes an original conceptual model of organizational resilience in H&T (Figure 0.1) substantiated in the study's theoretical foundation (conservation of resources theory and a capital-based view of organizations). The model is embedded in outcome and process views on organizational resilience and reflects the adaptation and anticipation perspectives, positive psychology, and organizational development perspectives. It presents a human capital-based view on H&T organizations' resilience since the H&T sector is a service industry that relies heavily on people. The chapter also discusses other models and measures of organizational resilience from prior research in organizational studies and tourism management studies. Based on the conceptual model, the authors put forward seven hypotheses and explain the variables and measures used in the study. Their model predicts that resource-rich environments fuel better organizational resilience than when resources are scarce. The employee-level components (psychological and personal social capital, learning goal orientation, and employee resilience) and organizational learning culture drive organizational resilience, whereas learning goal orientation and employee resilience are mediators. They also explain the alternative model, where organizational resilience stimulates employee resilience.

Introduction   5

The following three chapters discuss research findings on H&T organizational resilience from Poland (*Chapter 4)*, Türkiye (*Chapter 5*), and the United States (*Chapter 6*). Each chapter describes the country-specific context of the study, namely the macro- and microenvironments. Further, details of the research sample and an assessment of organizational resilience in H&T organizations are given. The conceptual and alternative models are tested, and results and implications are discussed.

The concluding *Chapter 7* attempts to recap and integrate the research findings by comparing the results among the countries analyzed to identify the degree of generalizability of the model and country-specific differences. It also comments on the theoretical and practical contributions of the research to organizational studies and tourism management studies and how it can be further developed.

We have found similarities and differences in the results obtained in Poland, Türkiye, and the United States, which let us revise the comprehensive conceptual model of organizational resilience and its alternative version (see Chapter 3). Regarding similarities and differences, in the Polish and U.S. samples, for instance, we have observed that psychological capital was critical for employee learning goal orientation, and both were vital for employee resilience. Surprisingly, employee resilience did not affect organizational resilience in the Polish sample. In all organizations studied, organizational learning culture influenced employee resilience and enhanced learning goal orientation. Furthermore, an organizational learning culture was the foundation of organizational resilience in H&T in Poland, Türkiye, and the United States.

Since prior research regarding antecedents of organizational resilience in H&T organizations has been insufficiently developed (Chowdhury et al., 2019; Rodríguez-Sánchez et al., 2019), with our monograph, we augment the H&T literature on organizational resilience and respond to the call of other authors, e.g., Jiang et al. (2019), Ngoc Su et al. (2021), and Prayag (2018). While constructing our conceptual model, we have fused the perspectives of two disciplines to explain organizational resilience in the H&T sector. Consequently, we add to the underdeveloped empirical studies in organizational psychology and organizational studies. To the best of our knowledge, it is one of the first applications of the conservation of resources theory to the research on organizational resilience in H&T organizations. Moreover, we add to organizational studies a conceptual model of organizational resilience in H&T grounded in the capital-based view of organizations that has emphasized personal predictors instrumental for human capital, which shape organizational resilience. As these factors have not yet been examined quantitatively in a single model with regard to organizational resilience (Bhaskara & Filimonau, 2021; Chowdhury et al., 2019; Pathak & Joshi, 2020), our empirical quantitative investigation in three distinct countries is novel and fills a significant gap. Finally, our comparative analysis has let us

6 *Introduction*

indicate similarities and differences regarding factors that affect organizational resilience in H&T in Poland, Türkiye, and the United States.

Note

1 Actually, some researchers believe that the Fifth Industrial Revolution, which embraces human-machine collaboration, has already emerged in 2020, see Noble et al. (2022).

References

Bhaskara, G. I., & Filimonau, V. (2021). The COVID-19 pandemic and organisational learning for disaster planning and management: A perspective of tourism businesses from a destination prone to consecutive disasters. *Journal of Hospitality and Tourism Management*, *46*(November 2020), 364–375. https://doi.org/10.1016/j.jhtm.2021.01.011

Chowdhury, M., Prayag, G., Orchiston, C., & Spector, S. (2019). Postdisaster social capital, adaptive resilience and business performance of tourism organizations in Christchurch, New Zealand. *Journal of Travel Research*, *58*(7), 1209–1226. https://doi.org/10.1177/0047287518794319

Filimonau, V., & De Coteau, D. (2020). Tourism resilience in the context of integrated destination and disaster management (DM2). *International Journal of Tourism Research*, *22*(2), 202–222. https://doi.org/10.1002/jtr.2329

Hobfoll, S. E., Halbesleben, J., Neveu, J.-P., & Westman, M. (2018). Conservation of resources in the organizational context: The reality of resources and their consequences. *Annual Review of Organizational Psychology and Organizational Behavior*, *5*, 103–128. https://doi.org/10.1146/annurev-orgpsych-

Jiang, Y., Ritchie, B. W., & Verreynne, M. L. (2019). Building tourism organizational resilience to crises and disasters: A dynamic capabilities view. *International Journal of Tourism Research*, *21*(6), 882–900. https://doi.org/10.1002/jtr.2312

Levey, J., & Levey, M. (2019). Mindful leadership for personal and organisational resilience. *Clinical Radiology*, *74*(10), 739–745. https://doi.org/10.1016/j.crad.2019.06.026

Lewin, P., & Baetjer, H. (2011). The capital-based view of the firm. *Review of Austrian Economics*, *24*(4), 335–354. https://doi.org/10.1007/s11138-011-0149-1

Luthans, F., & Broad, J. D. (2020). Positive psychological capital to help combat the mental health fallout from the pandemic and VUCA environment. *Organizational Dynamics*, *2019*, 100817. https://doi.org/10.1016/j.orgdyn.2020.100817

Ngoc Su, D., Luc Tra, D., Thi Huynh, H. M., Nguyen, H. H. T., & O'Mahony, B. (2021). Enhancing resilience in the Covid-19 crisis: Lessons from human resource management practices in Vietnam. *Current Issues in Tourism*, *24*(22), 1–17. https://doi.org/10.1080/13683500.2020.1863930

Noble, S. M., Mende, M., Grewal, D., & Parasuraman, A. (2022). The Fifth Industrial Revolution: How harmonious human–machine collaboration is triggering a retail and service [r]evolution. *Journal of Retailing*, *98*(2), 199–208. https://doi.org/10.1016/j.jretai.2022.04.003

Orth, D., & Schuldis, P. M. (2021). Organizational learning and unlearning capabilities for resilience during COVID-19. *Learning Organization, 28*(6), 509–522. https://doi.org/10.1108/TLO-07-2020-0130

Pathak, D., & Joshi, G. (2020). Impact of psychological capital and life satisfaction on organizational resilience during COVID-19: Indian tourism insights. *Current Issues in Tourism, 24*(17), 1–18. https://doi.org/10.1080/13683500.2020.1844643

Prayag, G. (2018). Symbiotic relationship or not? Understanding resilience and crisis management in tourism. *Tourism Management Perspectives, 25*(November), 133–135. https://doi.org/10.1016/j.tmp.2017.11.012

Prayag, G., Spector, S., Orchiston, C., & Chowdhury, M. (2020). Psychological resilience, organizational resilience and life satisfaction in tourism firms: Insights from the Canterbury earthquakes. *Current Issues in Tourism, 23*(10), 1216–1233. https://doi.org/10.1080/13683500.2019.1607832

Rodríguez-Sánchez, A., Guinot, J., Chiva, R., & López-Cabrales, Á. (2019). How to emerge stronger: Antecedents and consequences of organizational resilience. *Journal of Management and Organization, 2019*, 1–18. https://doi.org/10.1017/jmo.2019.5

Tasic, J., Amir, S., Tan, J., & Khader, M. (2020). A multilevel framework to enhance organizational resilience. *Journal of Risk Research, 23*(6), 713–738. https://doi.org/10.1080/13669877.2019.1617340

World Tourism Organization. (2021). *International Tourism Highlights International Tourism Trends. 2020 Edition.* https://doi.org/10.18111/978928

1 Organizational resilience, related constructs, and the VUCA concept in organizational studies

Organizational resilience

Organizational resilience and related concepts

The number of studies on organizational resilience is growing; however, the phenomenon still requires greater recognition and is certainly not a settled matter. There are still conceptual inconsistencies about resilience concerning its definition, level of analysis, the different contexts in which it occurs, or the theoretical roots (Frigotto et al., 2022; Powley, 2020). For instance, the main focus of prior research on resilience has been the individual as opposed to the organization. Nevertheless, resilience is a characteristic of not only an individual but also a collective capacity; thus, it can be studied from either the group perspective or organizational perspective (Lee et al., 2013; Orth & Schuldis, 2021; Rodríguez-Sánchez et al., 2021). Therefore, studies on resilience "[have] developed steadily over the years and the understanding of resilience has evolved from it being a personality trait, a state, a process or outcome and a dynamic capability" (Teng-Calleja et al., 2020). Overall, resilience assumes a certain ability to overcome difficulties and setbacks. It is "the ability of a system to return to a stable state after a disruptive condition" (Santoro et al., 2020, p. 143) or to absorb changes and persist (Holling, 1973). The topic has been studied from different perspectives and disciplines such as ecology, engineering, psychology, organizational studies, medical and health sciences, and so on, since the 1970s (Burnard & Bhamra, 2011; Holling, 1973; Jiang et al., 2019; Kantabutra & Ketprapakorn, 2021; Mousa et al., 2020) after its adaptation from physics in the 1950s (Sulphey, 2020).

In the organizational studies literature, interest in *organizational resilience* has grown enormously in the 21st century; however, it still gives rise to confusion (Britt & Sawhney, 2020; Dhoopar et al., 2021; Duchek, 2020; Hillmann, 2021; Hillmann & Guenther, 2021). First of all, a review conducted by Duchek (2020) shows three evolving approaches to organizational resilience. It has been conceptualized either as an organizational ability to resist adversity,

DOI: 10.4324/9781003291350-2

recover and return to a normal state (*the defensive approach*); to improve organizational functioning after a crisis via active and purposeful coping with the unexpected (*the adaptation perspective*); or to anticipate problems that may occur and to adapt to a new normal (*the anticipation perspective*). Consequently, organizational resilience is perceived as a crucial competence of today's organizations, their dynamic capability, and the utmost priority that enables them to prosper in volatile, uncertain, complex, and ambiguous environments (Duchek, 2020; Levey & Levey, 2019; Seville, 2018). The VUCA[1] environment brings about both threats to and opportunities for organizations, which compels them to function in a wiser and more sustainable way as well as to build extraordinary capabilities to manage crises (Levey & Levey, 2019). Organizations need to be prepared for and manage natural or man-made hazards, as such disasters impact their viability and affect employee performance, causing a risk of significant losses (Teng-Calleja et al., 2020). Resilient organizations successfully embrace their VUCA environment, which requires them to engage in transformative actions that reduce potential threats. Such organizations respond quickly to adversity by inventing new ways of doing business under conditions of stress and change (Santoro et al., 2020). They use defense mechanisms against internal and external hardships (Mousa et al., 2020). The concept describes organizations which are able to adapt to unexpected events. Such an organization sees and avails opportunities out of adversity. In addition, resilient organizations may not only bounce back from various crises but even become stronger in the aftermath. All these aspects make organizational resilience a distinct concept from flexibility, agility, or robustness, which do not assume adaptation to the unexpected and improvements after successfully coping with disaster (Duchek, 2020; Jiang et al., 2019; Rodríguez-Sánchez, 2021; Seville, 2018).

In addition to the abovementioned perspectives, Hillmann (2021) provides a different classification based on the disciplinary background. This classification indicates the ontological origin of the concept, the need for organizational resilience, its contributions, and potential applications. Against this backdrop, *the ecological perspective* derives from system thinking and describes organizational resilience as a survival ability. It makes it possible to derive an understanding of organizations in connection to their environment. *The safety and reliability perspective* locates the need for organizational resilience in the necessity to deal with failures and mitigate their impact on organizations. It is specifically present in crisis management. *The resilience engineering perspective* derives from system design and sees organizational resilience as a restore function. It may be applied in supply chain management. *The positive psychology and organizational development* perspective perceives organizational resilience as a developmental state by means of which to cope with crises and stress. In this view, employee and team resilience contribute to organizational resilience. Finally, *the strategic perspective* considers the need for organizational resilience

10 *Organizational resilience, related constructs, and the VUCA in OS*

from the competitive advantage angle and recommends investment in building resilience-related capabilities.

Ambiguity regarding organizational resilience is also reflected in how it is conceptualized, i.e., as an outcome or demonstration, a process or a capability (Britt & Sawhney, 2020; Duchek, 2020; Orth & Schuldis, 2021). Organizational resilience as an outcome means that organizations are able to prosper during and after hazardous events. Research in this stream tries to identify distinct characteristics of resilient organizations, i.e., specific resources, enhancing behaviors, strategies, and processes. Studies on organizational resilience as a process describe how it develops in stages, the numbers of which vary among researchers. They offer a dynamic view on resilience and suggest investigating it over the long term. Finally, research on organizational resilience as a capability attempts to identify which capabilities developed by organizations can support resilience. Resilient organizations are capable of solving current problems and availing themselves of opportunities for a prosperous future (Chowdhury et al., 2019).[2] Organizational resilience is also conceptualized as *planned resilience* or *adaptive resilience*. The former refers to pre-disaster preparedness and is a proactive approach (Conz & Magnani, 2020; Prayag, 2018), whereas the latter occurs during and after disasters when organizations "respond effectively, recover quickly, and successfully renew in the face of adverse events".

Britt and Sawhney (2020) and Hillmann (2021) assert that the theoretical studies on organizational resilience have outpaced its empirical investigation. Moreover, the number of qualitative studies exceeds quantitative research (Mousa et al., 2020). In organizational studies, the concept can be explained on the basis of *resource dependency theory* that sees organizations in its wider environment dependent on the resources provided by the actors of the environment. The dependency helps organizations to flexibly respond to both expected and unexpected disruptions in their environment (van den Berg et al., 2022). Organizational resilience can then be perceived as organizational adaptations to environmental pressures by securing resources and reducing environmental uncertainty, which can be achieved, among other things, by developing internal capabilities and resources that other organizations may be dependent on (Nandi et al., 2021). This leads to another theoretical underpinning of organizational resilience, conceptualized as a capability. This idea is rooted in *resource-based theory* and its extension, *dynamic capability theory*. The former states that certain internal resources of an organization may become the basis of its competitive advantage, while the latter suggests that an organization needs to know how to use, adapt, extend, or integrate its resources to meet market demands in order to survive on the market. Therefore, resilient organizations possess a number of useful resources that may help them cope quickly and adequately with disruption. They also possess the necessary capabilities to alter, combine, and reconfigure various resources to respond to changing circumstances (Duchek, 2020; Jiang et al., 2019; Karman & Savanevičienė, 2021; Zahari et al., 2022). Furthermore,

Organizational resilience, related constructs, and the VUCA in OS 11

the concept of organizational resilience derives from *evolutionary theory*, which focuses attention on certain superior routines that enable organizations to outperform others when they are faced with adversity, learn from disruptions, and modify their routines or create new ones (Jiang et al., 2019).[3]

Based on previous studies, we can delineate some factors that help to build organizational resilience. Among these, Seville (2018) lists leadership and culture, networks and relationships, and readiness for change. Tasic et al. (2020) highlight trustful relationships included in social capital as critical antecedents of organizational resilience. Likewise, Britt and Sawhney (2020) refer to social capital as a contributing factor to organizational resilience, whereas Rodriguez-Sanchez et al. (2021) mention organizational citizenship behaviors supported by HR practices and corporate social responsibility. Based on previous research, Tasic et al. (2020) mention various capabilities that help to enhance resilience such as cognitive, behavioral, emotional, relational (both with internal and external stakeholders), or socio-material (e.g., buildings, physical resources, procedures, communication). In her review of previous studies on organizational resilience, Duchek (2020) portrays other contributing or typical factors that describe resilient organizations. These are, e.g., access to adequate resources, positive relationships and collective behaviors, redundancy, solution-seeking behaviors directed toward goals, avoidance, critical approach, dependence in role performance, and reliance on sources. Furthermore, by applying the adaptation and anticipation perspectives on organizational resilience, she conceptualizes it as a meta-capability and proposes to develop it through three consecutive stages, i.e., anticipation, coping, and adaptation, and the related capabilities.[4]

The interrelated concepts of organizational resilience include the following: employee resilience, psychological resilience, and team resilience. Resilient organizations derive from resilient employees and groups (Rodríguez-Sánchez & Perea, 2015). Yet, organizational resilience is also an important antecedent of employee resilience (Teng-Calleja et al., 2020). Furthermore, organizational resilience is not the mere sum of individual and team resilience due to the fact that it also depends on the interaction between employees, teams, and managers (van den Berg et al., 2022). However, the multilevel influences across the three types of resilience have attracted insufficient academic interest to date. Thus, Britt and Sawhney (2020) call for more research that would combine the three and their interlinkages.[5]

Effectively leading people during hazardous times is the most important challenge. In such circumstances, employee resilience becomes a priority (Seville, 2018). *Employee resilience*, though applied to an individual, needs to be distinguished from psychological resilience. A resilient employee, while facing difficult events at work, attaches meaning to them and has an uncanny ability to improvise. Such an individual perceives even negative experiences in a constructive manner and is able to adapt to an adverse and uncertain situation in

12 *Organizational resilience, related constructs, and the VUCA in OS*

a workplace, make the necessary decisions, and use various resources and roles to cope (Rodríguez-Sánchez, 2021). S/he has the capacity to develop personal and organizational resources in the face of adversity and heightened demands. Employee resilience is not a trait but a developable quality with growing relevance to HRM; as such, it has the potential to grow when people interact or when it is supported by organizational resources (Plimmer et al., 2021; Teng-Calleja et al., 2020). It is a personal resource that people can use in both stable and tricky conditions (Plimmer et al., 2021; Santoro et al., 2020; Seville, 2018). The concept is rooted in positive psychology and *conservation of resources theory*, which implies that people attempt to gather, maintain, and protect the resources which are critical to their survival (Hobfoll et al., 2018). It allows for the assumption that resilient individuals have certain dispositions, motivations, and skillsets, and they exhibit behavior to find and deploy organizational resources to properly manage emergencies (Plimmer et al., 2021). In a study by Teng-Calleja et al. (2020), resilience-building organizational initiatives helped to build employee resilience, yet the effect was small. These initiatives included interventions directed toward three stages of the *resilience building process*, i.e., resistance, resilience, and recovery. It shows that in order to support employee resilience, organizations should design and implement programs which stimulate personnel immunity toward crisis (i.e. resistance), bouncing back (i.e., resilience) and regaining capacity (i.e., recovery) for further functioning. They may include disaster preparedness training, social support, psychological first aid, or therapy. In a study by Plimmer et al. (2021), factors that related positively to employee resilience were motivation, pro-social workplace skills, constructive leadership, and an innovative climate. Britt and Sawhney (2020) contend that resources embedded in social connections, organizations, and the community can help individuals become resilient employees.

Psychological or personal resilience means that an individual uses positive coping and adaptation strategies when adversity or risk occurs (Luthans et al., 2007; Shoss et al., 2018). It is a bounce-back capacity, as is employee resilience; however, the former is a broader concept than the latter and refers to various life domains, whereas employee resilience merely relates to the work domain. Psychological resilience is a precondition for employee resilience, yet the psychologically resilient employee may decide not to exhibit employee resilience (Seville, 2018). Moreover, it has been studied separately (Connor & Davidson, 2003; Hall et al., 2017; Wagnild & Young, 1993) and as one of four components of a higher-order construct of psychological capital along with hope, optimism, and self-efficacy (Fang et al., 2020; Luthans et al., 2007; Luthans & Broad, 2020). Prior research identifies enablers of personal resilience such as certain practices in organizations that reduce risks and stressors, build resources that help to face adversity (e.g., social capital and leadership), and enhance preparedness for a crisis (such as strategic planning and organizational learning) (Luthans & Youssef, 2004).

Organizational resilience, related constructs, and the VUCA in OS 13

Resilient employees can create resilient groups or teams. In defining team resilience, however, there are some ambiguities, whether it is a capacity, demonstration, or the process. Therefore, *team resilience* can be interpreted as a belief held by the team members concerning their collective ability to address adversity in a constructive way. It is then a capacity of a team, which suggests that it is only exposed when a crisis arises and the team successfully copes with it (Rodríguez-Sánchez, 2021). However, Britt and Sawhney (2020) quote prior studies that have approached team resilience as an emergent state which demonstrates resilience in the face of adversity or as the dynamic team process that follows when the team is confronted with significant hardships. Furthermore, it needs to be stressed that team resilience is not the mere sum of resilient individuals, since the team can be "either more or less resilient than its members on their own" depending on the group dynamics (Seville, 2018, p. 16). Previous, rather scarce studies show which factors may trigger team resilience (Fietz et al., 2021). These are transactive memory, shared mental models and communication among teammates, explicit behavioral norms, psychological safety, team identity, transformational leadership, structured empowerment, organizational practices such as work-life balance or career development, or collective efficacy (Britt & Sawhney, 2020; Hartmann et al., 2020; Rodríguez-Sánchez & Perea, 2015; van den Berg et al., 2022). Moreover, the resources possessed by each member may build team resilience as well (Britt & Sawhney, 2020).

Organizational resilience is conceptually closely related to *crisis management*, which can be characterized as a change management process in response to a crisis that consists of unlearning, relearning, and learning to increase preparedness for future hazards at each level in organizations, including group and individual levels. It assumes that organizations are capable of detecting weak signals of potential risks before initiating events occur, reacting wisely and recovering (Tasic et al., 2020; Wang, 2008). Effective crisis management is a prerequisite of organizational resilience. Nevertheless, Prayag (2018) indicates differences between these two concepts with regard to the types of change they refer to. Organizational resilience is connected to extraordinary or incremental and cumulative change, whereas crisis management frequently refers to change as a result of extraordinary circumstances. The same author also claims that organizational resilience is a complementary, but perhaps superior, perspective than crisis management when it comes to comprehending how organizations deal with any scale of disturbances. Moreover, resilient organizations are able to self-organize, while this aspect is not necessarily emphasized in crisis management thinking.

Organizational resilience shows significant parallels with the concept of *sustainability* as the long-term viability of organizations that strive toward balance among their economic, environmental, and social goals.[6] In their analysis of both constructs in the tourism context, Espiner et al. (2017) note that sustainable destinations also display greater resilience. They further argue that resilience

14 *Organizational resilience, related constructs, and the VUCA in OS*

is an essential – yet not entirely sufficient in itself – factor for sustainability; in other words, it is possible to "be resilient without being sustainable" (p. 1396). Resilient organizations that comply with the sustainability ideal effectively respond to perturbations affecting the socio-ecological system (Miceli et al., 2021). Thus, the resilience measure should be incorporated into sustainability demands. However, as Espiner et al. (2017) warn, immediate responses to actual and anticipated disturbances can result in maladaptive strategies that run counter to sustainability. Still, efforts to build organizational resilience can help to maintain sustainability. On the other hand, sustainable business practices may also contribute to higher levels of organizational resilience (Kantabutra & Ketprapakorn, 2021; Ortiz-de-Mandojana & Bansal, 2015; Rai et al., 2021). Hence, Kantabutra and Ketprapakorn (2021) propose a conceptual model (or an organizational theory of resilience, as they claim) that incorporates sustainability into the organizational resilience system. It is normative in its essence and has not yet been verified; nevertheless, some empirical trials have been conducted to test the interlinkages between sustainability and organizational resilience (Ortiz-de-Mandojana & Bansal, 2015; Rai et al., 2021).

To summarize, organizational resilience is necessary for organizations to survive and prosper. Notwithstanding the growing interest in this issue in organizational studies, it is still unclear how it should be approached and operationalized. A comprehensive theory of organizational resilience is also lacking. Yet, organizational resilience draws on individual and team resilience, and developing different resources and capabilities may strengthen it. As an organizational idea, resilience is related to crisis management or sustainability, albeit it remains a separate concept.

Organizational resilience as a learning approach

The links between organizational resilience and learning are complex and ambiguous; while, as a result, they are not fully recognized in prior studies, they are nevertheless extremely vital (Mousa et al., 2020). Organizational resilience is linked to learning and can be treated as a learning approach, which is also emphasized in its definitions and various perspectives. In particular, a learning aspect of organizational resilience is emphasized in more recent studies (Van Trijp et al., 2018). Empirical research shows a vague picture concerning the complex relationship between learning and resilience. To date it has been examined with regard to organizational learning, its forms and mechanisms, learning organization, unlearning, and organizational learning capabilities.

With regard to definitions of organizational resilience, Wildavsky (2017) describes it as the capacity which makes it possible to cope with unforeseen hazards after they have become apparent, and learning to recover. In a similar manner, Orth and Schuldis (2021) portray it as the "ability to anticipate and absorb external disruptions, learn from them and adapt for future challenges,

Organizational resilience, related constructs, and the VUCA in OS 15

while still pursuing their core objectives". It is highlighted that such disruptions create learning opportunities (Bhaskara & Filimonau, 2021). Van den Berg et al. (2022) indicate that resilient organizations not only cope with change but also learn how to become better through times of crisis. Rodriguez-Sanchez et al. (2021) stress that learning from past disruptions to emerge stronger from them is the fundamental nature of organizational resilience. Such an approach is allocated by Teo et al. (2017) to the developmental perspective of organizational resilience, where resilience is a form of organizational learning. As far as other perspectives of organizational resilience are concerned, it is an outcome of processes that trigger organizational learning and coping with the unexpected, and it can be learned (Santoro et al., 2020; Teng-Calleja et al., 2020). It may also be seen as a process in which learning is included. For instance, Burnard and Bhamra (2011) identify three stages of organizational resilience, namely detection and activation, response, and organizational learning. Likewise, employee resilience requires learning, adaptation, and network-leveraging (Plimmer et al., 2021). To further complicate the issue, organizational learning is a capability (an input) necessary for developing organizational resilience (Duchek, 2020; Koronis & Ponis, 2018; Orth & Schuldis, 2021; Tasic et al., 2020), but organizational learning capability, i.e., certain characteristics of organizations that stimulate organizational learning, can also be the outcome of resilience (Rodriguez-Sanchez et al., 2021). Lessons learned from previous crises can inform and guide responses to the current disruptions, and how organizations approach the present hazards changes routines and beliefs concerning future challenges (Orth & Schuldis, 2021). In Duchek's (2020) model of organizational resilience, organizational learning is a capability which is critical to the completion of the adaptation stage. Burnard and Bhamra (2011) contend that resilient organizations possess the adaptive capacity in response to a hazard and learning is its component. Similarly, in their review paper concerning the evolution of the concept of resilience, Van Trijp et al. (2018) note that learning is part of adaptive capacities, which when "embedded in strong network relationships are of vital importance for resilience" (p. 303).

Organizational resilience demonstrates a resemblance to organizational learning as it also tackles values, routines, models, and capabilities developed by organizational members to confront uncertainty in order to survive (Frigotto et al., 2022; Mousa et al., 2020). In general, *organizational learning* is a collective process of acquiring, using, and transforming knowledge and developing the skills of organizational members. It can occur at the individual, team or group, and organizational level (Yang et al., 2004). Rowland and Hall (2014) contend that organizational learning is less spontaneous than individual learning and more responsive; additionally, it is deliberate and formal. It can also be a source of sustainable competitive advantage. Burnard and Bhamra (2011) presented organizational learning in their conceptual framework as a result of resilient response (adjustment) to threatening events detected by an enhanced

16 *Organizational resilience, related constructs, and the VUCA in OS*

monitoring system in an organization. Stewart and O'Donnell (2007) examined technological changes in a public agency and explained the higher level of organizational resilience in some parts thereof through substantial organizational learning and strong leadership. A study by Mousa et al. (2020) conducted in the Egyptian academic environment revealed that organizational learning was positively related to organizational resilience and additionally mediated by multi-stakeholder networks. With regard to employee resilience, in their study of working experiences of professionals in the Middle East during COVID-19, Blaique et al. (2023) found that employee resilience was a mediator in the relationship between organizational learning and work engagement.

Based on the *evolutionary theory of the firm*, organizations need routines that help them to deal with environmental turbulence in order to survive. Thus, they have to revise existing routines or even produce new ones in response to disruptions. The process of adaptation of organizational routines involves organizational learning (Jiang et al., 2019), which, in view of *organizational learning theory*, can be single-, double-, or even triple-loop learning (Argyris, 1976; Rowland & Hall, 2014). *Single-loop learning* is concerned with the efficiency of actions and the improvements thereto. It is aimed at correcting errors with known and established routines. Concerning organizational resilience, single-loop learning facilitates the solution of an existing crisis. In their qualitative study on organizational learning from past disasters in the tourism sector in Bali and its resilience in the aftermath of the COVID-19 pandemic, Bhaskara and Filimonau (2021) found only single-loop learning among the studied sample. It served short-term income generation and played a limited role in strengthening organizational resilience. These authors attributed the reasons behind insufficient learning to the underdeveloped social and human capital of tourism in Bali. They further recommended that enterprises enhance *double-loop learning*, which is about questioning the assumptions behind actions (whether the actions make it possible to achieve the right aims). It modifies and adapts organizational routines and touches on the causes of problems (Azadegan et al., 2019). In the case of disasters, it means critical reflection on events to build preparedness for the future and recover from the current adversity (Bhaskara & Filimonau, 2021). Finally, *triple-loop learning* refers to the context where actions occur and assumptions are grounded. It states how organizations decide what the right thing to do is (Lau et al., 2019; Rowland & Hall, 2014). To the best of our knowledge, triple-loop learning has not been studied in the organizational resilience literature. Theoretically, it can refer to critical changes in the value system that govern routines needed to anticipate, respond, adapt, and recover from disasters. Beyond different types of learning, the organizational learning literature distinguishes *learning mechanisms* which are facilitators of learning, i.e., routines or arrangements for gathering, distributing, evaluating, accumulating, retrieving, and applying information that is useful for an organization (Derwik & Hellström, 2021; Schechter et al., 2021). Battisti et al. (2019) carried out a longitudinal study of resilience of small firms and the role of learning mechanisms, which at the level of organizational learning included proactive posture, whereas at the owner-manager level these pertained to learning goal orientation and knowledge acquisition. They found that links between learning mechanisms and resilient performance measured as stability, survival, and sustained performance are complex and nonlinear.

It needs to be stressed that organizations can learn only through their learning employees. Keyes and Yoon (2020) refer to individual learning routines as the building blocks of organizational resilience. These learning routines include openness to experience and learning identity (or a learning mindset),[7] social support through team learning, flexibility, focused action, and continuous improvement. Though not every employee learning will lead to organizational learning, those organizations that have features of learning organizations are capable of learning from their members. In the context of organizational studies, *learning organizations* are portrayed as having "the capacity to learn, adapt, and change" (Yang et al., 2004, p. 32). They present an adaptive capacity but can also make up alternative futures (Senge, 1990). They facilitate the learning of their employees and are prone to continuous transformations to reach their strategic goals. These organizations are capable of producing, obtaining, and sharing knowledge; what is more, they are willing to adapt their routines if the circumstances require it (Yang et al., 2004). We need to stress that we did not trace any empirical study on learning organization and organizational resilience. Yet, with regard to employee resilience in organizational settings, Caniëls and Baaten (2019) found that it was a mediator in the relationships between a learning-oriented organizational climate, a feature of a learning organization, and proactive work behaviors. Likewise, Malik and Garg (2020) studied IT organizations in India, observing that learning organizations have a positive impact on employee resilience and work engagement. Moreover, employee resilience partially mediated the influence of learning organization on work engagement. Malik and Garg (2017) also found that employee resilience partially mediates between learning culture (another characteristic of learning organizations) and change-supportive responses of employees, e.g., inquiry and dialogue or affective commitment to change.

An important aspect of organizational learning and a learning organization is *unlearning*, which is "the reversible process of intentionally discarding routines based on mental models" (Orth & Schuldis, 2021). It requires one to abandon obsolete mental models and routines as well as devising new ones in response to exogenous disruptions (Morais-Storz & Nguyen, 2017; Wong & Lam, 2012) and, in the view of Wang (2008), is a manifestation of double-loop learning. Unlearning is especially emphasized as a prerequisite of learning when tremendous problems occur (Orth & Schuldis, 2021; Wang, 2008). However, learning may happen without prior unlearning. Furthermore, unlearning may not result in the implementation of new routines. The relationship between unlearning and

18 *Organizational resilience, related constructs, and the VUCA in OS*

organizational resilience was the subject of a conceptual study by Morais-Storz and Nguyen (2017), who treat unlearning as "a constituent component of the metamorphosis cycle" (p. 96), composed of repeatable phases of learning and unlearning. The cycle is crucial in organizational or, more precisely, strategic resilience. The only traced empirical study on the links between unlearning, organizational learning, and organizational resilience, by Orth and Schuldis (2021), revealed a positive effect of organizational learning on organizational resilience, in particular its adaptive capacity. However, these authors did not prove the moderating effect of unlearning on the aforementioned relationship.

Learning and resilience are also intertwined through *organizational learning capabilities*, defined as the attributes of an organization and its managers that facilitate organizational learning (Rodriguez-Sanchez et al., 2021). Such a capability includes experimentation, tolerance for risk, uncertainty and mistakes, interactions with the external environment, dialogue, and participative decision making. Rodriguez-Sanchez et al. (2021) argue that organizational resilience supports each component of organizational learning capability, as when times are tricky, organizational members have to experiment with new routines or adapt them to embrace the volatility, uncertainty, complexity, and ambiguity present in their environments. To become resilient, organizations have to exploit new areas, so they must encourage risk-taking behaviors and accept possible errors arising from inferior experimentation. To successfully respond to disturbances, organizations frequently need to attract partners from their surroundings. Working out urgent problems may also require open communication and empowering employees to enable them to suggest solutions. Thus, in their research into small- and medium-sized companies in Spain, organizational resilience triggered organizational learning capability and had a positive impact on performance. Likewise, qualitative research by Zighan et al. (2022) on Jordanian small- and medium-sized enterprises revealed that learning capabilities, as one of the components of entrepreneurial orientation, were vital for the resilience of these companies in response to the COVID-19 pandemic.

Recapitulating, organizational resilience and organizational learning are inherently intertwined and resilient organizations are learning organizations. Nevertheless, research on the learning component of organizational resilience should be developed further to offer more conclusive results.

Organizational resilience, related concepts, and cross-cultural differences

In the numerous conceptualizations of organizational resilience, one may also find that it is the accumulated cultural capacity which organizations have developed to understand adversity and adapt to it (Koronis & Ponis, 2018). Organizational resilience requires the proper cultural and social basis, which in the view of Koronis and Ponis (2018) comprises trust, a strong perceived identity, and error-friendliness. They point to attention to a resilient culture, which has the features of a learning culture, as an antecedent of a resilient organization (Dhoopar et al., 2021). Such a culture should facilitate preparedness, responsiveness, adaptation, and learning (Koronis & Ponis, 2018). Culture at different levels (nations, within-country, organizations) encompasses the values and beliefs of organizational members which determine how they manage uncertainty. It also shapes expectations about how to cope with adversity (Dhoopar et al., 2021; Ungar, 2013). Organizational members may not accept actions which contradict their national cultural beliefs, values, and norms. Hence, Fietz et al. (2021) assert that the effect of national culture on internal stakeholders cannot be completely erased by a strong organizational culture. In addition, the impact of national culture on individuals is stronger than the influence of organizational culture. They further argue that organizational resilience depends on the cultural context, which should not be ignored in studies. Yet, to date it has not been sufficiently recognized with regard to national cultures, cross-cultural differences, or within-country differences (Fietz et al., 2021; Hillmann & Guenther, 2021).

One of the most commonly used concepts of *culture* and cultural frameworks in research is that proposed by Hofstede (Zhou & Kwon, 2020), who created a metaphor of a collective software that influences the way people think and act through a shared value system and norms (Hofstede, 1980). Although every culture faces the same underlying problems, the way various cultures approach them varies. Accordingly, national culture may cause differences in organizational structures and routines among countries that determine responses to a crisis. It impacts the decision-making process, problem-solving approaches, and attitudes toward a crisis (Fietz et al., 2021). National culture may also favor the values of resilience that underpins the organizational resilience of entities in a country, as Low Kim Cheng (2007) found with regard to Singaporeans and their businesses. Furthermore, there are different *cultural dimensions*, which describe national preferences for certain values (Hofstede & Minkov, 2010), and they can be linked with organizational resilience. Although there are studies which have analyzed cultural differences in individual or team responses to hazards (Hechanova et al., 2020; Hechanova & Waelde, 2017; Liu et al., 2021; Sulphey, 2020), to date few authors have examined the impact of cultural dimensions on organizational resilience (Fietz et al., 2021; Horn et al., 2021). Table 1.1 describes how these dimensions may affect organizational resilience. It needs to be stressed that the hypothesized associations do not show unequivocal direction in every case; put another way, a dimension may both support and harm organizational resilience. It seems that cultural orientations may have opposite effects on planned and adaptive resilience. Hence, more studies should be conducted to better understand the role of the cultural context in shaping organizational resilience.[8]

Horn et al. (2021), based on a literature review of Asian companies' responses to shocks, inferred that uncertainty avoidance – if combined with the universalism-particularism dimension – can better explain variances in the level

20 *Organizational resilience, related constructs, and the VUCA in OS*

Table 1.1 Hofstede's cultural dimensions and organizational/individual resilience

Cultural dimension	Predicted relationships to organizational resilience
Power distance	The dimension portrays differences in the degree of acceptance for power disparities among members of society. It is reflected in organizational hierarchies and structures and determines whether employees want and are empowered to make decisions. In times of crisis, high power distance may support the swift implementation of solutions by employees, without questioning top-down directives. Yet, it may also hinder innovative responses to hazards, as such a response requires a more participative organizational environment.
Individualism vs. collectivism	This orientation describes the relative value of individual and group interests in society and the importance it places on interpersonal relationships. Individualistic societies manifest in a loose connection to groups and value individual accomplishments; individuals pursue their own goals and think independently. Collectivistic societies tend to be more tightly linked with various networks, display a greater propensity to achieve common goals, and have a stronger sense of group identity, which are critical to building organizational resilience.
Masculinity vs. femininity	Values praised in masculine societies include being assertive, competitive, performance-oriented, and acquiring material success, while genders have distinct roles. Feminine societies prefer high-quality relationships and lives, stress-free and supportive workplaces, shared goals, and do not differentiate between male and female roles. Avoiding failure matters in masculine cultures and is less important in feminine ones. From the perspective of organizational resilience, avoiding failures may support preparedness but a stronger relationship oriented toward the feminine can also be supportive.
Uncertainty avoidance	The dimension reflects how members of a given culture approach the uncertain future, what they think of uncertainty, what they feel about it, and how they behave when they encounter it. Organizations confronted with the uncertainty caused by disruptions may behave defensively to minimize negative outcomes, or aggressively to avail shock and try new ways of doing things, or use a combination of defensive and aggressive approaches. Cultures high on this dimension will establish measures and formalize procedures to prevent crises. Thus, they may put more emphasis on preparedness and use a defensive approach. On the other hand, cultures low on uncertainty avoidance are open to change and do not feel threatened by ambiguity, so they will likely show more adaptive responses.

Organizational resilience, related constructs, and the VUCA in OS 21

Table 1.1 (Continued)

Cultural dimension	Predicted relationships to organizational resilience
Long-term orientation	The dimension exhibits the degree of focus on the future. Long-term oriented societies value saving, long-term planning, persistence, dedication, thrift and diligence and favor trust in relationships. Short-term oriented cultures are focused on the present and the past. They look for quick responses and manage time. Since long-term orientation prefers sustainable business embedded in strong social ties over short-term profits, it may enhance organizational resilience through preparedness. Nevertheless, managing shocks may also require immediate action, so short-term orientation can also be instrumental to organizational resilience through the capacity for adaptation.
Indulgence vs. restraint	This orientation shows the extent of control a society has over the desires, behavior, and emotions of its members. Indulgent cultures display a preference for pleasure over duty and are optimistic and extroverted. They create a relaxed workplace which is conducive to teamwork and commitment. Restraint cultures are more dedicated to fulfilling duties, work hard, are more pessimistic, and introvert. Their dedicated work ethic may mobilize employees when a crisis arises and trigger organizational resilience as a result. It may also support preparedness for the unexpected. On the other hand, this value orientation makes people more susceptible to vulnerabilities, as when individuals feel pessimistic, it becomes harder for them to recover.

Sources: Based on Andersson et al. (2019); van den Berg et al. (202s); Fietz et al. (2021); Hofstede and Minkov (2010); Horn et al. (2021).

of organizational resilience among Asian states, and Asian organizations and the rest of the world. Fietz et al. (2021) studied the organizational resilience of companies from the NAFTA region, discovering that high power distance, high uncertainty avoidance, and collectivism were positively associated with organizational resilience. However, time orientation and masculinity vs. femininity were not related to organizational resilience.

Organizations cannot be resilient until their employees and teams prove their resilience. Therefore, studies on cross-cultural differences in individual/ team resilience may enrich comprehension of the issue. Concerning teams, Liu et al. (2021) examined whether collectivism moderates the relationship between team learning and team resilience in the context of the COVID-19 pandemic. They showed that teams with a collectivist orientation exhibit a greater propensity to interact, which may enhance team learning, resulting in an abundance of resources that can be used to cope with stressful situations, and thus team resilience. As for individuals, Sulphey (2020) found that long-term orientation had a

22 *Organizational resilience, related constructs, and the VUCA in OS*

positive impact on psychological resilience. Hechanova and Waelde (2017) and Hechanova et al. (2020) analyzed how the cultural characteristics of Southeast Asian countries account for improvements in the effectiveness of provision of disaster mental health and psychosocial support to help build individual resilience. They inferred that collectivism, while having a primarily positive impact on resilience, can also be a risk factor due to the feelings of self-blame, guilt, and shame common in collectivistic societies when their relatives have suffered from trauma. Nevertheless, collectivistic societies form strong communities, institutions, and support groups that foster disaster preparedness and recovery. Moreover, the power distance dimension was identified as a factor which may have an impact on recovery processes, since members of high power distance societies expect health professionals to be experts. To recap, prior research, although sparse, confirms that cultural context plays a role in resilience.

The VUCA concept

The VUCA concept in organizational studies

Dramatic events of the past and present, such as the fourth industrial revolution, the COVID-19 pandemic, the rise of national protectionism and nationalistic sentiments, prolonged economic recessions, endangered democracy, the energy crisis, disruptions in the global supply chain, climate change, etc. have changed the world in which we live today. This reality is frequently portrayed as volatile, uncertain, complex, and ambiguous, frequently abbreviated to VUCA (Cavusgil et al., 2021). Although, the term is by no means new, it seems that the issue of VUCA today has never been more relevant. Risk and uncertainty have always been present in business, but today there is a broader set of risks that need to be managed. For instance, organizations around the world face the risk of technological obsolescence, are expected to run sustainable business and respond to a circular business model, and should be prepared for potential cyberattacks or disruptions caused by trade wars, such as the one between the United States and China. Moreover, they are all affected by the consequences of the recent pandemic (Cavusgil et al., 2021).[9] Understanding what a VUCA world means is therefore critical, especially with regard to organizational resilience.

The term VUCA originated with the U.S. military, which first used it in the 1990s to reflect on the new reality it faced after the end of the Cold War (Baran & Woznyj, 2021; Minciu et al., 2019). Over the years, the term was steadily borrowed by business practitioners and later by academics. The VUCA phenomenon describes conditions where entities struggle to define their future based on their accumulated past experience. Their environments are *volatile* and significant changes and fluctuations occur tumultuously, and vagueness concerning the size of alterations is considerable and unprecedented. Deterministic models of problematic situations do not work and implemented solutions quickly become

Organizational resilience, related constructs, and the VUCA in OS 23

obsolete. Turbulence has intensified in the 21st century due to financial turmoil, digitization, connectivity, globalization, innovation, etc., and volatility has increased the level of *uncertainty*. When environments become uncertain, the future is highly unpredictable, as organizational problems are not predefined and structured. Then, environments appear *complex*, and their intertwined subsystems can react in a different manner to the same external conditions. Hence, understanding connections and interrelationships is challenging. Finally, environments are *ambiguous*, so it is hard to discern clear patterns of underlying trends or to infer their causes and effects (Johansen & Euchner, 2013; Mack & Khare, 2016; Minciu et al., 2019). Although this description has prevailing negative overtones, VUCA environments create both threats and opportunities for organizations. VUCA conditions should not be viewed as unwelcome threats but as triggers for progress (Cavusgil et al., 2021; Johansen & Euchner, 2013; Minciu et al., 2019; Nandram & Bindlish, 2017a).

The VUCA concept, though borrowed, has been incorporated into organizational studies to reflect on the salient peculiarities of modern organizational environments and how to navigate within them. The authors made an effort to identify major VUCA challenges and remedies.[10] VUCA environments appear to represent "the new normal" conditions, "a more or less state of instability at the edge of chaos" (Mack & Khare, 2016, p. 5). Bennett and Lemoine (2014) conceptualize VUCA in their portfolio approach as a joint effect of the degree of predictability of actions and knowledge of the situations. They infer four VUCA categories:

- high predictability, little knowledge means complexity,
- high predictability, a lot of knowledge describes volatility,
- low predictability, little knowledge is ambiguity,
- low predictability, a lot of knowledge implies uncertainty.

For each of the four VUCA categories, they suggest implementing different responses. Drawing on their conceptualization and theoretical inspirations from *system theory* and *complexity theory*,[11] Mack and Khare (2016) present complexity as the core concept that affects the extent of ambiguity through the combined effects of volatility and uncertainty. Complexity is a derivate of *the complex system structure*, in which its different components are linked to one another in a nonlinear way, and *complex system behavior*, where interactions of its parts are also nonlinear. Against this backdrop, volatility and uncertainty are observable consequences of complexity. Additionally, these are attributes of environments ascribed to them by observers, not their objective properties. When decisions in organizations are made, these observable attributes of their environments contribute to ambiguity, where there are many solutions to problems and their expected results are not clear. In the view of Mack and Khare (2016), the VUCA phenomenon makes the traditional mechanistic worldview obsolete

24 *Organizational resilience, related constructs, and the VUCA in OS*

and inefficient. Thus, they recommend reflecting environmental complexity at individual and organizational levels. An organizational approach to the VUCA issue is addressed in the book *Managing in a VUCA World* (Mack et al., 2016). Its authors referred to problems such as change management, risk management, adaptation to complexity, customer relationships, pricing, corporate communication, supply chain management, agility, and corporate social responsibility. An individual approach to dealing with the VUCA phenomenon is presented in the book *Managing VUCA Through Integrative Self-Management* (Nandram & Bindlish, 2017b). The contributors propose an integrative paradigm, which draws on Indian philosophy, to help individuals embrace and live in a VUCA world. They claim that an integrative paradigm is a holistic view with a focus on integral unity in which "[a]ll purposes and perspectives are brought together to arrive at a coherent understanding and subsequent framework of action" (Bindlish et al., 2017, p. 326). They discuss issues of spirituality in workplaces and beyond, sense-making in change management processes, transformational management education and leadership, technological change, mindfulness, intuition, and integrating simplification theory.

Drawing on a review of organizational studies on the VUCA concept by Popova et al. (2018), several themes of concern can be identified. These are:

- problems generated by VUCA conditions for managing organizations and their impact on system behavior,
- the role of leadership in organizations that face VUCA challenges,
- personnel development for the VUCA times,
- organizational change in the VUCA context.

Furthermore, there is a growing perspective, conceptual, descriptive, or case study literature on management approaches and strategies to deal with VUCA conditions (e.g., Baran & Woznyj, 2021; Cavusgil et al., 2021; Mack et al., 2016; Minciu et al., 2019; Nandram & Bindlish, 2017b; Popova et al., 2018; Schoemaker et al., 2018). Other topics that have been inspired by VUCA environments include innovation, agility, and supply chain management (Gao et al., 2021; Reid et al., 2016; Troise et al., 2022). The VUCA issue, albeit to a limited extent, has also been plotted into research in hospitality and tourism (H&T). In a cross-sectional study of Indian Generation Z female hospitality students, Kautish et al. (2021) examined whether career belief, career self-efficacy, and social support are positively related to VUCA skills, e.g., immersive learning, smart-mob organizing, or commons creating. They found that career self-efficacy and social support enhance VUCA skills. Wakelin-Theron et al. (2019) made an attempt to construct a tourism employability model in the VUCA context. Based on a mixed methods study in South Africa, they observed that there are significant relationships among professional skills (e.g., multitasking), personality traits (e.g., flexibility), knowledge skills (e.g., research skills), and operational skills (e.g., critical thinking) that enhance employability in the sector. Major and Clarke (2021) recommend a regenerative tourism model as a remedy for VUCA conditions in the H&T sector. A regenerative model considers the tourism business to be a living system embedded in place and community.

The subject literature affirms that organizations cannot limit VUCA factors; thus, they must learn continuously (Ferrari et al., 2016; Minciu et al., 2019). They should expect significant disruptions and be able to respond quickly by adopting appropriate strategies. Consequently, they have to be resilient. As Frigotto et al. (2022) contend, "resilience embodies a holistic response that is appropriate to the VUCA [...] world of today" (p. 8) and can be perceived as an organizational remedy for a VUCA world. Various authors have documented the role of organizational or personal resilience in the VUCA times, yet there is a vacuum in the H&T literature in that respect. For example, Reid et al. (2016) studied SMEs' agility as their dynamic capability required for organizational resilience in the VUCA context. They propose a framework for the assessment of the areas affected by VUCA turbulence in SMEs, which should be further covered in their strategic plans to increase agility. Li (2020) analyzed loose coupling as a solution to the global interdependence paradox in VUCA environments, indicating that it can foster organizational resilience. Rimita et al. (2020) found that recovery management for organizational resilience was one of 11 strategies applied by Nigerian executives to deal with the VUCA phenomenon in their businesses. Bhattacharjee and Singh (2017) put forward the concept of karmic leadership that may, in their view, promote organizational resilience. They describe karmic leaders as being able to adapt to different circumstances due to their mindful understanding of the continual evolution of the context that occurs in different action-reaction cycles. Likewise, Moss Breen (2017) considers leaders with resilience capability to be properly equipped to navigate in a VUCA world. Lepeley (2021) indicates resilience and agility as complementary master soft skills in her Human Centered Management model, which are required by people and organizations in order to handle VUCA conditions. Luthans and Broad (2020) imply that VUCA factors in workplaces nowadays are the consequences of the COVID-19 pandemic and the fourth industrial revolution. They consider the VUCA context a threat to employee mental health and associate with it such negative outcomes as anxiety, substance abuse, stress, depression, and suicide. Thus, they recommend interventions as well as wearable technology and gamulation training enabled by the fourth industrial revolution to support psychological capital (which includes a state of resilience) alongside medical measures to combat mental health crises. Levey and Levey (2019) indicate that when challenged by VUCA conditions, mindfulness training programs may foster personal and organizational resilience.

Recapitulating, the environment in which organizations operate today has become more volatile, uncertain, complex, and ambiguous; thus, the VUCA phenomenon is attracting growing academic interest. It is associated with both

26 *Organizational resilience, related constructs, and the VUCA in OS*

tremendous threats and opportunities. The complexity of the world appears to be its central feature and volatility, uncertainty, and ambiguity are the consequences. The literature provides recommendations concerning management in the VUCA times; organizational resilience is proposed as one of the possible answers, yet in studies on the H&T sector the problem seems to be neglected.

Current VUCA challenges, opportunities, and remedies

Minciu et al. (2019) note that "VUCA represents a world of dilemmas without general solutions" (p. 1144) where threats prevail but opportunities are also available (Johansen & Euchner, 2013). Although the present and future are volatile, uncertain, complex, and ambiguous, various authors have attempted to detect the fundamental trends that define the terms of VUCA and will continue to do so. On the one hand, they have identified various mechanisms to effectively manage VUCA challenges and avail oneself of opportunities arising out of this new normal. On the other hand, due to the innate nature of the VUCA issue, the future cannot be fully anticipated, and confusion is a part of this. Moreover, it may be questioned whether the VUCA phenomenon is entirely new, since VUCA conditions can also be traced back to the past. However, what makes the present different from the past is the scale, intensity, and rate of VUCA changes (Johansen & Euchner, 2013).

Johansen and Euchner (2013) recognized the following trends that have been instrumental in shaping the VUCA world, i.e., climate change, terrorism (including bioterrorism), cyber warfare, digitalization, connectivity, the globalization of R&D and technology, innovation, and generation of digital natives. Cavusgil et al. (2021) add increasing nationalism, economic recession, black swan events such as COVID-19, trade wars, sustainability, and social tensions. Overall, they divide trends that affect the world into long-term and short- to medium-term trends. The former include digitalization and resource shortages, whereas the latter include challenges caused by the natural, geopolitical, and financial environment (see Table 1.2).

Johansen and Euchner (2013) claim that organizations and their leaders can successfully work in VUCA conditions. They should combat volatility with a clear vision for their organizations. To counter uncertainty they ought to look from the outside to gain an understanding of the unknown through learning and collaboration with others. Complexity can be managed through the clarity of the actions taken and ambiguity with agility, which enables one to move quickly from one course of action to another. Cavusgil et al. (2021) recommend various coping mechanisms and strategies for dealing with VUCA challenges related to the supply chain, people and relationships, business agility, sustainability and governance, and technology (Table 1.3). Additionally, Baran and Woznyj (2021) suggest three interrelated steps with regard to agility: (1) to identify VUCA, (2) to implement agility-enhancing practices, and (3) to define obstacles

Organizational resilience, related constructs, and the VUCA in OS 27

Table 1.2 World trends and VUCA

Long-term trends	
Digitalization and the fourth industrial revolution	Digitalization began in the 1950s and the fourth industrial revolution in the 2010s. They have resulted in technological innovations that are forcing organizations to redefine their business models. Thanks to them, the importance of physical location has diminished, e-commerce is growing, the ability to collect and analyze Big Data has increased globally, and cryptocurrencies and blockchain technologies have emerged. Artificial intelligence enables the management of supply chains on a global scale, and 3D printing and automation, e.g., have reduced production costs and the need for low-cost labor locations, making nearshoring and reshoring a viable option for multinational companies. This has also affected the policy environment, which has shifted toward greater digital protectionism since 2017, and further attempts and pressures on technology companies may continue in the future. The fourth industrial revolution is creating new types of human-machine interactions that are changing the workplace through the emergence of new roles and jobs, which demand new skills.
Climate change and resource scarcity	These phenomena have been present in public discussion for the last 30 years, but their role is growing. They are affecting many sectors, including H&T, and require a wider implementation of circular or sustainable business models, putting more pressure on sustainability, overcoming bottlenecks in global supply chains, and changing economic and environmental policies to further enable the green transition. A complex paradigm shift that calls for a reduction in the use of fossil fuels and an increase in renewables could increase the current volatility of energy markets, which are inherently global and subject to geopolitical tensions.
The Fifth Industrial Revolution	The Fifth Industrial Revolution brings changes in the way human-machine interaction is viewed. It will put more emphasis on synergistic cooperation instead of competition between the two (as in the Fourth Industrial Revolution). Humans are to cooperate with machines, exploit their strengths and offset their weaknesses with the help of technology. The emphasis will be on societal well-being and the servant role of technology in achieving this and sustainability.

(Continued)

28 *Organizational resilience, related constructs, and the VUCA in OS*

Table 1.2 (Continued)

Short- to medium-term trends

Natural disruptions and health economy	Natural disruptions, such as natural disasters or pandemics, are to some extent inevitable, unavoidable, and unpredictable. They have always affected various sectors, destroying infrastructure, long and complex supply chains and damaging people's health and mental condition. H&T are particularly vulnerable in this regard. Moreover, due to climate change, the occurrence of natural hazards may increase in the future. If the world remains physically connected, pandemics may also occur more frequently, raising concerns about people's health. As a result, more attention will need to be paid to the interplay of the environment, health, and the economy.
Geopolitical/financial disruptions	Protectionist and nationalist movements are on the rise around the world, democracies are under threat, and a retreat from regional integration and globalization (referred to as slowbalization) is evident. These factors negatively affect global supply chains, trade, and foreign investment. Prices, stocks, and currencies are volatile, and political tensions only increase this instability.
Social changes	Social media has significantly altered the business landscape and will continue to do so in the future, affecting other environmental domains as well. Engaged citizens, self-customization, grassroots initiatives, smart social networks, digital natives, and polarizing extremes are all outcomes of the emergence of new media that increase the complexity of connections between individuals.

Sources: Based on Bichler et al. (2022); Cavusgil et al. (2021); Filimonau and De Coteau (2020); Ivaldi et al. (2022); Major and Clarke (2021); Olivié and Gracia (2020); Worzala and Wyman (2022); Noble et al. (2022).

to agility. Alternatively, Troise et al. (2022) identified antecedents of organizational agility in SMEs, such as their dynamic capabilities (relational capability, innovation capability, and digital technologies capability). Popova et al. (2018) propose a model for enterprise management, which includes eight managerial approaches, namely, the system, project, marketing, situational, stakeholder, scenario, logistics, and behavioral approaches, as well as the implementation of modern techniques and tools such as digital technologies, adaptability, proactiveness, etc. Other authors add the following measures: developing dynamic capabilities (e.g., sensing change, seizing opportunities, transforming

Organizational resilience, related constructs, and the VUCA in OS 29

Table 1.3 Coping mechanisms and strategies for VUCA conditions

Strategy	Description
Supply chain resilience	Supply chain strategies need to be redefined in the face of the VUCA era. Efficiency must be balanced with sustainability, just-in-case approaches must replace just-in-time management, and supply chains should become simpler and shorter. Industry 4.0 helps streamline today's overly rigid supply chains. Reconfigured supply chains should be more resilient, and artificial intelligence and Big Data analytics can help achieve this goal.
People, relationships, and leadership	Virtual teams and remote work may become more common in the future so people and leaders will have to develop their communication and digital skills, emotional intelligence, mindfulness, and cross-cultural competence. Shared, participative, distributed, relational, moral, and charismatic leadership can help deal with the VUCA times. In addition, the authors note the role of philosophical and artistic leadership. As a coping mechanism, people must be engaged in continuous learning. There is a compelling need for personal and professional networks that can provide information or resources when adversity strikes.
Agility	Ever-changing conditions that are difficult to anticipate and understand require swift moves and adaptability; thus, agility has become a crucial factor in the capacity of today's organizations to respond to VUCA conditions. There are several practices that promote agility: effective communication, including bottom-up communication, and transparency, knowledge sharing and teamwork, fostering agile behaviors through training, iterative improvement and continuous learning, customer focus, leadership, strategic alignment, and attracting agile candidates.
Sustainability and governance	Organizational stakeholders, including politicians, expect organizations to take responsibility for a better future. Sustainability and governance strategies respond to this demand. They can also contribute to the greater resilience of organizations under VUCA conditions.
Technology leveraging	Digitalization may promote agility and affect expectations toward leaders who should be able to effectively manage the information overload caused by digitalization and social media. Industry 4.0 has the potential to improve supply chains to better adapt to various hazards; it may also inspire innovations in organizations, industries, and societies. Industry 5.0 presents even greater potential.

Sources: Based on Cavusgil et al. (2021); Gao et al. (2021); Jamil and Humphries-Kil (2017); Miceli et al. (2021); Rath et al. (2021); Rees (2017).

30 *Organizational resilience, related constructs, and the VUCA in OS*

the firm), business model innovation, and leadership skills, such as anticipation and learning (Schoemaker et al., 2018). Nonaka and Takeuchi (2021), in analyzing the role of organizational strategy for properly dealing with VUCA, argue that it should be "more future-oriented, society-focused, dynamic, and human-centric". This means that while organizational leaders cannot predict the future, they can shape it. Such a strategy cannot be directed only at shareholders but must include a wide group of stakeholders. It should be based on dynamic capabilities and practical wisdom. Finally, it has to put people at the core of the strategy developed through an inside-out approach, which is driven by people's beliefs, ideals, and intuition. The authors contend that organizations in the VUCA world should be evaluated on the basis of resilience, longevity, and sustainability.

It is also worth mentioning the intersection between *organizational agility* and resilience, which share commonalities yet remain distinct concepts. Cavusgil et al. (2021) indicate that agility is the capacity of organizations to be responsive in the face of rapid, ambigous changes; conceptually, this overlaps with ideas such as resilience as well as adaptability, rapidity, flexibility, iteration, or ambidexterity. However, organizational resilience refers to tremendous, substantial changes that may threaten organizations but can also lead to improvements, whereas agility treats changes as opportunities and emphasizes responsiveness. Both concepts put the emphasis on flexibility, scenerio prediction, adaptability, and improvements of competitive advantage (Abdelaziz Elgamal, 2018; Miceli et al., 2021). Moreover, through its proactive approach and consideration of time, agility can support the strategic dimension of organizational resilience as a basis for organizational transformation and renewal (Miceli et al., 2021). To further complicate the issue, some authors view organizational agility as one dimension of organizational resilience alongside robustness and integrity, or adaptive capacity (Bouaziz & Smaoui Hachicha, 2018). Regardless how both concepts are approached, agility is linked to resilience, and both can better prepare organizations to deal with the new VUCA era.

In summary, some of the challenges and opportunities of VUCA have been present for years and will emerge in the future, while others will remain unclear, so organizations need to sense their weak signals to respond wisely. Among the many recommended strategies for managing under VUCA, agility is often mentioned in the literature. Since it is closely related to organizational resilience, strengthening the latter can be seen as a wise response to the VUCA era.

Notes

1 We discuss the VUCA concept in the next subchapter.
2 In our model (Chapter 3) we combine the outcome and process views on organizational resilience as well as the adaptation and anticipation perspectives. Our model also incorporates the positive psychology and organizational development perspective.

Organizational resilience, related constructs, and the VUCA in OS   31

3 We also refer to evolutionary theory in the subsequent subchapter to expose a learning component of resilience thinking.
4 We describe these capabilities in Chapter 3.
5 In our model of organizational resilience, we include linkages between individual and organizational resilience. See Chapter 3.
6 See also Chapter 2.
7 Keyes and Yoon (2020), while describing a learning mindset, contrast it with a performance mindset which resembles learning goal orientation and performance goal orientation included in our model of organizational resilience (see Chapter 3).
8 Studies concerning cross-cultural differences of organizational resilience in H&T are presented in Chapter 2.
9 More about current VUCA challenges, opportunities, and remedies in the subsequent subchapter.
10 See the next subchapter.
11 System theory sees organizations as open systems of interconnected parts, and complexity theory claims that organizations are complex adaptive systems in which internal and external interactions constantly alter organizations in order to cope with environmental changes, to ensure a proper degree of stability and flexibility (Lewin, 1999).

References

Abdelaziz Elgamal, M. (2018). Dynamic organizational capabilities: The joint effect of agility, resilience and empowerment. *Journal of Human Resource Management*, *6*(2), 44. https://doi.org/10.11648/j.jhrm.20180602.11

Andersson, T., Cäker, M., Tengblad, S., & Wickelgren, M. (2019). Building traits for organizational resilience through balancing organizational structures. *Scandinavian Journal of Management*, *35*(1), 36–45. https://doi.org/10.1016/j.scaman.2019.01.001

Argyris, C. (1976). Single-loop and double-loop models in research on decision making. *Administrative Science Quarterly*, *21*(3), 363. https://doi.org/10.2307/2391848

Azadegan, A., Srinivasan, R., Blome, C., & Tajeddini, K. (2019). Learning from near-miss events: An organizational learning perspective on supply chain disruption response. *International Journal of Production Economics*, *216*(May), 215–226. https://doi.org/10.1016/j.ijpe.2019.04.021

Baran, B. E., & Woznyj, H. M. (2021). Managing VUCA: The human dynamics of agility. *Organizational Dynamics*, *50*(2), 100787. https://doi.org/10.1016/j.orgdyn.2020.100787

Battisti, M., Beynon, M., Pickernell, D., & Deakins, D. (2019). Surviving or thriving: The role of learning for the resilient performance of small firms. *Journal of Business Research*, *100*(March), 38–50. https://doi.org/10.1016/j.jbusres.2019.03.006

Bennett, N., & Lemoine, G. J. (2014). What VUCA really means for you. *Harvard Business Review*, *9*(1/2) https://hbr.org/2014/01/what-vuca-really-means-for-you, *Jan-Feb*.

Bhaskara, G. I., & Filimonau, V. (2021). The COVID-19 pandemic and organisational learning for disaster planning and management: A perspective of tourism businesses from a destination prone to consecutive disasters. *Journal of Hospitality*

32 *Organizational resilience, related constructs, and the VUCA in OS*

and Tourism Management, 46(November 2020), 364–375. https://doi.org/10.1016/j.jhtm.2021.01.011

Bhattacharjee, A., & Singh, S. (2017). Karmic leadership for a mindful existence. In S. S. Nandram & P. K. Bindlish (Eds.), *Managing VUCA through integrative self-management* (pp. 161–170). Springer International Publishing.

Bichler, M., Buhl, H. U., Knörr, J., Maldonado, F., Schott, P., Waldherr, S., & Weibelzahl, M. (2022). Electricity markets in a time of change: A call to arms for business research. *Schmalenbach Journal of Business Research.* https://doi.org/10.1007/s41471-021-00126-4

Bindlish, P. K., Nandram, S. S., & Joshi, A. (2017). Integrativeness through pursuing integrative intelligence as the way forward. In S. S. Nandram & P. K. Bindlish (Eds.), *Managing VUCA through integrative self-management* (pp. 321–330). Springer International Publishing.

Blaique, L., Ismail, H. N., & Aldabbas, H. (2023). Organizational learning, resilience and psychological empowerment as antecedents of work engagement during COVID-19. *International Journal of Productivity and Performance Management, 72*(6), pp. 1584–1607. https://doi.org/10.1108/ijppm-04-2021-0197

Bouaziz, F., & Smaoui Hachicha, Z. (2018). Strategic human resource management practices and organizational resilience. *Journal of Management Development, 37*(7), 537–551. https://doi.org/10.1108/JMD-11-2017-0358

Britt, T. W., & Sawhney, G. (2020). Resilience capacity, processes and demonstration at the employee, team and organizational levels: A multilevel perspective. In E. H. Powley, B. Barker Caza, & A. Caza (Eds.), *Research handbook on organizational resilience* (pp. 10–24). Edward Elgar Publishing.

Burnard, K., & Bhamra, R. (2011). Organisational resilience: Development of a conceptual framework for organisational responses. *International Journal of Production, 49*(18), 5581–5599. https://doi.org/10.1080/00207543.2011.563827

Caniëls, M. C. J., & Baaten, S. M. J. (2019). How a learning-oriented organizational climate is linked to different proactive behaviors: The role of employee resilience. *Social Indicators Research, 143*(2), 561–577. https://doi.org/10.1007/s11205-018-1996-y

Cavusgil, S. T., Liu, L. A., & Wang, E. Y. (2021). International business in an accelerated VUCA world: Trends, disruptions, and coping strategies. *Rutgers Business Review, 6*(3), 219–243.

Chowdhury, M., Prayag, G., Orchiston, C., & Spector, S. (2019). Postdisaster social capital, adaptive resilience and business performance of tourism organizations in Christchurch, New Zealand. *Journal of Travel Research, 58*(7), 1209–1226. https://doi.org/10.1177/0047287518794319

Connor, K. M., & Davidson, J. R. T. (2003). Development of a new resilience scale: The Connor-Davidson Resilience Scale (CD-RISC). *Depression and Anxiety, 18*(2), 76–82. https://doi.org/10.1002/da.10113

Conz, E., & Magnani, G. (2020). A dynamic perspective on the resilience of firms: A systematic literature review and a framework for future research. *European Management Journal, 38*(3), 400–412. https://doi.org/10.1016/j.emj.2019.12.004

Derwik, P., & Hellström, D. (2021). How supply chain professionals learn at work: An investigation of learning mechanisms. *International Journal of Physical Distribution and Logistics Management, 51*(7), 738–763. https://doi.org/10.1108/IJPDLM-11-2019-0335

Organizational resilience, related constructs, and the VUCA in OS 33

Dhoopar, A., Sihag, P., Kumar, A., & Suhag, A. K. (2021). Organizational resilience and employee performance in COVID-19 pandemic: The mediating effect of emotional intelligence. *International Journal of Organizational Analysis*. https://doi.org/10.1108/IJOA-06-2020-2261

Duchek, S. (2020). Organizational resilience: A capability-based conceptualization. *Business Research, 13*(1), 215–246. https://doi.org/10.1007/s40685-019-0085-7

Espiner, S., Orchiston, C., & Higham, J. (2017). Resilience and sustainability: A complementary relationship? Towards a practical conceptual model for the sustainability–resilience nexus in tourism. *Journal of Sustainable Tourism, 25*(10), 1385–1400. https://doi.org/10.1080/09669582.2017.1281929

Fang, S. (Echo), Prayag, G., Ozanne, L. K., & de Vries, H. (2020). Psychological capital, coping mechanisms and organizational resilience: Insights from the 2016 Kaikoura earthquake, New Zealand. *Tourism Management Perspectives, 34*(March 2019), 100637. https://doi.org/10.1016/j.tmp.2020.100637

Ferrari, E., Sparrer, I., & Von Kibed, M. V. (2016). Simply more complex: A SySt ® approach to VUCA. In O. Mack, A. Khare, A. Krämer, & T. Burgartz (Eds.), *Managing in a VUCA world* (pp. 21–40). Springer International Publishing.

Fietz, B., Hillmann, J., & Guenther, E. (2021). Cultural effects on organizational resilience: Evidence from the NAFTA region. *Schmalenbach Journal of Business Research, 73*(1), 5–46. https://doi.org/10.1007/s41471-021-00106-8

Filimonau, V., & De Coteau, D. (2020). Tourism resilience in the context of integrated destination and disaster management (DM2). *International Journal of Tourism Research, 22*(2), 202–222. https://doi.org/10.1002/jtr.2329

Frigotto, M. L., Young, M., & Pinheiro, R. (2022). Resilience in organizations and societies: The state of the art and three organizing principles for moving forward. In R. Pinheiro, M. L. Frigotto, & M. Young (Eds.), *Towards resilient organizations and societies: A cross-sectoral and multi-disciplinary perspective* (pp. 3–42). Palgrave Macmillan. https://doi.org/10.1007/978-3-030-82072-5

Gao, Y., Feng, Z., & Zhang, S. (2021). Managing supply chain resilience in the era of VUCA. *Frontiers of Engineering Management, 8*(3), 465–470. https://doi.org/10.1007/s42524-021-0164-2

Hall, C. M., Prayag, G., & Amore, A. (2017). Tourism and resilience: Individual, organisational and destination perspectives. *Tourism and Resilience: Individual, Organisational and Destination Perspectives, November*, 1–189. https://doi.org/10.21832/HALL6300

Hartmann, S., Weiss, M., & Hoegl, M. (2020). Team resilience in organizations: A conceptual and theoretical discussion of a team-level concept. In E. H. Powley, B. Barker Caza, & A. Caza (Eds.), *Research handbook on organizational resilience* (pp. 39–52). Edward Elgar Publishing.

Hechanova, M. R. M., Waelde, L. C., & Torres, A. N. (2020). Cultural implications for the provision of disaster mental health and psychosocial support in southeast Asia. In M.R.M. Hechanova & L. C. Waelde (Eds.), *Community, environment and disaster risk management* (Vol. 21, pp. 3–13). Emerald Publishing Limited. https://doi.org/10.1108/S2040-726220200000021001

Hechanova, R., & Waelde, L. (2017). The influence of culture on disaster mental health and psychosocial support interventions in Southeast Asia. *Mental health, religion and culture, 20*(1), 31–44. https://doi.org/10.1080/13674676.2017.1322048

34 *Organizational resilience, related constructs, and the VUCA in OS*

Hillmann, J. (2021). Disciplines of organizational resilience: Contributions, critiques, and future research avenues. *Review of Managerial Science, 15*. https://doi.org/10.1007/s11846-020-00384-2

Hillmann, J., & Guenther, E. (2021). Organizational resilience: A valuable construct for management research? *International Journal of Management Reviews, 23*(1), 7–44. https://doi.org/10.1111/ijmr.12239

Hobfoll, S. E., Halbesleben, J., Neveu, J.-P., & Westman, M. (2018). Conservation of resources in the organizational context: The reality of resources and their consequences. *Annual Review of Organizational Psychology and Organizational Behavior, 5*, 103–128. https://doi.org/10.1146/annurev-orgpsych-

Hofstede, G. (1980). *Culture's consequences: International differences in work related values*. SAGE.

Hofstede, G., & Minkov, M. (2010). *Cultures and organizations: Software of the mind*. McGraw-Hill Professional.

Holling, C. S. (1973). Resilience and stability of ecological systems. *Annual Review of Ecological Systems, 4*, 1–23.

Horn, S., Sekiguchi, T., & Weiss, M. (2021). Thrown off track? Adjustments of Asian business to shock events. *Asian Business and Management, 20*(4), 435–455. https://doi.org/10.1057/s41291-021-00158-y

Ivaldi, S., Scaratti, G., & Fregnan, E. (2022). Dwelling within the fourth industrial revolution: Organizational learning for new competences, processes and work cultures. *Journal of Workplace Learning, 34*(1), 1–26. https://doi.org/10.1108/JWL-07-2020-0127

Jamil, N., & Humphries-Kil, M. (2017). Living and leading in a VUCA world: Response-ability and people of faith. In S. S. Nadram & P. K. Bindlish (Eds.), *Managing VUCA through integrative self-management* (pp. 65–79). Springer International Publishing. https://doi.org/10.1007/978-3-319-52231-9

Jiang, Y., Ritchie, B. W., & Verreynne, M. L. (2019). Building tourism organizational resilience to crises and disasters: A dynamic capabilities view. *International Journal of Tourism Research, 21*(6), 882–900. https://doi.org/10.1002/jtr.2312

Johansen, B., & Euchner, J. (2013). Navigating the VUCA world: An interview with Bob Johansen. *Research Technology Management, 56*(1), 10–15. https://doi.org/10.5437/08956308X5601003

Kantabutra, S., & Ketprapakorn, N. (2021). Toward an organizational theory of resilience: An interim struggle. *Sustainability (Switzerland), 13*(23), 1–28. https://doi.org/10.3390/su132313137

Karman, A., & Savanevičienė, A. (2021). Enhancing dynamic capabilities to improve sustainable competitiveness: Insights from research on organisations of the Baltic region. *Baltic Journal of Management, 16*(2), 318–341. https://doi.org/10.1108/BJM-08-2020-0287

Kautish, P., Hameed, S., Kour, P., & Walia, S. (2021). Career beliefs, self-efficacy and VUCA skills: A study among generation Z female students of tourism and hospitality. *Journal of Hospitality, Leisure, Sport and Tourism Education, 30*, 100340. https://doi.org/10.1016/j.jhlste.2021.100340

Keyes, D. C., & Yoon, J. (2020). Learning routines that build organizational resilience. In E. H. Powley, B. A. Caza, & A. Caza (Eds.), *Research handbook on organizational resilience* (pp. 203–213). Edward Elgar Publishing.

Organizational resilience, related constructs, and the VUCA in OS 35

Koronis, E., & Ponis, S. (2018). Better than before: The resilient organization in crisis mode. *Journal of Business Strategy*, *39*(1), 32–42. https://doi.org/10.1108/JBS-10-2016-0124

Lau, K. W., Lee, P. Y., & Chung, Y. Y. (2019). A collective organizational learning model for organizational development. *Leadership and Organization Development Journal*, *40*(1), 107–123. https://doi.org/10.1108/LODJ-06-2018-0228

Lee, A. V., Vargo, J., & Seville, E. (2013). Developing a tool to measure and compare organizations' resilience. *Natural Hazards Review*, *14*(1), 29–41. https://doi.org/10.1061/(asce)nh.1527-6996.0000075

Lepeley, M.-T. (2021). Soft skills in human centered management: Operational HCM and the resilience – agility umbrella. In M.-T. Lepeley, N. J. Beutell, N. Abarca, & N. Majluf (Eds.), *Soft skills for human centered management and global sustainability* (pp. 1–38). Routledge.

Levey, J., & Levey, M. (2019). Mindful leadership for personal and organisational resilience. *Clinical Radiology*, *74*(10), 739–745. https://doi.org/10.1016/j.crad.2019.06.026

Lewin, A. Y. (1999). Application of complexity theory to organization science. *Organization Science*, *10*(3), 215–215. https://doi.org/10.1287/orsc.10.3.215

Li, P. P. (2020). Organizational resilience for a new normal: Balancing the paradox of global interdependence. *Management and Organization Review*, *16*(3), 503–509. https://doi.org/10.1017/mor.2020.30

Liu, L., Ren, X., & Li, L. (2021). Research on civil engineering project team management under adverse conditions. *IOP Conference Series: Earth and Environmental Science*, *791*(1). https://doi.org/10.1088/1755-1315/791/1/012054

Low Kim Cheng, P. (2007). The cultural value of resilience: The Singapore case study. *Cross Cultural Management: An International Journal*, *14*(2), 136–149. https://doi.org/10.1108/13527600710745741

Luthans, F., Avolio, B. J., Avey, J. B., & Norman, S. M. (2007). Positive psychological capital: Measurement and relationship with performance and satisfaction. *Personnel Psychology*, *60*(3), 541–572. https://doi.org/10.1111/j.1744-6570.2007.00083.x

Luthans, F., & Broad, J. D. (2020). Positive psychological capital to help combat the mental health fallout from the pandemic and VUCA environment. *Organizational Dynamics*, *2019*, 100817. https://doi.org/10.1016/j.orgdyn.2020.100817

Luthans, F., & Youssef, C. M. (2004). Human, social, and now positive psychological capital management: Investing in people for competitive advantage. *Organizational Dynamics*, *33*(2), 143–160. https://doi.org/10.1016/j.orgdyn.2004.01.003

Mack, O., & Khare, A. (2016). Perspectives on a VUCA world. In O. Mack, A. Khare, A. Krämer, & T. Burgartz (Eds.), *Managing in a VUCA world* (pp. 3–20). Springer International Publishing. https://doi.org/10.1007/978-3-319-16889-0

Mack, O., Khare, A., Krämer, A., & Burgartz, T. (Eds.). (2016). *Managing in a VUCA world*. Springer International Publishing.

Major, J., & Clarke, D. (2021). Regenerative tourism in Aotearoa New Zealand – A new paradigm for the VUCA world. *Journal of Tourism Futures*, *8*(2), 194–199. https://doi.org/10.1108/JTF-09-2021-0233

Malik, P., & Garg, P. (2017). The relationship between learning culture, inquiry and dialogue, knowledge sharing structure and affective commitment to change. *Journal of Organizational Change Management*, *30*(4), 610–631. https://doi.org/10.1108/JOCM-09-2016-0176

36 *Organizational resilience, related constructs, and the VUCA in OS*

Malik, P., & Garg, P. (2020). Learning organization and work engagement: The mediating role of employee resilience. *International Journal of Human Resource Management, 31*(8), 1071–1094. https://doi.org/10.1080/09585192.2017.1396549

Miceli, A., Hagen, B., Riccardi, M. P., Sotti, F., & Settembre-Blundo, D. (2021). Thriving, not just surviving in changing times: How sustainability, agility and digitalization intertwine with organizational resilience. *Sustainability (Switzerland), 13*(4), 1–17. https://doi.org/10.3390/su13042052

Minciu, M., Berar, F. A., & Dima, C. (2019). The opportunities and threats in the context of the VUCA world. *13th International Management Conference*, 1142–1150.

Morais-Storz, M., & Nguyen, N. (2017). The role of unlearning in metamorphosis and strategic resilience. *Learning Organization, 24*(2), 93–106. https://doi.org/10.1108/TLO-12-2016-0091

Moss Breen, J. (2017). Leadership resilience in a VUCA world. In R. Elkington, M. Van Der Steege, J. Glick-Smith, & J. Moss Breen (Eds.), *Visionary leadership in a turbulent world: Thriving in the new VUCA context* (pp. 39–58). Emerald Publishing Limited.

Mousa, M., Abdelgaffar, H. A., Chaouali, W., & Aboramadan, M. (2020). Organizational learning, organizational resilience and the mediating role of multi-stakeholder networks: A study of Egyptian academics. *Journal of Workplace Learning, 32*(3), 161–181. https://doi.org/10.1108/JWL-05-2019-0057

Nandi, S., Sarkis, J., Hervani, A., & Helms, M. (2021). Do blockchain and circular economy practices improve post COVID-19 supply chains? A resource-based and resource dependence perspective. *Industrial Management and Data Systems, 121*(2), 333–363. https://doi.org/10.1108/IMDS-09-2020-0560

Nandram, S. S., & Bindlish, P. K. (2017a). Introduction to VUCA. In S. S. Nandram & P. K. Bindlish (Eds.), *Managing VUCA through integrative self-management* (pp. 3–14). Springer International Publishing. http://www.springer.com/series/10101

Nandram, S. S., & Bindlish, P. K. (Eds.). (2017b). *Managing VUCA through integrative self-management* (management). Springer International Publishing.

Noble, S. M., Mende, M., Grewal, D., & Parasuraman, A. (2022). The Fifth Industrial Revolution: How harmonious human–machine collaboration is triggering a retail and service [r]evolution. *Journal of Retailing, 98*(2), 199–208. https://doi.org/10.1016/j.jretai.2022.04.003

Nonaka, I., & Takeuchi, H. (2021). Humanizing strategy. *Long Range Planning, 54*(4), 102070. https://doi.org/10.1016/j.lrp.2021.102070

Olivié, I., & Gracia, M. (2020). Is this the end of globalization (as we know it)? *Globalizations, 17*(6), 990–1007. https://doi.org/10.1080/14747731.2020.1716923

Orth, D., & Schuldis, P. M. (2021). Organizational learning and unlearning capabilities for resilience during COVID-19. *Learning Organization.* https://doi.org/10.1108/TLO-07-2020-0130

Ortiz-de-Mandojana, N., & Bansal, P. (2015). The long-term benefits of organizational resilience through sustainable business practices. *Strategic Management Journal, 37*(8), 1615–1631. https://doi.org/10.1002/smj

Plimmer, G., Berman, E. M., Malinen, S., Franken, E., Naswall, K., Kuntz, J., & Löfgren, K. (2021). Resilience in public sector managers. *Review of Public Personnel Administration, 42*(2), 338–367. https://doi.org/10.1177/0734371X20985105

Organizational resilience, related constructs, and the VUCA in OS 37

Popova, N., Kryvoruchko, O., Shynkarenko, V., & Zéman, Z. (2018). Enterprise management in VUCA conditions. *Economic Annals-XXI*, *170*(3–4), 27–31. https://doi.org/10.21003/ea.V170-05

Powley, E. H. (2020). Introduction: Framing resilience research. In E. H. Powley, B. Barker Caza, & A. Caza (Eds.), *Research handbook on organizational resilience* (pp. 2–9). Edward Elgar Publishing.

Prayag, G. (2018). Symbiotic relationship or not? Understanding resilience and crisis management in tourism. *Tourism Management Perspectives*, *25*(November), 133–135. https://doi.org/10.1016/j.tmp.2017.11.012

Rai, S. S., Rai, S., & Singh, N. K. (2021). Organizational resilience and social-economic sustainability: COVID-19 perspective. *Environment, Development and Sustainability*, *23*(8), 12006–12023. https://doi.org/10.1007/s10668-020-01154-6

Rath, C. R., Grosskopf, S., & Barmeyer, C. (2021). Leadership in the VUCA world – a systematic literature review and its link to intercultural competencies. *European Journal of Cross-Cultural Competence and Management*, *5*(3), 195. https://doi.org/10.1504/ejccm.2021.116890

Rees, B. (2017). The use of mindfulness in a traumatic VUCA world. In S. S. Nandram & P. K. Bindlish (Eds.), *Managing VUCA through integrative self-management* (pp. 193–206). Springer International Publishing. https://doi.org/10.1007/978-3-319-52231-9

Reid, I., Ismail, H., & Sharifi, H. (2016). A framework for operational agility: How SMEs are evaluating their supply chain integration. In O. Mack, A. Khare, A. Krämer, & T. Burgartz (Eds.), *Managing in a VUCA world* (pp. 151–168). Springer International Publishing.

Rimita, K., Hoon, S. N., & Levasseur, R. (2020). Leader readiness in a volatile, uncertain, complex, and ambiguous business erenvironment. *Journal of Social Change*, *12*(1), 10–18. https://doi.org/10.5590/josc.2020.12.1.02

Rodríguez-Sánchez, A. (2021). Organizational resilience. In R. Chiva (Ed.), *Change and development in organisations: Towards consciousness, humanity and innovation* (pp. 25–35). Routledge.

Rodriguez-Sanchez, A., Guinot, J., Chiva, R., & Lopez-Cabrales, A. (2021). How to emerge stronger: Antecedents and consequences of organizational resilience. *Journal of Management and Organization*, *27*(3), 442–459. https://doi.org/10.1017/jmo.2019.5

Rodríguez-Sánchez, A. M., & Perea, M. V. (2015). The secret of organisation success: A revision on organisational and team resilience. *International Journal of Emergency Services*, *4*(1), 27–36.

Rowland, C., & Hall, R. (2014). Management learning, performance and reward: Theory and practice revisited. *Journal of Management Development*, *33*(4), 342–356. https://doi.org/10.1108/JMD-08-2012-0110

Santoro, G., Bertoldi, B., Giachino, C., & Candelo, E. (2020). Exploring the relationship between entrepreneurial resilience and success: The moderating role of stakeholders' engagement. *Journal of Business Research*, *119*(April), 142–150. https://doi.org/10.1016/j.jbusres.2018.11.052

Schechter, C., Qadach, M., & Da'as, R. (2021). Organizational learning mechanisms for learning schools. *Learning Organization*. https://doi.org/10.1108/TLO-10-2018-0169

Schoemaker, P. J. H., Heaton, S., & Teece, D. (2018). Innovation, dynamic capabilities, and leadership. *California Management Review*, *61*(1), 15–42. https://doi.org/10.1177/0008125618790246

Senge, P. M. (1990). *The fifth discipline: The art & practice of the learning organization.* Random House.

Seville, E. (2018). Building resilience: How to have a positive impact at the organizational and individual employee level. *Development and Learning in Organizations, 32*(3), 15–18. https://doi.org/10.1108/DLO-09-2017-0076

Shoss, M. K., Jiang, L., Probst, T. M., & Shoss, M. K. (2018). Bending without breaking: A two-study examination of employee resilience in the face of job insecurity. *Journal of Occupational Health Psychology, 27*(1), 112–126. doi: 10.1037/ocp0000060.

Stewart, J., & O'Donnell, M. (2007). Implementing change in a public agency: Leadership, learning and organisational resilience. *International Journal of Public Sector Management, 20*(3), 239–251. https://doi.org/10.1108/09513550710740634

Sulphey, M. M. (2020). A study on the effect of long-term orientation and risk propensity on resilience. *International Journal of Sociology and Social Policy, 40*(11–12), 1585–1610. https://doi.org/10.1108/IJSSP-09-2019-0192

Tasic, J., Amir, S., Tan, J., & Khader, M. (2020). A multilevel framework to enhance organizational resilience. *Journal of Risk Research, 23*(6), 713–738. https://doi.org/10.1080/13669877.2019.1617340

Teng-Calleja, M., Hechanova, M. R. M., Sabile, P. R., & Villasanta, A. P. V. P. (2020). Building organization and employee resilience in disaster contexts. *International Journal of Workplace Health Management, 13*(4), 393–411. https://doi.org/10.1108/IJWHM-09-2019-0122

Teo, W. L., Lee, M., & Lim, W. S. (2017). The relational activation of resilience model: How leadership activates resilience in an organizational crisis. *Journal of Contingencies and Crisis Management, 25*(3), 136–147. https://doi.org/10.1111/1468-5973.12179

Troise, C., Corvello, V., Ghobadian, A., & O'Regan, N. (2022). How can SMEs successfully navigate VUCA environment: The role of agility in the digital transformation era. *Technological Forecasting and Social Change, 174*(April 2021), 121227. https://doi.org/10.1016/j.techfore.2021.121227

Ungar, M. (2013). Resilience, trauma, context, and culture. *Trauma, Violence, and Abuse, 14*(3), 255–266. https://doi.org/10.1177/1524838013487805

van den Berg, J., Alblas, A., Blanc, P. Le, & Romme, A. G. L. (2022). How structural empowerment boosts organizational resilience: A case study in the Dutch home care industry. *Organization Studies, 43*(9), 1425–1451. https://doi.org/10.1177/01708406211030659

Van Trijp, J., Boersma, K., & Groenewegen, P. (2018). Resilience from the real world towards specific organisational resilience in emergency response organisations. *International Journal of Emergency Management, 14*(4), 303–321. https://doi.org/10.1504/IJEM.2018.097358

Wagnild, G., & Young, H. (1993). Development and psychometric evaluation of the Resilience Scale. *Journal of Nursing Measurement, 1*(2), 165–178.

Wakelin-Theron, N., Ukpere, W. I., & Spowart, J. (2019). Determining tourism graduate employability, knowledge, skills, and competencies in a VUCA world: Constructing a tourism employability model. *African Journal of Hospitality, Tourism and Leisure, 8*(3).

Wang, J. (2008). Developing organizational learning capacity in crisis management. *Advances in Developing Human Resources, 10*(3), 425–445. https://doi.org/10.1177/1523422308316464

Wildavsky, A. (2017). *Searching for safety*. Routledge. https://doi.org/10.4324/978135 1316248

Wong, P. S. P., & Lam, K. Y. (2012). Facing turbulence: Driving force for construction organizations to regain unlearning and learning traction. *Journal of Construction Engineering and Management, 138*(10), 1202–1211. https://doi.org/10.1061/(asce)co.1943-7862.0000523

Worzala, E., & Wyman, D. (2022). The human factor: The "unknown unknowns" in the real estate development process. *Journal of Property Investment and Finance, 40*(3), 300–305. https://doi.org/10.1108/JPIF-11-2021-0099

Yang, B., Watkins, K. E., & Marsick, V. J. (2004). The construct of the learning organization: Dimensions, measurement, and validation. *Human Resource Development Quarterly, 15*(1), 31–55. https://doi.org/10.1002/hrdq.1086

Zahari, A. I., Mohamed, N., Said, J., & Yusof, F. (2022). Assessing the mediating effect of ieadership capabilities on the relationship between organisational resilience and organisational performance. *International Journal of Social Economics, 49*(2), 280–295. https://doi.org/10.1108/IJSE-06-2021-0358

Zhou, Y., & Kwon, J. W. (2020). Overview of Hofstede-inspired research over the past 40 years: The network diversity perspective. *SAGE Open, 10*(3). https://doi.org/10.1177/2158244020947425

Zighan, S., Abualqumboz, M., Dwaikat, N., & Alkalha, Z. (2022). The role of entrepreneurial orientation in developing SMEs resilience capabilities throughout COVID-19. *International Journal of Entrepreneurship and Innovation, 23*(4), 227–239. https://doi.org/10.1177/14657503211046849

2 Organizational resilience and related concepts in hospitality and tourism management studies

Hospitality and tourism organizational resilience versus hospitality and tourism crisis/disaster management

Crises and disasters are undeniably among the greatest threats to hospitality and tourism (H&T). Although the sector has been relatively immune to turbulence for many years, the events of the 21st century have clearly shown that an increasing number of threats are directly endangering the H&T industry. The global tourism industry has recently encountered numerous significant challenges and adversities, such as political instability, terrorist attacks, economic recessions, biosecurity threats, and natural disasters (Boniface et al., 2020).

The terms "crisis" and "disaster" are visible in virtually all societies today. The terms are often used interchangeably, which is a fundamental error (Berbekova et al., 2021). These terms have distinct conceptual debates and carry different legal implications in various countries, for instance, in the context of the declaration of a state of emergency or accessing funds to respond to a disaster (Aliperti et al., 2019). In general, a *crisis* is viewed as "a dangerous and extraordinary situation in which a decision must be made under time pressure" (Glaesser, 2006, p. 12) or "an unpredictable event that threatens important expectancies of stakeholders related to health, safety, environmental, and economic issues, which can seriously impact an organization's performance and generate negative outcomes" (Coombs, 2007, pp. 2–3). Faulkner (2001) highlighted that crisis is broadly defined and encompasses occurrences resulting from technical or man-made errors and disasters. He made a distinction between disasters and crises regarding their origin, scale, or magnitude. Thus, a crisis stems from unproductive actions by an organization or multiple organizations, whereas disasters are consequences of external factors, natural or created by humans. Disasters typically refer to events organizations cannot control, e.g., natural disasters (Wut et al., 2021).

The concept of a *tourism crisis* is an indispensable aspect related to the functioning of this sector. It is conceptualized as "an event of major proportions that disrupts orderly tourism operations and requires immediate managerial

DOI: 10.4324/9781003291350-3

Organizational resilience and related concepts in H&T studies   41

action to overcome the resulting problems" (Laws et al., 2007, p. 3). Conversely, a "tourism disaster" is viewed as a worsening of the "tourism crisis", which encompasses the repercussions resulting from a sudden and impactful event in the tourism sector, affecting booking trends, hotel occupancy rates, economic losses in the tourism industry, and more (Aliperti et al., 2019). Regardless of the division and differences in terms, both phenomena are dangerous for the H&T sector due to the scope and scale of their influence. One can even assume that they concern all subsectors of the H&T sector, such as:

- tour operators/travel agencies–terrorism, political events, financial crisis, issues regarding health, natural disasters,
- hotel operators–natural disasters, political events, human error events,
- airline industry–natural disasters, human error-airplane crashes,
- restaurant industry–health issues,
- ocean cruising industry–human error services.

(Wut et al., 2021)

Only relatively recently, Faulkner (2001) noted a need for more research concerning crisis and disaster occurrences in the H&T industry. Yet, in the last two decades, this situation has changed. Several interesting works have appeared in the scientific literature relating to crises and disasters in H&T. This has been influenced by several disturbing events that occurred in the first two decades of the 21st millennium, including the 9/11 terrorist attacks (e.g., Adams et al., 2001; Blake & Sinclair, 2003; Fall & Massey, 2006; Goodrich, 2002), the global economic crisis (Cohen & Neal, 2010; Papatheodorou et al., 2010; Perles-Ribes et al., 2016), and the COVID-19 pandemic. Especially during the latter era, there has been a definite rise in interest in the subject of crises in the tourism sector (e.g., Baum & Hai, 2020; Dube et al., 2020; Hall et al., 2020; Sigala, 2020). This is understandable, as the tourism industry had not previously encountered a crisis of such magnitude. As it is widely recognized, the pandemic profoundly affected virtually all tourism subsectors, and its impact was felt across the globe. Moreover, tourism has never experienced such a drastic drop in the number of tourists and revenue. The latest crisis has received considerable attention in academic studies. Nevertheless, it is also vital to mention events that had a national dimension and greatly affected the H&T sector. The events of 2015, such as the terrorist attack in Paris, and 2016, including floods and the tragic incident where 86 people lost their lives during Bastille Day celebrations in Nice, resulted in a substantial decrease in visitor arrivals to France. Consequently in 2016, France witnessed a 7% decline in tourist visits (Agence France, 2016). Crises may also have a local dimension, where the negative effect of crises on local communities is evident, thus affecting the economies there (e.g., Cushnahan, 2004; Gurtner, 2008). Beyond crises, disasters also affect H&T. Recently, due to global warming, natural disasters, e.g., earthquakes, tsunamis, occur more frequently

42 *Organizational resilience and related concepts in H&T studies*

than before. These phenomena negatively affected the H&T industry and caused a marked fall in demand for tourism (Chu, 2008; Lanouar & Goaied, 2019).

The subject areas addressed by researchers in the context of crises and disasters in H&T are manifold. An interesting overview was compiled by Utkarsh and Sigala (2021) based on 177 papers published between January 2020 and January 2021 related to the impact of the COVID-19 pandemic on H&T. At the same time, they identified topics that addressed the effect of COVID-19 on H&T:

- the impact of COVID-19 on tourist decision-making, destination marketing, and technology adoption (e.g., Bae & Chang, 2021; Jarratt, 2021),
- the future of tourism post-COVID-19: crisis, recovery and future (e.g., Cardoso, 2020; Yeh, 2021),
- managing change in the tourism industry: change, resilience, and transformation (e.g., Chemli et al., 2022; Zenker & Kock, 2020),
- the effect of COVID-19 on H&T stakeholders (e.g., Filimonau et al., 2020; Vo-Thanh et al., 2021).

Because of their often disruptive, sudden, and unforeseen nature, tourism crises demand swift and targeted interventions (Monterrubio, 2017). Since tourism growth can be intermittently interrupted, the significance of crisis and disaster management and mitigation in the industry has consequently increased (Broshi-Chen & Mansfeld, 2021). Therefore, from the angle of the emergence of crises and disasters in the tourism and hospitality sector, it is crucial to take appropriate and measurable actions to reduce the effects of or mitigate these phenomena. Hence, in broader terms, *tourism crisis and disaster management* come into play. The concept can be defined as a broad organizational function that aims to understand, prevent, or deal with crises while taking stakeholder interests into account (Santana, 2004). The initial experience in this area was relatively poor, albeit the scholarly literature on crisis management in H&T has evolved from documenting global crises to identifying and distinguishing different types of crises and stages (e.g., Faulkner, 2001; Ritchie, 2009). For decades, crisis and disaster management have received insufficient attention in H&T studies (Pforr & Hosie, 2007). The literature on the subject has reached a maturity phase but still needs more crisis strategies and tactics beyond the repeatable linear ex-post-crisis approaches. These conventional strategies might not align adequately with tourism crises' intricate, unpredictable, and complex nature (Broshi-Chen & Mansfeld, 2021). Even though the issue of tourism crises has attracted scholars for some time, crisis and disaster management remains relatively new as a H&T industry practice (Ghaderi et al., 2012). Still, it grew after the events of 9/11 (Broshi-Chen & Mansfeld, 2021). Nevertheless, in subsequent years, it has been observed that H&T organizations should be better prepared to manage adversities (Wang &

Organizational resilience and related concepts in H&T studies 43

Ritchie, 2012). Indeed, interest in the topic has significantly grown since 2020, mainly because of the outbreak of the last pandemic, COVID-19. The global impact of the pandemic and the subsequent economic downturn experienced by numerous countries have refocused attention on crisis and disaster management. Organizations and researchers are again showing keen interest in understanding and developing effective strategies to navigate such unprecedented crises (Gössling et al., 2020; Qiu et al., 2020). The years 2020–2022 have resulted in an increased interest in crisis and disaster management among practitioners in the H&T sector and academic researchers. Moreover, the issue of crisis management used to be dominant in studies addressing tourism crises (Cohen & Neal, 2010).

Decision-makers involved in crisis and disaster management within the H&T sector have multiple options and tools at their disposal for implementation. However, it is notable that crisis and disaster management should be seen as an ongoing process rather than a single isolated action (Cioccio & Michael, 2007). In this regard, a fundamental issue is whether and how they should respond to an unexpected and sudden decline in tourism demand (Blake & Sinclair, 2003), which is an inevitable consequence of crisis situations in tourism. In such circumstances, when a tourism crisis arises, H&T managers must undertake specific and measurable actions to address the situation effectively: (a) respond immediately to the crisis; (b) address the concerns and needs of those directly influenced by the crisis; (c) minimize the harm resulting from negative publicity and subsequent decrease of incomes; (d) resolve problems with contractors and other stakeholders (Laws et al., 2007). This issue is even approached differently by Ritchie and Jiang (2019), who list three stages of crisis management and corresponding actions (p. 4):

- "preparedness and planning: proactive crisis management/response, disaster reaction to reduction, mitigation, and preparedness, crisis management plan and strategies, tourism crisis/disaster planning strategies, influencing factors and predictors of tourism crisis planning, human resource development in crisis preparation (internal stakeholders), crisis leadership (internal stakeholders), tourism integration with emergency agency and disaster risk reduction (external stakeholders), risk analysis, forecasting tools, pre-assessment and detection, crisis prevention methods, risk assessment mechanism, crisis learning,
- response and recovery: tourism response and recovery strategies, government policy response actions, physical and financial recovery, tourism reconstruction, crisis/disaster communication/public relationships, post-crisis/disaster marketing strategies and campaign, tourism market recovery, tourists' misperception/destination image/(re)-positioning, press response/media and marketing, marketing message, new market segmentation, resource management (HR, finance), community collaboration,

44 *Organizational resilience and related concepts in H&T studies*

small business recovery/business resilience, measurement of recovery strategies,
- resolution and reflection: crisis/disaster learning, organizational learning, knowledge management, destination/enterprise resilience".

In a world that is increasingly susceptible to crises and disasters, there is a general expectation for businesses and destinations to concentrate on these stages. This approach aims to diminish their vulnerability to such events and enhance their resilience (Ritchie & Jiang, 2019). This matter holds significance since, although tourism researchers have extensively studied crisis and disaster management, it might be the appropriate moment to investigate the correlation between crisis/disaster management and resilience (Prayag, 2018). Research on resilience in crisis and disaster management is important for destinations and businesses that directly or indirectly depend on tourism and should be continuous and in-depth. Because of its distinctiveness, this industry requires continuous monitoring, particularly because crises/disasters pose a significant challenge to the H&T sector (Williams & Baláž, 2015). Consequently, there could be substantial economic and employment losses due to a decline in tourism demand (Boukas & Ziakas, 2013). Previous research on resilience in tourism has mainly been based on significant crises and disasters (Becken, 2013; Hall et al., 2017). In addition, as revealed by Chen et al. (2021) in their literature review on crisis/disaster management in H&T, only 5% of the research has analyzed resilience. It is primarily theoretical, and empirical studies are still scarce.

Building organizational resilience as part of crisis management should be a critical aspect of H&T operations (Wut et al., 2021). However, unlike crisis management, resilience thinking suggests that systems (e.g., ecological, social-ecological) can adapt, respond, and evolve in the face of extraordinary circumstances and gradual changes (Lew, 2014). As such, resilience thinking provides a complementary, if not better, perspective on crisis management in understanding how systems cope with adversity of any scale. Resilient systems can self-organize, whereas in crisis management thinking, this can only happen sometimes (Carpenter et al., 2001; Prayag, 2018). From the crisis management stream perspective, three different accounts of resilience exist. The initial approach suggests reverting to a previous state of perceived "normalcy". The second perspective considers resilience as the capacity to rebound from a crisis through a series of rescue operations, reconstructing damaged infrastructure, and subsequently revitalizing markets (Scott & Laws, 2006). Finally, the third approach to resilience predicts that a crisis can lead to a fundamentally different state (Dahles & Susilowati, 2015).

Building resilience in tourism and hospitality has many advantages, mainly in the context of exposure to potential crises and disasters. For instance, a resilience framework can be employed to gain deeper insights into exposure to crises/disasters during the phase of planning and prevention. Moreover, it can aid in comprehending response strategies and contribute to future planning efforts to build resilience for the times ahead. Having a more profound understanding of resilience, its various levels (individual, organizational), and the factors that impact it (e.g., social or financial capital) is valuable. Additionally, researching the emergence of dynamic capabilities due to crises and disasters is essential to advancing knowledge in this field (Ritchie & Jiang, 2019). For organizations involved in crisis/disaster management, resilience should be seen as a crucial aspect of their culture (Sawalha, 2015). They should strive to build the capacity to transition from previous practices to adapt and respond to adversities effectively (Duarte Alonso et al., 2018). This issue seems particularly important for the H&T sector, as achieving organizational resilience in the event of disruption is vital for the sustainable development of H&T organizations (Orchiston et al., 2016).

Presently, researchers show growing interest in the area of crisis/disaster management. Though, a gap in research remains that connects disaster response to the resilience, sustainability, and strength of a local community reliant on tourism (Cartier & Taylor, 2020). Hence, there is a clear need for further research and analysis relating to resilience and crisis management in H&T. In particular, there is a need for further research that investigates the disaster event in direct relation to the various resilience process stages. Diverse research is essential to better understand crisis management in a destination and help the industry effectively mitigate crises both before and during times of need (Pennington-Gray, 2018). Prayag (2018) infers that future H&T studies should be directed at resilience rather than crises because "if a system is resilient, it is implicit that it has the capacity not only to overcome crises and disasters, but also to better adapt to change in general" (p. 3). This is particularly important for research on H&T organizations. Although resilience is a topic extensively considered and researched from the community and destination angles, organizational resilience in H&T has a shorter track record in the literature, with research efforts limited to the last 20 years (Annarelli & Nonino, 2016; Hall, 2018).

To sum up, the issues of crisis and disasters, and consequently crisis and disaster management in H&T, are becoming the subject of increasing debate. This is mainly the result of numerous threats that have affected the industry in the 21st century, e.g., the COVID-19 pandemic. In particular, the concept of resilience is becoming a considerable challenge. The discussion demonstrated the need for research and action in this area.

Hospitality and tourism organizational resilience versus hospitality and tourism organizational sustainability

The term "sustainability" was initially coined to address the deterioration of the natural environment and its adverse effects on human health, social cohesion, and economic progress. In recent times, sustainability has evolved to encompass

46 *Organizational resilience and related concepts in H&T studies*

a more comprehensive array of concerns, representing an amalgamation of social, economic, and environmental aspects. It has gained significant prominence in various spheres, including the media, company boardrooms, political domains, and universities (Mohrman & Worley, 2010). An increasing number of companies are incorporating sustainability considerations into their strategies and operations with more typical business goals (Thomas & Lamm, 2012). Increasingly, this is independent of the fashion for the concept or the popularity thereof. Organizations are implementing sustainability policies because they reflect meaningful changes in business processes rather than they improve their public image (Eccles et al., 2012).

According to many researchers (e.g., Hart et al. 2003), a sustainable enterprise can significantly further sustainable development by concurrently delivering economic, social, and environmental values – often referred to as the "triple bottom line". This involves adopting a well-balanced organizational approach that considers economic, environmental, and social aspects holistically (Florea et al., 2013). Unfortunately, organizational solutions to sustainability have mainly addressed one or two of these values (Greenfield, 2004). In many organizations, sustainability was initially linked mainly to the economic aspect, focusing on factors like financial prosperity, robust products, and quality services (Florea et al., 2013). Recently, there have been increasing efforts in other areas related to organizational sustainability. In addition, there is a growing focus on new areas in ongoing research. For example, organizational sustainability is progressively focused on managing new knowledge, inventing ideas, and developing practices that can improve the business (Lopes et al., 2017). Furthermore, every innovation is related to organizational sustainability, involving amendments in management, technology, and environmental operations. This relates to both companies and public sector organizations (Kozioł-Nadolna & Beyer, 2021). Additionally, it may be perceived as a business approach that fosters the organization's long-term economic success while considering the well-being of other constituencies impacted by the company's operations (Ulus & Hatipoglu, 2016).

For many years, most environmental engagement and sustainability research has been directed at the manufacturing industry (Graci & Dodds, 2008). Within this framework, studies focusing on the service industry, such as H&T, have yet to receive much interest in the literature (Ulus & Hatipoglu, 2016). However, H&T is increasingly becoming one of the industries with the highest contribution to climate change globally, primarily due to significant anthropogenic CO_2 emissions (Gössling & Peeters, 2015; Scott et al., 2016). Consequently, there is an increasing concern regarding sustainability challenges of the H&T sector (Miththapala et al., 2013). The issue of organizational sustainability is crucial for H&T. It can even be assumed that it goes beyond the classical understanding of organizational sustainability. From the angle of tourism and hospitality operations, other sector-specific factors also come into play, e.g.,

Organizational resilience and related concepts in H&T studies 47

significant emphasis is placed on the human factor. This is confirmed, for example, by the research of Kim et al. (2019), which infers that the social identity view provides solid implications regarding the sustainability behaviors of employees. Rezapouraghdam et al. (2019) argue that the utmost critical task for organizations refers to involving every staff member in sustainability processes and practices, which is crucial for a mutual effort to achieve sustainability. This concern becomes even more pressing in the H&T industry, which heavily relies on natural resources while also being a labor-intensive sector with a large workforce. From an employee perspective, it is also important to fully engage everyone. Embedding sustainability is more than simply the agenda of top managers or sustainability officers; it is also the concern of middle managers (Ulus & Hatipoglu, 2016). Cohesive, top-down messaging, integration of sustainability into central job functions and decision-making processes, and enterprise-wide sustainability goals are suggested to engage employees in the adoption process (Moran & Tame, 2013; Savitz & Weber, 2013). By contrast, a study by Oriade et al. (2021) found that sustainability management practices are substantially linked with organizational culture and staff's awareness of sustainability. Efficient learning and proper knowledge acquisition play a crucial role in comprehending and addressing sustainability issues, as many managers currently miss the essential knowledge and interest needed to fulfill the fundamental goals of responsibility in social and environmental aspects (Erdogan & Baris, 2007; Mensah, 2006). This indicates that to progress sustainability in the H&T sector, there is a requirement for approaches that encourage stakeholder collaboration and organizational learning (Schianetz et al., 2007). The ultimate objective of an organization regarding human factor management is to minimize change resistance and involve staff in sustainability practices at work (Verhulst & Boks, 2014).

As mentioned, an understanding of sustainability is increasingly evident in H&T. Both businesses and the public sector are increasingly implementing solutions incorporating social, economic, and environmental elements. For instance, Leslie (2007) observed that hotels implement programs and initiatives to encourage responsible environmental practices. Additionally, Mensah (2014) highlighted that hotels have progressed in their environmental management practices from focusing solely on the conservation of water and energy to encompassing voluntary environmental programs that extend the scope of sustainability considerations. Nevertheless, there are numerous other areas to integrate organizational sustainability, such as exploring ownership patterns and advancing sustainable development, adopting sustainable H&T supply chain management practices, considering the sustainability pillars and competitive synergy within H&T organizations, examining hotels' environmental policies in conjunction with employees' environmental beliefs, and embracing corporate social responsibility within the H&T industry (Melissen et al., 2016; Xu & Gursoy, 2015). At the same time, H&T businesses should be regarded as

48 *Organizational resilience and related concepts in H&T studies*

organizations that foster the well-being of their people (Pandey et al., 2009) and actively support social and environmental welfare. True sustainability can only be attained by transforming and moving from materialism to a spiritual value orientation (Dhiman, 2016).

Despite the growing interest of researchers in sustainability in H&T, the current body of scientific knowledge still needs to be improved. This is supported by research, including Pushpakumara et al. (2019), who showed a significant dearth in the literature and highlighted the lack of sufficient findings and a suitable theoretical framework to explain "how, why, and when" being green can enhance the performance of tourism organizations, aligned with three pillars of sustainability. Furthermore, the majority of research on sustainability practices in the H&T sector is confined to bigger organizations, such as star-class hotels (Alonso-Almeida et al., 2018). Therefore, sustainability should be more widely studied by researchers and applied by practitioners in the sector, especially given that scholars suggest that sustainability is a profitable path to pursue irrespective of the size, category, or available funds of business organizations in the H&T sector (Hellmeister & Richins, 2019). Sustainable organization and operation should be developed by something other than market orientation. Instead, it should stem from a comprehensive understanding of the interplay between various factors, leading to a continuous state of sustainability (Núñez-Ríos et al., 2020). Thus, it is necessary to include not only the perception of H&T enterprises concerning the potential economic and social gains of the activity of H&T organizations but also the perception of key actors or community representatives (Rasoolimanesh et al., 2017).

The considerations presented earlier are a starting point for analyzing the relationship between H&T organizational resilience and tourism organizational sustainability. This is an essential issue because organizations can play a critical role in guiding societies toward sustainable, resilient, and regenerative development paths (Hestad et al., 2021). Moreover, one of the objectives of studying resilience is to explore how enhancing it can align with sustainability objectives (Becken, 2013). Sustainability and resilience are intricate concepts, and their relationship can be conceptualized and applied in various ways (Saarinen & Gill, 2018). While some researchers see sustainability and resilience as slightly different perspectives of the same phenomenon, others say they have distinct differences. They perceive conservation goals of sustainability as contrasting with resilience's focus on adaptation. The confusion arises from the fact that both terms are described and utilized in diverse ways to serve various political objectives, which may only sometimes manifest their genuine definitions. Additionally, they both share common aims and perspectives, such as addressing climate change and searching for a harmonious balance between people and nature (Lew et al., 2016). Compared to sustainability, which is linked to stability, resilience is portrayed as an idea associated with a necessity to transform and adapt (Davidson, 2010). It is viewed as a valuable abstract tool, handy for analyzing how organizations respond to changes (Berkes & Ross, 2013). Discussions in the field regarding the linkages between resilience and sustainability are taking intriguing turns. Some attempts aim to unify the two approaches (Walker & Salt, 2006), incorporating resilience into the sustainability concept as its new dimension (Strickland-Munro et al., 2010), and others suggest entirely replacing sustainability with resilience (Butler, 2018). In general, the concept of resilience is gaining increasing attention across various academic disciplines and business sectors (Jones & Comfort, 2018). Espiner et al. (2017) implied that although sustainability remains a crucial concept for H&T scholars, the interest in resilience has grown in recent times within H&T scholarship as a term that may encompass the critical sustainability aspects.

Regarding the linkages between organizational resilience and sustainable tourism development, we see several factors that influence it. These factors were presented by Fatoki (2018) based on the example of small enterprises. They included internal (e.g., planning, managers' skills, and innovation) and external ones, such as government support and the country's economic performance. Business planning, including the development thereof, is essential from the angle of resilience and sustainability. In their study on small hospitality enterprises, this has been corroborated by Sobaih et al. (2021). They suggest that owner-managers should give greater importance to strategic planning to cultivate well-designed resilience, which contributes to adaptive resilience both directly and indirectly. It also supports the performance of the firm and sustainable tourism development. The authors examined two aspects of organizational resilience, namely planned and adaptive, and found that while adaptive resilience is critical for business recovery during and after crises, planned resilience significantly enhances adaptive resilience and furthers the performance and sustainable development of tourism firms. Resilience planning offers socio-ecological adaptation and an alternative view on community development in contrast to more perspectives on sustainable development (Lew, 2014). In the H&T industry, more specifically, Cheer and Lew (2017) argue that "a paradigmatic shift is taking place in the long-term planning of tourism development, in which the prevailing focus on sustainability is being enhanced with the practical application of resilience planning".

Despite the growing interest in the issue, state-of-the-art knowledge is still insufficient in this regard. The integration of sustainability and resilience has yet to be extensively explored, despite several authors advocating for more research in this area (Cheer et al., 2019; Innerhofer et al., 2018). The resilience concept is gaining increasing interest from scholars investigating sustainability in the H&T sector. Though this study area is still developing, several interconnected themes are emerging, offering a loose framework for this growing field. These themes include the following: the development of conceptual and theoretical frameworks, sensitive environments, destination resilience, community resilience, disaster resilience in the H&T industry, climate change, and leadership

50 *Organizational resilience and related concepts in H&T studies*

(Jones & Comfort, 2020). This issue becomes even more significant in the post-COVID-19 pandemic era. One may posit that the tourism system is more susceptible to disruptions compared to other sectors, in which connections between resilience and sustainability are more advanced in terms of social, political, economic, and environmental aspects (Espiner et al., 2017). Organizational resilience in H&T can help achieve financial goals, sustainability, and competitive advantage in a rapidly changing environment (Akgün & Keskin, 2014). Souza et al. (2017) contended that developing business resilience toward sustainability requires long-term plans and benchmarking. Resilience reflects the organizational capacity to recover from adversities through appropriate decision-making support and infrastructure that ensure sustainable development (Faber et al., 2020). Drawing upon resilience theory, the H&T sector necessitates organizations to cultivate adaptive capacities, foster being flexible and self-efficient, and prioritize innovations to enhance their scope of resilience and sustainability. Those lacking resources for innovation resort to adaptive strategies to ensure their survival in the future (Khan et al., 2021).

In conclusion, further studies concerning links between resilience and sustainability in the H&T sector are important not only for developing enterprises in the sector but also for the perception of regional and country social and economic development. As we showed, this issue is becoming increasingly popular among researchers. However, given the vulnerability of the H&T sector, further research in this area is highly recommended.

Hospitality and tourism organizational resilience versus destination resilience

The *destination* concept holds significant importance in the literature as it globally influences the selection of tourist trips (Díaz & Espino-Rodríguez, 2016). *Destinations* are central places where tourism activities coincide (Fyall & Garrod, 2020). These are geographic areas with tourism and other economic activities, occupied by communities and with diverse land use. For instance, these can be regions characterized by cultural or environmental coherence, governed by local or regional tourism organizations cooperating with other institutions (Becken, 2013). Pavlovich (2003) noticed: "the tourism destination generally comprises different types of complementary and competing organizations, multiple sectors, infrastructures, and an array of public/private linkages that create a diverse and highly fragmented supply structure" (p. 205). Hence, it is necessary to talk about the complexity of the destination concept due to the multiplicity of entities forming it. A crucial success factor for destinations is their capacity to offer visitors a protected, predictable, and safe place (Volo, 2007). Safety and security issues have constantly been essential prerequisites for H&T (Kővári & Zimányi, 2010). Travelers generally feel averse to risk; therefore, any actual or potential danger that possibly affects their safety and security or health will

Organizational resilience and related concepts in H&T studies 51

probably impact their decision to visit a specific destination (Lepp & Gibson, 2003; Sonmez & Graefe, 1998). Therefore, the occurrence of different kinds of crises and disasters is a key threat to destinations. This was undeniably visible in the era of the last global pandemic, which practically more or less influenced most of the world's destinations. This issue has already been the topic of several studies and papers relating to the functioning of destinations in times of pandemics (e.g., Ahmad et al., 2021; Avraham, 2015; Benjamin et al., 2020; Hassan & Soliman, 2021; Li et al., 2021; Rasoolimanesh et al., 2021).

It is a vital challenge for a destination to cope with diverse, frequently unpredictable events. Therefore, it is reasonable to consider the assumptions of *destination resilience*. The concept of destination resilience presents conceptual challenges, as defining destinations can be complex. Moreover, destination resilience is frequently interconnected with the resilience of its various constituents, e.g., communities, organizations, and others (Hall et al., 2017). Destination resilience is an emerging research field aiding tourism managers and policymakers in how to devise more adaptive strategies to address vulnerabilities, uncertainty, and heightened risks posed by multiple crises and disasters (Bethune et al., 2022). Prayag (2018) contends that effectively conceptualized resilience thinking can offer a superior angle for comprehending how tourism destinations tackle adversities. From a tourism development and resilience perspective, more research is still needed (Luthe & Wyss, 2014). Despite the increased interest in this topic, we still see insufficiently developed research on tourism management related to the crisis management process (Khazai et al., 2018) and destination resilience (Schroeder & Pennington-Gray, 2018). This holds especially true for the five gaps recognized concerning destination resilience: the necessity to develop both theoretical and empirical models, to understand the linkages of destination resilience to sustainable tourism development, to study smart tourism, and to comprehend tourism recovery (Schroeder & Pennington-Gray, 2018). We need to understand not only if and how destinations recover from a crisis but also how they rebound from it and foster future resilience (Ritchie & Jiang, 2019).

Interest in destination resilience has been markedly heightened during periods of crisis. The last pandemic has undoubtedly contributed to this. Destinations were looking for ways to build resilience after the fact of facing the new reality of COVID-19 and its related impacts (McCartney et al., 2021). However, it is vital to note that destination resilience must be equated, or expanded, to emergency and disaster management. Crisis/disaster management, while essential, is insufficient in itself to increase our understanding of how organizations, communities, and destinations prepare for, respond to, and bounce back from events that are growing in scale and have significant social, economic, and environmental consequences for people and entire societies (Prayag, 2018). Therefore, from a destination perspective, the concept of resilience takes on an additional, significant meaning. Destination resilience enables handling crises/disasters in

52 Organizational resilience and related concepts in H&T studies

a more strategic and integrated way (Lee et al., 2013; Prayag, 2018). Basurto-Cedeño and Pennington-Gray (2018) claim that destination resilience helps to deal with the growing regularity and size of disasters affecting the H&T sector. They coined a scalable resilience model applicable to different sources of risks and destinations' sizes (Basurto-Cedeño & Pennington-Gray, 2018). To create effective strategies and manage and secure long-term sustainable development, we need to comprehend better the systemic linkages between destinations and resilience (Hall et al., 2017).

The engagement of different groups of constituencies is a critical aspect regarding the operation of a destination. The same principle applies to destination resilience, where the efforts and actions of all stakeholders should be considered, including those functioning in the destination and those contributing to its development. The level of collaboration among tourism businesses, their staff, destination management organizations (DMOs), disaster management professionals, and other stakeholders is also meaningful (Jiang et al., 2019). The destination can be viewed as an ecosystem. Thus, destination resilience should be established on the resilience of all its stakeholders (Amore et al., 2018). Destination resilience aims to balance various interests and recognizes that stakeholders attain greater benefits in ecosystems by pursuing a common goal (Gretzel et al., 2015). However, the destination can extend beyond the H&T businesses operating there and encompasses the H&T industry, non-tourism sectors, and the community (Amore et al., 2018). Destination resilience is a crucial function of destination management. The soundness of resilience can instill trust in a destination's ability to protect both its residents and its visitors (Bethune et al., 2022). The capacity of employees, organizations, and destinations to preserve their identity and effectively bounce back from recurrent crises is an enduring process (Prayag, 2018). This matter has lastly gained particular significance, especially during the COVID-19 pandemic, and many destinations and tourism entities needed to make substantial progress in this regard (Bhaskara & Filimonau, 2021).

While all stakeholders should be engaged in fostering destination resilience, DMOs, specifically established to oversee tourism, should play a significant role (Borzyszkowski, 2013). DMOs and tourism organizations should enhance the marketing effectiveness of destinations by adopting suitable strategies for risk communication in regard to the regional crisis stage (Han et al., 2022). While DMOs usually function proactively in the marketing domain, they are also tasked with assuming leadership to manage crises and assist the local H&T sector in responding to and recovering from adversities (Cartier & Taylor, 2020). Moreover, building destination resilience must become one of the core activities of DMOs. The evolving role of these organizations points to a potential direction for future research, linking destination strategy with insights into leadership and governance of a destination (Beritelli & Bieger, 2014; Hristov & Zehrer, 2015). There needs to be more involvement with policymakers and

DMO professionals, as they can foster organizational learning and foster organizational resilience in H&T businesses (Ruiz-Ballesteros, 2011).

It is important to remember that DMOs are directed at the coordination of their stakeholder in the pursuit of a shared vision (R.-Toubes et al., 2020). The effectiveness of this task relies on the number and quality of the DMO's interactions with all its constituencies (Paraskevas & Arendell, 2007). Both DMOs and policymakers can assess whether strategies aimed at adaptation and mitigation derived from such evaluations genuinely aid in reducing vulnerability and enhancing resilience. Therefore, it is crucial to conceptualize and analyze H&T's vulnerability and resilience, which is extensively impacted by many factors (e.g., climatic, social, economic, and political aspects). This approach is needed for devising viable strategies regarding adaptation and mitigation on a macro and a micro scale (Dogru et al., 2019). From the perspective of resilience and the DMOs' role in creating it for the benefit of the destination, the participation of individual stakeholders is crucial. This aligns with the findings of Blackman et al. (2011), who emphasize the significance of DMOs in fostering the learning of local H&T organizations. However, they also recognize the challenges posed by the complexity and diversity of the H&T sector, along with organizational inertia, which can hinder learning. The proper composition of capabilities and resources strengthens organizational resilience (Faulkner, 2001) and stakeholder collaboration (Nguyen et al., 2017), as any associated shortages, should teach H&T organizations to look for lacking capital, either social, human, financial, or physical, from other stakeholders, consequently enhancing organizational learning. Of course, the scale of their involvement may be relatively different. It is contingent on many factors, e.g., the size of the company or its importance to local tourism. Based on research conducted by R.-Toubes et al. (2020), hotels seem to be most significant in this regard. These entities and DMOs play a distinctive role in establishing social networks among tourism stakeholders, which serves as a foundation for developing destination resilience (Timur & Getz, 2008).

As is well known, in numerous locations, the local economy highly depends on H&T organizations, their prosperity, and their resilience (Prasad et al., 2015; Thomas et al., 2011). Specifically, the last pandemic has intensified the pursuit of H&T-wide consensus to incorporate a resilience perspective into daily operations and decision-making (Bethune et al., 2022). Hence, there is a need to bring all stakeholder forces together. Several empirical researches have highlighted that if there is marketing collaboration among multiple H&T organizations, which indicates bridging networks, and between them and DMOs, which implies linking networks, synergy can be achieved (Orchiston & Higham, 2016). It is essential for smaller businesses. Previous studies investigating resilience have primarily concentrated on large businesses, neglecting small or family firms. Considering the prevalence of small organizations in the H&T sector, future research is undoubtedly necessary to gain a better understanding of and

54   *Organizational resilience and related concepts in H&T studies*

provide guidelines on how to transform management and capabilities necessary for resilience building within these small establishments (Utkarsh & Sigala, 2021). Micro and small organizations are essential for delivering H&T services in numerous places, making it crucial to examine their resilience in the face of external shocks closely (Pham et al., 2021). Implementing innovative solutions is particularly important. For instance, social networks can offer them improved access to various business resources, influencing their likelihood of surviving and recovering from disasters and crises. Consequently, the enhanced resilience of small H&T businesses results in alterations in their social networks. It creates double loops of learning and transformation that enable coping with the potential external shocks and turbulences (Pham et al., 2021).

These considerations are certainly important for both organizations and destinations. The research conducted and the solutions suggested on that basis should contribute to the implementation of specific instruments that enable better handling of crises, thus building the resilience of the destination and the organization. As we progress toward a phased exit from lockdowns and the relaunch of the H&T organizations, scholars, governments, and tourism managers and owners must learn from the past. Reflecting on past experiences will help them learn and make better decisions while reinforcing their resilience to thrive in the highly unpredictable and turbulent world (Gretzel et al., 2020). Given the immense disruptions and crises the H&T sector faces, displaying resilience is essential. Therefore, exploring resilience from the angle of destinations and various stakeholders becomes a significant topic for scientific investigation and practical implementation (Prayag, 2020). From the perspective of destination operations, it is imperative to include research on the resilience of individual organizations. An interesting view on this issue is presented by Sharma et al. (2021), who propose a broader approach to building resilience in the H&T industry, pointing to four factors: government response, local belongingness, technology innovation, and employee and consumer confidence. According to these authors, if we adopt inclusive resilience in the H&T sector, we can achieve a novel economic order globally simultaneously based on sustainable H&T, the well-being of society, reduced climate risk, and the active participation of grassroots communities.

In conclusion, from a destination resilience perspective, the actions of the H&T industry need to be strengthened. Resilience is widely considered and studied at the level of community and destination. Nonetheless, organizational resilience has received less attention in tourism research and needs further development.

Cross-cultural differences in hospitability and tourism and organizational resilience

The H&T sector relies on people. It is also a labor-intensive industry that significantly impacts other sectors of the economy. Koc (2021) suggests that the

Organizational resilience and related concepts in H&T studies   55

social interactions between employees, subordinates and managers, staff and customers, and the general characteristics of H&T services (such as tangibility, inseparability, or heterogeneity) render this sector susceptible to cultural influences. Therefore, culture and cultural differences may determine business success and the resilience of H&T organizations. However, we could only find a few studies that emphasized the cultural context of organizational resilience in the discussed sector. To this end, we examine research on cultural factors in H&T and whether similar concepts or characteristics and selected antecedents of organizational resilience[1] in relation to culture have attracted the interest of H&T scholars.[2]

Research on cross-cultural H&T dates back to at least the 1990s and covers numerous themes (Li, 2014; Sun & Luo, 2021). The demand side of the sector is reflected in studies on service quality, perception or image, tourist attitudes/ intentions, their travel motivation and information-seeking, travel, and destination/restaurant selection behavior (Li, 2014). There are also studies that have examined the impact of black swan events (such as terrorism or pandemics) on tourism in terms of cultural distance/proximity or cultural factors (Cuomo et al., 2021; Juárez et al., 2011; Liu et al., 2021; Peter et al., 2014; Sun & Luo, 2021). For example, Sun and Luo (2021) investigated tourism development in low-risk and high-risk country groups in Asia in terms of terrorist attacks, observing differences between the two groups. Six of Hofstede's dimensions were control variables in this research. They discovered that two dimensions positively impacted tourism development in the low-risk group, namely masculinity and long-term orientation. The same cultural factors had a negative effect on the high-risk group. Moreover, uncertainty avoidance negatively influenced tourism development in the low-risk group. Mattila (2019), in her commentary on cross-cultural research in H&T, provides examples of studies conducted from the customer/marketing perspective and the service provider/management perspective that considered either a single cultural dimension or several or each of the six of Hofstede's dimensions. The demand side was represented in issues such as loyalty programs, pricing, risk perception, volunteer tourism, or tourist complaints, whereas the supply side included topics such as leadership styles, workplace issues, corporate strategies, organizational commitment, or compensation practices. This stream is represented by a research carried out by Sun et al. (2020), which investigated the effect of cultural values on the adoption of technology among hotel employees. The findings revealed that long-term orientation and collectivism positively influenced the perceived usefulness of technology and ease of use of technology, while power distance had an effect only on the perceived usefulness. Moreover, masculinity was negatively related to the technology perceived usefulness. A meta-analysis by Ouyang et al. (2021) on creativity in H&T studies showed partial support for the hypothesis that uncertainty avoidance and long-term orientation are moderators in the association between the examined antecedents and employee creativity. These examples

56 *Organizational resilience and related concepts in H&T studies*

prove that research on cultural differences in H&T has been conducted, and culture influences various aspects of functioning of H&T organizations; it can also shape their resilience.

With respect to resilience, van Strien (2018) holds that resilience in tourism is a product of the social system, having analyzed tourism resilience in the aftermath of two disruptive events in Nepal. He noted that the culture of mistrust in Nepal was left over from short-term collaborative efforts among various tourism stakeholders in response to the disruptions and could prevent transformative resilience in the sector. Ngoc Su et al. (2021) suggested, interpreting the outcomes of their qualitative study, that Vietnamese collectivistic values enabled businesses in this sector to develop organizational resilience struggling with the first wave of the COVID-19 pandemic. Posch et al. (2019) adopted an actor-centered perspective on organizational resilience in their study of lodge owners to explain the relationship between owners' values and disaster resilience in Nepal. They found that the types of disaster risk reduction activities undertaken by lodge owners were strongly correlated with their values. For example, owners who showed the least commitment to preparedness and support for prevention presented above-average fatalistic value orientation. Liu-Lastres et al. (2020) explored the destination resilience of an Indonesian island, discovering that its local culture and Muslim religion helped the island recover and laid the groundwork for tsunami tourism which honors spiritual values.

Regarding the relative scarcity of studies on cultural aspects of organizational resilience in H&T, we looked for scholarly works on crisis/disaster management in the discipline. In their bibliometric analysis of the crisis/disaster management literature, Jiang et al. (2019) imply that resilience is among those topics that are attracting increased scholarly attention and are likely to be noticeable in future studies. This observation is also true for the behavior of consumers in relation to crises/disasters, whose perception of risk is culture specific. Tourists' perceptions of risk may determine whether H&T organizations can quickly bounce back to once again grow their consumer base and return to business after a hazard (Duan et al., 2021). Similarly, the risk perception of service providers/managers in the sector also matters, because it can influence organizational emergency preparedness. Regarding the former, Seabra et al. (2013) obtained inconclusive results for international travelers from countries with different levels of uncertainty avoidance and their perception of risk. Concerning the latter, Peter et al. (2014) examined preparedness for terrorist attacks by assessing the attitudes and risk management approaches of New Zealand hotel managers. They found that managers were not concerned about security, which these authors explained by New Zealand's low score on the uncertainty avoidance index.[3] In their research of crisis management in Jordanian hotels, Sawalha et al. (2013) found that certain characteristics of Arab culture (such as short-term orientation, centralization of power, and others) could slow down the adoption of crisis management best practices. Attitudes and perceptions concerning hotel crisis planning were

Organizational resilience and related concepts in H&T studies 57

also explored by Wang and Wu (2018) in their comparative study of Chinese and Australian managers. They discovered that intentions to undertake crisis planning were driven by different factors in the two national groups due to their association with values of collectivism/individualism and the dimension of power distance. For individualistic and low power distance Australians, attitudes were a significant determinant of intention to implement crisis planning, while for collectivistic, high power distance Chinese, it was perceived control. The cultural background of members of H&T organizations can also affect the way they perceive and respond to adversity, and consequently how they manage crises. Regarding the perception of hazards, Shapoval et al. (2021) studied whether the COVID-19 pandemic was seen differently by hospitality leaders from Israel, Sweden, and the U.S. These authors identified cross-cultural differences in participants' perceptions of the pandemic, but these differences were not always consistent with a country's cultural profile. For example, Swedish participants were significantly worried about the future of the sector, which translated to their personal and professional lives, despite Sweden having a low uncertainty avoidance score and a high indulgence score.

To better comprehend the role of cross-cultural differences in organizational resilience in H&T, we also looked at how culture affects its selected antecedents, namely organizational citizenship behavior, social capital, empowerment, business strategy, and transformational leadership in H&T organizations. With regard to organizational citizenship behavior, we have found that cultural values may directly influence or moderate such behavior. In a study by Magnini et al. (2013), the collectivistic values of society supported the organizational citizenship behavior of South Korean hospitality workers. In another study by Kim et al. (2017), six out of nine cultural values (i.e., uncertainty avoidance, assertiveness, collectivism I, collectivism II, power distance, and gender egalitarianism) moderated the relationship between self-efficacy and reciprocity and four antecedents of organizational citizenship behaviors (i.e., conscientiousness, consideration, civic virtue, and sportsmanship) of South Korean hospitality employees. With respect to social capital, Chon et al. (2020) discussed the so-called Asian paradigm in H&T and pointed out that Asian countries have a relationship-oriented environment conducive to cooperation, which supports social capital development in the sector and its stakeholders. Zoghbi-Manrique-de-Lara and Ruiz-Palomino (2019) explained the mediating effect of social interactions between servant leadership and personal social capital through the collectivistic values of respondents that favor linking their identities to others. Concerning empowerment, Magnini et al. (2013) found that collectivism diminished the comfort level of hotel employees with empowerment, whereas Raub and Robert (2013) showed that the mediating effect of psychological empowerment between empowering leadership and organizational commitment and voice behavior was weaker for cultures of strong power distance in the Middle East and Asia Pacific. As far as business strategy is concerned, the way it is formulated reflects the cultural values of managers (Hofstede & Minkov,

58 *Organizational resilience and related concepts in H&T studies*

2010). A business strategy may show a degree of openness to change, and organizational change is intrinsically linked with organizational resilience (Duchek, 2020; Tasic et al., 2020). The business strategy formulation process in hotels with respect to cultural differences has been investigated in several studies. Ayoun and Moreo (2008) and Ayoun et al. (2010) compared the approaches of top managers to business strategy in the U.S., Malaysia, Thailand, and Türkiye, and discovered a minimal effect of uncertainty avoidance on openness to change but a significant effect of individualism. Regarding transformational leadership, it has not been studied as an antecedent of organizational resilience in H&T with respect to cultural issues. Nevertheless, a meta-analysis conducted by Gui and Zhang (2020) for studies in this discipline uncovered a stronger correlation between transformational leadership and extra activities in collectivistic cultures than individualistic ones, as well as a stronger correlation between organizational climate, satisfaction, and performance in individualistic societies than in collectivistic ones.

In summary, cultural factors in H&T research have been used as independent variables, mediators or moderators, and control variables. Studies have not always reached consistent conclusions. There are studies suggesting resilience links to national/local culture, but this issue appears to be under-recognized. Similarly, a review of work on selected antecedents of organizational resilience in H&T in relation to culture reveals gaps but also shows that these determinants can be modeled by culture. This subchapter argues that it is reasonable to conduct research on organizational resilience in H&T organizations in different countries and to compare results between them. They may also need to examine the measurement properties of the instruments to see if they are culturally loaded.

Notes

1 The subject literature has identified many antecedents of organizational resilience (see Chapter 1); an analysis of each is beyond the scope of this subchapter.
2 Koc (2021) studied the impact of culture on H&T from the demand side (the customer/marketing perspective) and supply side (the service provider/management perspective). Cultural studies concerning the former are more numerous than investigations on the impact of culture on the service provider/management in the H&T sector (Cuomo et al., 2021; Juárez et al., 2011; Liu et al., 2021; Mattila, 2019; Sun & Luo, 2021).
3 It should be noted that, according to Golets et al. (2021), the effect of uncertainty avoidance on H&T is not sufficiently recognized in current research.

References

Adams, P. D., Dixon, P. B., & Rimmer, M. T. (2001). The September 11 shock to tourism and the Australian economy from 2001-02 to 2003-04. *Australian Bulletin of Labour*, *27*(4), 241–257.

Agence France (2016, August 23). France hit by drop in tourism in wake of strikes and terror attacks. *The guardian*. Retrieved 22 February 2022, from www.theguardian.com/world/2016/aug/23/france-hit-by-drop-in-tourism-strikes-terror-attacks

Ahmad, A., Jamaludin, A., Zuraimi, N. S. M., & Valeri, M. (2021). Visit intention and destination image in post-Covid-19 crisis recovery. *Current Issues in Tourism, 24*(17). https://doi.org/10.1080/13683500.2020.1842342

Akgün, A. E., & Keskin, H. (2014). Organisational resilience capacity and firm product innovativeness and performance. *International Journal of Production Research, 52*(23). https://doi.org/10.1080/00207543.2014.910624

Aliperti, G., Sandholz, S., Hagenlocher, M., Rizzi, F., Frey, M., & Garschagen, M. (2019). Tourism, crisis, disaster: An interdisciplinary approach. *Annals of Tourism Research, 79*, 102808. https://doi.org/10.1016/J.ANNALS.2019.102808

Alonso-Almeida, M. del M., Bagur-Femenias, L., Llach, J., & Perramon, J. (2018). Sustainability in small tourist businesses: The link between initiatives and performance. *Current Issues in Tourism, 21*(1). https://doi.org/10.1080/13683500.2015.1066764

Amore, A., Prayag, G., & Hall, C. M. (2018). Conceptualizing destination resilience from a multilevel perspective. *Tourism Review International, 22*(3). https://doi.org/10.3727/154427218X15369305779010

Annarelli, A., & Nonino, F. (2016). Strategic and operational management of organizational resilience: Current state of research and future directions. *Omega (United Kingdom), 62*. https://doi.org/10.1016/j.omega.2015.08.004

Avraham, E. (2015). Destination image repair during crisis: Attracting tourism during the Arab Spring uprisings. *Tourism Management, 47*. https://doi.org/10.1016/j.tourman.2014.10.003

Ayoun, B., & Moreo, P. J. (2008). The influence of the cultural dimension of uncertainty avoidance on business strategy development: A cross-national study of hotel managers. *International Journal of Hospitality Management, 27*(1), 65–75. https://doi.org/10.1016/j.ijhm.2007.07.008

Ayoun, B., Palakurthi, R., & Moreo, P. (2010). Individualism-collectivism insights into the strategic behavior of hotel managers. *Journal of Human Resources in Hospitality and Tourism, 9*(1), 47–70. https://doi.org/10.1080/15332840902942719

Bae, S. Y., & Chang, P.-J. (2021). The effect of coronavirus disease-19 (COVID-19) risk perception on behavioural intention towards 'untact' tourism in South Korea during the first wave of the pandemic (March 2020). *Current Issues in Tourism, 24*(7), 1017–1035. https://doi.org/10.1080/13683500.2020.1798895

Basurto-Cedeño, E. M., & Pennington-Gray, L. (2018). An applied destination resilience model. *Tourism Review International, 22*(3). https://doi.org/10.3727/154427218X153 69305779092

Baum, T., & Hai, N. T. T. (2020). Hospitality, tourism, human rights and the impact of COVID-19. *International Journal of Contemporary Hospitality Management, 32*(7). https://doi.org/10.1108/IJCHM-03-2020-0242

Becken, S. (2013). Developing a framework for assessing resilience of tourism subsystems to climatic factors. *Annals of Tourism Research, 43*. https://doi.org/10.1016/j.annals.2013.06.002

Benjamin, S., Dillette, A., & Alderman, D. H. (2020). "We can't return to normal": Committing to tourism equity in the post-pandemic age. *Tourism Geographies, 22*(3). https://doi.org/10.1080/14616688.2020.1759130

60 Organizational resilience and related concepts in H&T studies

Berbekova, A., Uysal, M., & Assaf, A. G. (2021). A thematic analysis of crisis management in tourism: A theoretical perspective. *Tourism Management, 86.* https://doi.org/10.1016/j.tourman.2021.104342

Beritelli, P., & Bieger, T. (2014). From destination governance to destination leadership – Defining and exploring the significance with the help of a systemic perspective. *Tourism Review, 69*(1). https://doi.org/10.1108/TR-07-2013-0043

Berkes, F., & Ross, H. (2013). Community resilience: Toward an integrated approach. *Society and Natural Resources, 26*(1). https://doi.org/10.1080/08941920.2012.736605

Bethune, E., Buhalis, D., & Miles, L. (2022). Real time response (RTR): Conceptualizing a smart systems approach to destination resilience. *Journal of Destination Marketing & Management, 23,* 100687. https://doi.org/10.1016/J.JDMM.2021.100687

Bhaskara, G. I., & Filimonau, V. (2021). The COVID-19 pandemic and organisational learning for disaster planning and management: A perspective of tourism businesses from a destination prone to consecutive disasters. *Journal of Hospitality and Tourism Management, 46,* 364–375. https://doi.org/10.1016/J.JHTM.2021.01.011

Blackman, D., Kennedy, M., & Ritchie, B. (2011). Knowledge management: The missing link in DMO crisis management? *Current Issues in Tourism, 14*(4). https://doi.org/10.1080/13683500.2010.489637

Blake, A., & Sinclair, M. T. (2003). Tourism crisis management US response to September 11. *Annals of Tourism Research, 30*(4). https://doi.org/10.1016/S0160-7383(03)00056-2

Boniface, M. A., B., Cooper, C., & Cooper, R. (2020). The future geography of travel and tourism. In *Worldwide destinations*. Routledge. https://doi.org/10.4324/9780080454917-34

Borzyszkowski, J. (2013). Destination management organizations (DMO's) and crisis management. *Journal of Tourism & Services, 4*(7), 6–17.

Boukas, N., & Ziakas, V. (2013). Impacts of the global economic crisis on Cyprus tourism and policy responses. *International Journal of Tourism Research, 15*(4). https://doi.org/10.1002/jtr.1878

Broshi-Chen, O., & Mansfeld, Y. (2021). A wasted invitation to innovate? Creativity and innovation in tourism crisis management: A QC&IM approach. *Journal of Hospitality and Tourism Management, 46.* https://doi.org/10.1016/j.jhtm.2021.01.003

Butler, R. (2018). Sustainable tourism in sensitive environments: A wolf in sheep's clothing? *Sustainability (Switzerland), 10*(6). https://doi.org/10.3390/su10061789

Cardoso, C. (2020). The contribution of tourism towards a more sustainable and inclusive society: Key guiding principles in times of crisis. *Worldwide Hospitality and Tourism Themes, 12*(6). https://doi.org/10.1108/WHATT-07-2020-0065

Carpenter, S., Walker, B., Anderies, J. M., & Abel, N. (2001). From metaphor to measurement: Resilience of what to what? *Ecosystems, 4*(8). https://doi.org/10.1007/s10021-001-0045-9

Cartier, E. A., & Taylor, L. L. (2020). Living in a wildfire: The relationship between crisis management and community resilience in a tourism-based destination. *Tourism Management Perspectives, 34.* https://doi.org/10.1016/j.tmp.2020.100635

Cheer, J. M., & Lew, A. A. (2017). *Tourism, resilience and sustainability: Adapting to social, political and economic change.* Routledge Advances in Tourism Series, *August 2017.* Routledge.

Organizational resilience and related concepts in H&T studies 61

Cheer, J. M., Milano, C., & Novelli, M. (2019). Tourism and community resilience in the Anthropocene: Accentuating temporal overtourism. *Journal of Sustainable Tourism, 27*(4). https://doi.org/10.1080/09669582.2019.1578363

Chemli, S., Toanoglou, M., & Valeri, M. (2022). The impact of Covid-19 media coverage on tourist's awareness for future travelling. *Current Issues in Tourism, 25*(2). https://doi.org/10.1080/13683500.2020.1846502

Chen, J., Guo, X., Pan, H., & Zhong, S. (2021). What determines city's resilience against epidemic outbreak: evidence from China's COVID-19 experience. *Sustainable Cities and Society, 70*. https://doi.org/10.1016/j.scs.2021.102892

Chon, K., Park, E., & Zoltan, J. (2020). The Asian paradigm in hospitality and tourism. *Journal of Hospitality and Tourism Research, 44*(8), 1183–1202. https://doi.org/10.1177/1096348020945370

Chu, F. L. (2008). A fractionally integrated autoregressive moving average approach to forecasting tourism demand. *Tourism Management, 29*(1). https://doi.org/10.1016/j.tourman.2007.04.003

Cioccio, L., & Michael, E. J. (2007). Hazard or disaster: Tourism management for the inevitable in Northeast Victoria. *Tourism Management, 28*(1). https://doi.org/10.1016/j.tourman.2005.07.015

Cohen, E., & Neal, M. (2010). Coinciding crises and tourism in contemporary Thailand. *Current Issues in Tourism, 13*(5). https://doi.org/10.1080/13683500.2010.491898

Coombs, W. T. (2007). Ongoing crisis communication: Planning, managing and responding, second edition. In *Physician sportsmedicine*. Sage Publications.

Cuomo, M. T., Tortora, D., Danovi, A., Festa, G., & Metallo, G. (2021). Toward a 'new normal'? Tourist preferences impact on hospitality industry competitiveness. *Corporate Reputation Review, 25*, 212–225. 0123456789. https://doi.org/10.1057/s41299-021-00123-7

Cushnahan, G. (2004). Crisis management in small-scale tourism. *Journal of Travel and Tourism Marketing, 15*(4). https://doi.org/10.1300/J073v15n04_06

Dahles, H., & Susilowati, T. P. (2015). Business resilience in times of growth and crisis. *Annals of Tourism Research, 51*. https://doi.org/10.1016/j.annals.2015.01.002

Davidson, D. J. (2010). The applicability of the concept of resilience to social systems: Some sources of optimism and nagging doubts. *Society and Natural Resources, 23*(12). https://doi.org/10.1080/08941921003652940

Dhiman, S. (2016). The case for eco-spirituality: Everybody can do something. In: S. Dhiman & J. Marques (Eds) *Spirituality and sustainability*. Springer. https://doi.org/10.1007/978-3-319-34235-1_1

Díaz, M. R., & Espino-Rodríguez, T. F. (2016). Determining the sustainability factors and performance of a tourism destination from the stakeholders' perspective. *Sustainability (Switzerland), 8*(9). https://doi.org/10.3390/su8090951

Dogru, T., Marchio, E. A., Bulut, U., & Suess, C. (2019). Climate change: Vulnerability and resilience of tourism and the entire economy. *Tourism Management, 72*, 292–305. https://doi.org/10.1016/J.TOURMAN.2018.12.010

Duan, J., Xie, C., & Morrison, A. M. (2021). Tourism crises and impacts on destinations: A systematic review of the tourism and hospitality literature. *Journal of Hospitality and Tourism Research, 46*(4), 1–29. https://doi.org/10.1177/1096348021994194

62 *Organizational resilience and related concepts in H&T studies*

Duarte Alonso, A., Kok, S., & O'Shea, M. (2018). Family businesses and adaptation: A dynamic capabilities approach. *Journal of Family and Economic Issues, 39*(4), 683–698. https://doi.org/10.1007/s10834-018-9586-3

Dube, K., Nhamo, G., & Chikodzi, D. (2020). COVID-19 cripples global restaurant and hospitality industry. *Current Issues in Tourism, 24*(11), 1487–1490, https://doi.org/10.1080/13683500.2020.1773416

Duchek, S. (2020). Organizational resilience: A capability-based conceptualization. *Business Research, 13*(1), 215–246. https://doi.org/10.1007/s40685-019-0085-7

Eccles, R. G., Ioannou, I., & Serafeim, G. (2012). The impact of a corporate culture of sustainability on corporate behavior and performance. *SSRN Electronic Journal, 60*(11), 2835–2857, https://doi.org/10.2139/ssrn.1964011

Erdogan, N., & Baris, E. (2007). Environmental protection programs and conservation practices of hotels in Ankara, Turkey. *Tourism Management, 28*(2). https://doi.org/10.1016/j.tourman.2006.07.003

Espiner, S., Orchiston, C., & Higham, J. (2017). Resilience and sustainability: A complementary relationship? Towards a practical conceptual model for the sustainability–resilience nexus in tourism. *Journal of Sustainable Tourism, 25*(10). https://doi.org/10.1080/09669582.2017.1281929

Faber, M. H., Miraglia, S., Qin, J., & Stewart, M. G. (2020). Bridging resilience and sustainability – Decision analysis for design and management of infrastructure systems*. *Sustainable and Resilient Infrastructure, 5*(1–2). https://doi.org/10.1080/23789689.2017.1417348

Fall, L. T., & Massey, J. E. (2006). The significance of crisis communication in the aftermath of 9/11: A national investigation of how tourism managers have re-tooled their promotional campaigns. *Journal of Travel and Tourism Marketing, 19*(2–3). https://doi.org/10.1300/J073v19n02_07

Fatoki, O. (2018). The impact of entrepreneurial resilience on the success of small and medium enterprises in South Africa. *Sustainability (Switzerland), 10*(7). https://doi.org/10.3390/su10072527

Faulkner, B. (2001). Towards a framework for tourism disaster management. *Tourism Management, 22*(2). https://doi.org/10.1016/S0261-5177(00)00048-0

Filimonau, V., Derqui, B., & Matute, J. (2020). The COVID-19 pandemic and organisational commitment of senior hotel managers. *International Journal of Hospitality Management, 91*. https://doi.org/10.1016/j.ijhm.2020.102659

Florea, L., Cheung, Y. H., & Herndon, N. C. (2013). For all good reasons: Role of values in organizational sustainability. *Journal of Business Ethics, 114*(3). https://doi.org/10.1007/s10551-012-1355-x

Fyall, A., & Garrod, B. (2020). Destination management: A perspective article. *Tourism Review, 75*(1). https://doi.org/10.1108/TR-07-2019-0311

Ghaderi, Z., Mat Som, A. P., & Henderson, J. C. (2012). Tourism crises and island destinations: Experiences in Penang, Malaysia. *Tourism Management Perspectives, 2–3.* https://doi.org/10.1016/j.tmp.2012.03.006

Glaesser, D. (2006). *Crisis management in the tourism industry.* Routledge. https://doi.org/10.4324/9780080454801

Golets, A., Farias, J., Pilati, R., & Costa, H. (2021). COVID-19 pandemic and tourism: The impact of health risk perception and intolerance of uncertainty on travel intentions. *Current Psychology, 42*, 2500–2513, https://doi.org/10.1007/s12144-021-02282-6

Organizational resilience and related concepts in H&T studies 63

Goodrich, J. N. (2002). September 11, 2001 attack on America: A record of the immediate impacts and reactions in the USA travel and tourism industry. *Tourism Management, 23*(6). https://doi.org/10.1016/S0261-5177(02)00029-8

Gössling, S., & Peeters, P. (2015). Assessing tourism's global environmental impact 1900–2050. *Journal of Sustainable Tourism, 23*(5). https://doi.org/10.1080/09669 582.2015.1008500

Gössling, S., Scott, D., & Hall, C. M. (2020). Pandemics, tourism and global change: A rapid assessment of COVID-19. *Journal of Sustainable Tourism, 29*(1), 1–20. https://doi.org/10.1080/09669582.2020.1758708

Graci, S., & Dodds, R. (2008). Why go green? The business case for environmental commitment in the Canadian hotel industry. *Anatolia, 19*(2). https://doi.org/10.1080/13032917.2008.9687072

Greenfield, W. M. (2004). Attention to people and principles is key to corporate governance and ethics. *Employment Relations Today, 30*(4). https://doi.org/10.1002/ert.10103

Gretzel, U., Fuchs, M., Baggio, R., Hoepken, W., Law, R., Neidhardt, J., Pesonen, J., Zanker, M., & Xiang, Z. (2020). e-Tourism beyond COVID-19: A call for transformative research. *Information Technology and Tourism, 22*(2). https://doi.org/10.1007/s40 558-020-00181-3

Gretzel, U., Werthner, H., Koo, C., & Lamsfus, C. (2015). Conceptual foundations for understanding smart tourism ecosystems. *Computers in Human Behavior, 50*. https://doi.org/10.1016/j.chb.2015.03.043

Gui, C., & Zhang, P. (2020). A meta-analysis of transformational leadership in hospitality research. *International Journal of Contemporary Hospitality Management, 32*(6), 2137–2154. https://doi.org/10.1108/IJCHM-05-2019-0507

Gurtner, Y. (2008). Understanding tourism crisis: Case studies of Bali and Phuket. *Tourism Review International, 10*(1). https://doi.org/10.3727/154427206779307286; www.taylorfrancis.com/chapters/edit/10.4324/9781315162157-3/resilience-theory-tourism-michael-hall

Hall, C. M. (2018). *Resilience theory and tourism.* Routledge. https://doi.org/10.4324/9781315162157-3

Hall, C. M., Prayag, G., & Amore, A. (2017). *Tourism and resilience: Individual, organisational and destination perspectives.* Channel View Publications, https://doi.org/10.21832/HALL6300

Hall, C. M., Scott, D., & Gössling, S. (2020). Pandemics, transformations and tourism: Be careful what you wish for. *Tourism Geographies, 22*(3). https://doi.org/10.1080/14616 688.2020.1759131

Han, S., Yoon, A., Kim, M. J., & Yoon, J.-H. (2022). What influences tourist behaviors during and after the COVID-19 pandemic? Focusing on theories of risk, coping, and resilience. *Journal of Hospitality and Tourism Management, 50*, 355–365. https://doi.org/10.1016/J.JHTM.2022.02.024

Hart, S. L., Milstein, M. B., & Caggiano, J. (2003). Creating sustainable value. *Academy of Management Executive, 17*(2). https://doi.org/10.5465/ame.2003.10025194

Hassan, S. B., & Soliman, M. (2021). COVID-19 and repeat visitation: Assessing the role of destination social responsibility, destination reputation, holidaymakers' trust and fear arousal. *Journal of Destination Marketing and Management, 19*. https://doi.org/10.1016/j.jdmm.2020.100495

64 *Organizational resilience and related concepts in H&T studies*

Hellmeister, A., & Richins, H. (2019). Green to gold: Beneficial impacts of sustainability certification and practice on tour enterprise performance. *Sustainability (Switzerland)*, *11*(3). https://doi.org/10.3390/su11030709

Hestad, D., Tàbara, J. D., & Thornton, T. F. (2021). The role of sustainability-oriented hybrid organisations in the development of transformative capacities: The case of Barcelona. *Cities*, *119*. https://doi.org/10.1016/j.cities.2021.103365

Hofstede, G., & Minkov, M. (2010). *Cultures and organizations: Software of the mind.* McGraw-Hill Professional.

Hristov, D., & Zehrer, A. (2015). The destination paradigm continuum revisited: DMOs serving as leadership networks. *Tourism Review*, *70*(2). https://doi.org/10.1108/TR-08-2014-0050

Innerhofer, E., Fontanari, M., & Pechlaner, H. (2018). Destination resilience: Challenges and opportunities for destination management and governance. In *Destination resilience: Challenges and opportunities for destination management and governance.* Routledge. https://doi.org/10.4324/9780203701904

Jarratt, D. (2021). An exploration of webcam-travel: Connecting to place and nature through webcams during the COVID-19 lockdown of 2020. *Tourism and Hospitality Research*, *21*(2). https://doi.org/10.1177/1467358420963370

Jiang, Y., Ritchie, B. W., & Benckendorff, P. (2019). Bibliometric visualisation: An application in tourism crisis and disaster management research. *Current Issues in Tourism*, *22*(16), 1925–1957. https://doi.org/10.1080/13683500.2017.1408574

Jones, P., & Comfort, D. (2018). Bouncing back: A commentary on resilience in sustainability narratives. *Journal of Public Affairs*, *18*(3). https://doi.org/10.1002/pa.1689

Jones, P., & Comfort, D. (2020). The role of resilience in research and planning in the tourism industry. *Athens Journal of Tourism*, *7*(1). https://doi.org/10.30958/ajt.7-1-1

Juárez, A., Sancho, A., & Gutiérrez, C. (2011). Cultural differences and interferences between China and Spain in the tourism industry. *Balance*, *12*(19.3). www.uv.es/=sancho/Cultural%20Differences%20between%20China%20and%20Spain%20in%20the%20Tourism%20Industry.pdf; https://scholar.google.com/scholar_lookup?title=Cultural+Differences+and+Interferences+between+China+and+Spain+in+the+Tourism+Industry&author=Ju%C3%A1rez,+A.&author=Sancho,+A.&author=Guti%C3%A9rrez,+C.&publication_year=2011&journal=Balance&volume=12&pages=14%E2%80%93879

Khan, A., Bibi, S., Lyu, J., Latif, A., & Lorenzo, A. (2021). COVID-19 and sectoral employment trends: Assessing resilience in the US leisure and hospitality industry. *Current Issues in Tourism*, *24*(7). https://doi.org/10.1080/13683500.2020.1850653

Khazai, B., Mahdavian, F., & Platt, S. (2018). Tourism Recovery Scorecard (TOURS) – Benchmarking and monitoring progress on disaster recovery in tourism destinations. *International Journal of Disaster Risk Reduction*, *27*. https://doi.org/10.1016/j.ijdrr.2017.09.039

Kim, S.-H., Kim, M.-S., Holland, S., & Han, H.-S. (2017). Hospitality employees' citizenship behavior: The moderating role of cultural values. *International Journal of Contemporary Hospitality Management*, *30*(2), 662–684. https://doi.org/10.1108/EUM0000000001079

Kim, Y. J., Kim, W. G., Choi, H. M., & Phetvaroon, K. (2019). The effect of green human resource management on hotel employees' eco-friendly behavior and environmental

Organizational resilience and related concepts in H&T studies 65

performance. *International Journal of Hospitality Management, 76.* https://doi.org/10.1016/j.ijhm.2018.04.007

Koc, E. (2021). *Cross-cultural aspects of tourism and hospitality. A services marketing and management perspective.* Routledge. https://doi.org/10.4324/9781003018193

Kővári, I., & Zimányi, K. (2010). Safety and security in the age of global tourism. *Applied Studies in Agribusiness and Commerce, 4*(5–6). https://doi.org/10.19041/apstract/2010/5-6/11

Kozioł-Nadolna, K., & Beyer, K. (2021). Barriers to innovative activity in the sustainable development of public sector organizations. *Procedia Computer Science, 192.* https://doi.org/10.1016/j.procs.2021.09.214

Lanouar, C., & Goaied, M. (2019). Tourism, terrorism and political violence in Tunisia: Evidence from Markov-switching models. *Tourism Management, 70.* https://doi.org/10.1016/j.tourman.2018.09.002

Laws, E., Prideaux, B., and Chon, K. (2007) Crisis management in tourism: Challenges for managers and researchers. In E. Laws, B. Prideaux, &, K. Chon (Eds.), *Crisis management in tourism* (pp. 1–12). CABI.

Lee, A. v., Vargo, J., & Seville, E. (2013). Developing a tool to measure and compare organizations' resilience. *Natural Hazards Review, 14*(1). https://doi.org/10.1061/(asce)nh.1527-6996.0000075

Lepp, A., & Gibson, H. (2003). Tourist roles, perceived risk and international tourism. *Annals of Tourism Research, 30*(3). https://doi.org/10.1016/S0160-7383(03)00024-0

Leslie, D. (2007). The missing component in the "greening" of tourism: The environmental performance of the self-catering accommodation sector. *International Journal of Hospitality Management, 26*(2). https://doi.org/10.1016/j.ijhm.2006.10.008

Lew, A. A. (2014). Scale, change and resilience in community tourism planning. *Tourism Geographies, 16*(1). https://doi.org/10.1080/14616688.2013.864325

Lew, A. A., Ng, P. T., Ni, C. Cheng (Nickel), & Wu, T. Chiung (Emily). (2016). Community sustainability and resilience: Similarities, differences and indicators. *Tourism Geographies, 18*(1). https://doi.org/10.1080/14616688.2015.1122664

Li, M. (2014). Cross-cultural tourist research: A meta-analysis. *Journal of Hospitality and Tourism Research, 38*(1). https://doi.org/10.1177/1096348012442542

Li, X., Gong, J., Gao, B., & Yuan, P. (2021). Impacts of COVID-19 on tourists' destination preferences: Evidence from China. *Annals of Tourism Research, 90.* https://doi.org/10.1016/j.annals.2021.103258

Liu, A., Fan, D. X. F., & Qiu, R. T. R. (2021). Does culture affect tourism demand? A global perspective. *Journal of Hospitality and Tourism Research, 45*(1), 192–214. https://doi.org/10.1177/1096348020934849

Liu-Lastres, B., Mariska, D., Tan, X., & Ying, T. (2020). Can post-disaster tourism development improve destination livelihoods? A case study of Aceh, Indonesia. *Journal of Destination Marketing and Management, 18*(October), 100510. https://doi.org/10.1016/j.jdmm.2020.100510

Lopes, C. M., Scavarda, A., Hofmeister, L. F., Thomé, A. M. T., & Vaccaro, G. L. R. (2017). An analysis of the interplay between organizational sustainability, knowledge management, and open innovation. *Journal of Cleaner Production, 142.* https://doi.org/10.1016/j.jclepro.2016.10.083

Luthe, T., & Wyss, R. (2014). Assessing and planning resilience in tourism. *Tourism Management, 44.* https://doi.org/10.1016/j.tourman.2014.03.011

66   *Organizational resilience and related concepts in H&T studies*

Magnini, V. P., Hyun, S. (Sean), Kim, B. C. (Peter), & Uysal, M. (2013). The influences of collectivism in hospitality work settings. *International Journal of Contemporary Hospitality Management*, *25*(6), 844–864. https://doi.org/10.1108/IJCHM-07-2012-0127

Mattila, A. S. (2019). A commentary on cross-cultural research in hospitality & tourism inquiry (invited paper for 'luminaries' special issue of *International Journal of Hospitality Management*). *International Journal of Hospitality Management*, *76*(June 2018), 10–12. https://doi.org/10.1016/j.ijhm.2018.06.007

McCartney, G., Pinto, J., & Liu, M. (2021). City resilience and recovery from COVID-19: The case of Macao. *Cities*, *112*. https://doi.org/10.1016/j.cities.2021.103130

Melissen, F., van Ginneken, R., & Wood, R. C. (2016). Sustainability challenges and opportunities arising from the owner-operator split in hotels. *International Journal of Hospitality Management*, *54*. https://doi.org/10.1016/j.ijhm.2016.01.005

Mensah, I. (2006). Environmental management practices among hotels in the greater Accra region. *International Journal of Hospitality Management*, *25*(3). https://doi.org/10.1016/j.ijhm.2005.02.003

Mensah, I. (2014). Different shades of green: Environmental management in hotels in Accra. *International Journal of Tourism Research*, *16*(5). https://doi.org/10.1002/jtr.1939

Miththapala, S., Jayawardena, C. (Chandi), & Mudadeniya, D. (2013). Responding to trends: Environmentally-friendly sustainable operations (ESO) of Sri Lankan hotels. *Worldwide Hospitality and Tourism Themes*, *5*(5). https://doi.org/10.1108/WHATT-05-2013-0027

Mohrman, S. A., & Worley, C. G. (2010). The organizational sustainability journey: Introduction to the special issue. *Organizational Dynamics*, *39*(4). https://doi.org/10.1016/j.orgdyn.2010.07.008

Monterrubio, C. (2017). Protests and tourism crises: A social movement approach to causality. *Tourism Management Perspectives*, *22*. https://doi.org/10.1016/j.tmp.2017.03.001

Moran, B., & Tame, P. (2013). Employee engagement: Advancing organizational sustainability. *Journal of Sustainability Education*, *5*(May). www.susted.com/wordpress/content/employee-engagement-advancing-organizational-sustainability_2013_06/

Ngoc Su, D., Luc Tra, D., Thi Huynh, H. M., Nguyen, H. H. T., & O'Mahony, B. (2021). Enhancing resilience in the Covid-19 crisis: Lessons from human resource management practices in Vietnam. *Current Issues in Tourism*, *24*(22), 1–17. https://doi.org/10.1080/13683500.2020.1863930

Nguyen, D. N., Imamura, F., & Iuchi, K. (2017). Public-private collaboration for disaster risk management: A case study of hotels in Matsushima, Japan. *Tourism Management*, *61*. https://doi.org/10.1016/j.tourman.2017.02.003

Núñez-Ríos, J. E., Sánchez-García, J. Y., Rojas, O. G., & Olivares-Benitez, E. (2020). Factors to foster organizational sustainability in tourism SMEs. *Sustainability (Switzerland)*, *12*(20). https://doi.org/10.3390/su12208657

Orchiston, C., & Higham, J. E. S. (2016). Knowledge management and tourism recovery (de)marketing: the Christchurch earthquakes 2010–2011. *Current Issues in Tourism*, *19*(1). https://doi.org/10.1080/13683500.2014.990424

Orchiston, C., Prayag, G., & Brown, C. (2016). Organizational resilience in the tourism sector. *Annals of Tourism Research*, *56*. https://doi.org/10.1016/j.annals.2015.11.002

Organizational resilience and related concepts in H&T studies 67

Oriade, A., Osinaike, A., Aduhene, K., & Wang, Y. (2021). Sustainability awareness, management practices and organisational culture in hotels: Evidence from developing countries. *International Journal of Hospitality Management, 92.* https://doi.org/10.1016/j.ijhm.2020.102699

Ouyang, X., Liu, Z., & Gui, C. (2021). Creativity in the hospitality and tourism industry: A meta-analysis. *International Journal of Contemporary Hospitality Management, 33*(10), 3685–3704. https://doi.org/10.1108/IJCHM-03-2021-0411

Pandey, A., Gupta, R. K., & Arora, A. P. (2009). Spiritual climate of business organizations and its impact on customers' experience. *Journal of Business Ethics, 88*(2). https://doi.org/10.1007/s10551-008-9965-z

Papatheodorou, A., Rosselló, J., & Xiao, H. (2010). Global economic crisis and tourism: Consequences and perspectives. *Journal of Travel Research, 49*(1). https://doi.org/10.1177/0047287509355327

Paraskevas, A., & Arendell, B. (2007). A strategic framework for terrorism prevention and mitigation in tourism destinations. *Tourism Management, 28*(6). https://doi.org/10.1016/j.tourman.2007.02.012

Pavlovich, K. (2003). The evolution and transformation of a tourism destination network: The Waitomo Caves, New Zealand. *Tourism Management, 24*(2). https://doi.org/10.1016/S0261-5177(02)00056-0

Pennington-Gray, L. (2018). Reflections to move forward: Where destination crisis management research needs to go. *Tourism Management Perspectives, 25.* https://doi.org/10.1016/j.tmp.2017.11.013

Perles-Ribes, J. F., Ramón-Rodríguez, A. B., Sevilla-Jiménez, M., & Moreno-Izquierdo, L. (2016). Unemployment effects of economic crises on hotel and residential tourism destinations: The case of Spain. *Tourism Management, 54*, 356–368. https://doi.org/10.1016/J.TOURMAN.2015.12.002

Peter, C., Poulston, J., & Losekoot, E. (2014). Terrorism, rugby, and hospitality: She'll be right. *Journal of Destination Marketing and Management, 3*(4), 253–261. https://doi.org/10.1016/j.jdmm.2014.03.001

Pforr, C., & Hosie, P. J. (2007). Crisis management in tourism: Preparing for recovery. *Journal of Travel and Tourism Marketing, 23*(2–4). https://doi.org/10.1300/J073v2 3n02_19

Pham, L. D. Q., Coles, T., Ritchie, B. W., & Wang, J. (2021). Building business resilience to external shocks: Conceptualising the role of social networks to small tourism & hospitality businesses. *Journal of Hospitality and Tourism Management, 48*, 210–219. https://doi.org/10.1016/J.JHTM.2021.06.012

Posch, E., Hoferl, K. M., Steiger, R., Bell, R., & Gurung, L. (2019). Ke garne? How values and worldviews influence resilience to natural hazards: A case study from Mustang, Nepal. *Mountain Research and Development, 39*(4), R10–R19. https://doi.org/10.1659/MRD-JOURNAL-D-19-00005.1

Prasad, S., Su, H. C., Altay, N., & Tata, J. (2015). Building disaster-resilient micro enterprises in the developing world. *Disasters, 39*(3). https://doi.org/10.1111/disa.12117

Prayag, G. (2018). Symbiotic relationship or not? Understanding resilience and crisis management in tourism. *Tourism Management Perspectives, 25.* https://doi.org/10.1016/j.tmp.2017.11.012

68 *Organizational resilience and related concepts in H&T studies*

Prayag, G. (2020). Time for reset? Covid-19 and tourism resilience. *Tourism Review International*, *24*(2–3). https://doi.org/10.3727/154427220X15926147793595

Pushpakumara, W. D. H., Atan, H., Khatib, A., Azam, S. M. F., & Tham, J. (2019). Developing a framework for scrutinizing strategic green orientation and organizational performance with relevance to the sustainability of tourism industry. *European Journal of Social Sciences Studies*, *4*(3), 1–18.

Qiu, R. T. R., Park, J., Li, S. N., & Song, H. (2020). Social costs of tourism during the COVID-19 pandemic. *Annals of Tourism Research*, *84*. https://doi.org/10.1016/j.annals.2020.102994

Rasoolimanesh, S. M., Jaafar, M., Kock, N., & Ahmad, A. G. (2017). The effects of community factors on residents' perceptions toward World Heritage Site inscription and sustainable tourism development. *Journal of Sustainable Tourism*, *25*(2). https://doi.org/10.1080/09669582.2016.1195836

Rasoolimanesh, S. M., Seyfi, S., Rastegar, R., & Hall, C. M. (2021). Destination image during the COVID-19 pandemic and future travel behavior: The moderating role of past experience. *Journal of Destination Marketing and Management*, *21*. https://doi.org/10.1016/j.jdmm.2021.100620

Raub, S., & Robert, C. (2013). Empowerment, organizational commitment, and voice behavior in the hospitality industry: Evidence from a multinational sample. *Cornell Hospitality Quarterly*, *54*(2), 136–148. https://doi.org/10.1177/1938965512457240

Rezapouraghdam, H., Alipour, H., & Arasli, H. (2019). Workplace spirituality and organization sustainability: A theoretical perspective on hospitality employees' sustainable behavior. *Environment, Development and Sustainability*, 21(4). https://doi.org/10.1007/s10668-018-0120-4

Ritchie, B. W. (2009). Crisis and disaster management for tourism. In *Crisis and disaster management for tourism*. Channel View Publications. https://doi.org/10.21832/9781845411077

Ritchie, B. W., & Jiang, Y. (2019). A review of research on tourism risk, crisis and disaster management: Launching the annals of tourism research curated collection on tourism risk, crisis and disaster management. *Annals of Tourism Research*, *79*. https://doi.org/10.1016/j.annals.2019.102812

R.-Toubes, D., Araújo-Vila, N., & Fraiz-Brea, J. A. (2020). Be water my friend: Building a liquid destination through collaborative networks. *Tourism Management Perspectives*, *33*, 100619. https://doi.org/10.1016/J.TMP.2019.100619

Ruiz-Ballesteros, E. (2011). Social-ecological resilience and community-based tourism. An approach from Agua Blanca, Ecuador. *Tourism Management*, *32*(3). https://doi.org/10.1016/j.tourman.2010.05.021

Saarinen, J., & Gill, A. M. (2018). *Resilient destinations and tourism: Governance strategies in the transition towards sustainability in tourism*. Routledge. https://doi.org/10.4324/9781315162157

Santana, G. (2004). Crisis management and tourism: Beyond the rhetoric. *Journal of Travel and Tourism Marketing*, *15*(4). https://doi.org/10.1300/J073v15n04_05

Savitz, A., & Weber, K. (2013). *Talent, transformation and the triple bottom line: How companies can leverage human resources to achieve sustainable growth*. Jossey-Bass.

Sawalha, I. H. S. (2015). Managing adversity: Understanding some dimensions of organizational resilience. *Management Research Review*, *38*(4). https://doi.org/10.1108/MRR-01-2014-0010

Sawalha, I. H. S., Jraisat, L. E., & Al-Qudah, K. A. M. (2013). Crisis and disaster management in Jordanian hotels: Practices and cultural considerations. *Disaster Prevention and Management: An International Journal, 22*(3), 210–228. https://doi.org/10.1108/DPM-09-2012-0101

Schianetz, K., Kavanagh, L., & Lockington, D. (2007). The learning tourism destination: The potential of a learning organisation approach for improving the sustainability of tourism destinations. *Tourism Management, 28*(6). https://doi.org/10.1016/j.tourman.2007.01.012

Schroeder, A., & Pennington-Gray, L. (2018). Resilience: The new paradigm for planning. What do we know and where do we need to go? *Tourism Review International, 22*(3). https://doi.org/10.3727/154427218X15369305778994

Scott, D., Gössling, S., Hall, C. M., & Peeters, P. (2016). Can tourism be part of the decarbonized global economy? The costs and risks of alternate carbon reduction policy pathways. *Journal of Sustainable Tourism, 24*(1). https://doi.org/10.1080/09669582.2015.1107080

Scott, N., & Laws, E. (2006). Tourism crises and disasters: Enhancing understanding of system effects. *Journal of Travel and Tourism Marketing, 19*(2–3). https://doi.org/10.1300/J073v19n02_12

Seabra, C., Dolnicar, S., Abrantes, J. L., & Kastenholz, E. (2013). Heterogeneity in risk and safety perceptions of international tourists. *Tourism Management, 36*(1), 502–510. https://doi.org/10.1016/j.tourman.2012.09.008

Shapoval, V., Hägglund, P., Pizam, A., Abraham, V., Carlbäck, M., Nygren, T., & Smith, R. M. (2021). The COVID-19 pandemic effects on the hospitality industry using social systems theory: A multi-country comparison. *International Journal of Hospitality Management, 94*(December 2020). https://doi.org/10.1016/j.ijhm.2020.102813

Sharma, G. D., Thomas, A., & Paul, J. (2021). Reviving tourism industry post-COVID-19: A resilience-based framework. *Tourism Management Perspectives, 37*, 100786. https://doi.org/10.1016/J.TMP.2020.100786

Sigala, M. (2020). Tourism and COVID-19: Impacts and implications for advancing and resetting industry and research. *Journal of Business Research, 117*. https://doi.org/10.1016/j.jbusres.2020.06.015

Sobaih, A. E. E., Elshaer, I., Hasanein, A. M., & Abdelaziz, A. S. (2021). Responses to COVID-19: The role of performance in the relationship between small hospitality enterprises' resilience and sustainable tourism development. *International Journal of Hospitality Management, 94*. https://doi.org/10.1016/j.ijhm.2020.102824

Sonmez, S. F., & Graefe, A. R. (1998). Determining future travel behavior from past travel experience and perceptions of risk and safety. *Journal of Travel Research, 37*(2). https://doi.org/10.1177/004728759803700209

Souza, A. A. A., Alves, M. F. R., Macini, N., Cezarino, L. O., & Liboni, L. B. (2017). Resilience for sustainability as an eco-capability. *International Journal of Climate Change Strategies and Management, 9*(5). https://doi.org/10.1108/IJCCSM-09-2016-0144

Strickland-Munro, J. K., Allison, H. E., & Moore, S. A. (2010). Using resilience concepts to investigate the impacts of protected area tourism on communities. *Annals of Tourism Research, 37*(2). https://doi.org/10.1016/j.annals.2009.11.001

Sun, S., Lee, P. C., Law, R., & Zhong, L. (2020). The impact of cultural values on the acceptance of hotel technology adoption from the perspective of hotel employees.

70 Organizational resilience and related concepts in H&T studies

Journal of Hospitality and Tourism Management, 44(September 2019), 61–69. https://doi.org/10.1016/j.jhtm.2020.04.012

Sun, Y., & Luo, M. (2021). Impacts of terrorist events on tourism development: Evidence from Asia. *Journal of Hospitality and Tourism Research, 46*(4), 1–28. https://doi.org/10.1177/1096348020986903

Tasic, J., Amir, S., Tan, J., & Khader, M. (2020). A multilevel framework to enhance organizational resilience. *Journal of Risk Research, 23*(6), 713–738. https://doi.org/10.1080/13669877.2019.1617340

Thomas, R., Shaw, G., & Page, S. J. (2011). Understanding small firms in tourism: A perspective on research trends and challenges. *Tourism Management, 32*(5). https://doi.org/10.1016/j.tourman.2011.02.003

Thomas, T. E., & Lamm, E. (2012). Legitimacy and organizational sustainability. *Journal of Business Ethics, 110*(2). https://doi.org/10.1007/s10551-012-1421-4

Timur, S., & Getz, D. (2008). A network perspective on managing stakeholders for sustainable urban tourism. *International Journal of Contemporary Hospitality Management, 20*(4). https://doi.org/10.1108/09596110810873543

Ulus, M., & Hatipoglu, B. (2016). Human aspect as a critical factor for organization sustainability in the tourism industry. *Sustainability (Switzerland), 8*(3). https://doi.org/10.3390/su8030232

Utkarsh, & Sigala, M. (2021). A bibliometric review of research on COVID-19 and tourism: Reflections for moving forward. *Tourism Management Perspectives, 40*. https://doi.org/10.1016/j.tmp.2021.100912

van Strien, M. (2018). Tourism business response to multiple natural and human-induced stressors in Nepal. *Community, Environment and Disaster Risk Management, 19*, 87–104. https://doi.org/10.1108/S2040-726220180000019005

Verhulst, E., & Boks, C. (2014). Employee empowerment for sustainable design. *Journal of Corporate Citizenship, 2014*(55). https://doi.org/10.9774/gleaf.4700.2014.se.00008

Volo, S. (2007). Communicating tourism crises through destination websites. *Journal of Travel and Tourism Marketing, 23*(2–4). https://doi.org/10.1300/J073v23n02_07

Vo-Thanh, T., Vu, T.-V., Nguyen, N. P., Nguyen, D. van, Zaman, M., & Chi, H. (2021). How does hotel employees' satisfaction with the organization's COVID-19 responses affect job insecurity and job performance? *Journal of Sustainable Tourism, 29*(6), 907–925. https://doi.org/10.1080/09669582.2020.1850750

Walker, B., & Salt, D. (2006). *Resilience thinking: Sustaining ecosystems and people in a changing world.* Island Press.

Wang, J., & Ritchie, B. W. (2012). Understanding accommodation managers' crisis planning intention: An application of the theory of planned behaviour. *Tourism Management, 33*(5). https://doi.org/10.1016/j.tourman.2011.12.006

Wang, J., & Wu, X. (2018). Top-down or outside-in? Culturally diverse approaches to hotel crisis planning. *Journal of Hospitality and Tourism Management, 36*(February), 76–84. https://doi.org/10.1016/j.jhtm.2018.08.002

Williams, A. M., & Baláž, V. (2015). Tourism risk and uncertainty: Theoretical reflections. *Journal of Travel Research, 54*(3). https://doi.org/10.1177/0047287514523334

Wut, T. M., Xu, J. (Bill), & Wong, S. mun. (2021). Crisis management research (1985–2020) in the hospitality and tourism industry: A review and research agenda. *Tourism Management, 85*. https://doi.org/10.1016/j.tourman.2021.104307

Xu, X., & Gursoy, D. (2015). A conceptual framework of sustainable hospitality supply chain management. *Journal of Hospitality Marketing and Management*, *24*(3). https://doi.org/10.1080/19368623.2014.909691

Yeh, S. S. (2021). Tourism recovery strategy against COVID-19 pandemic. *Tourism Recreation Research*, *46*(2). https://doi.org/10.1080/02508281.2020.1805933

Zenker, S., & Kock, F. (2020). The coronavirus pandemic – A critical discussion of a tourism research agenda. *Tourism Management*, *81*. https://doi.org/10.1016/j.tourman.2020.104164

Zoghbi-Manrique-de-Lara, P., & Ruiz-Palomino, P. (2019). How servant leadership creates and accumulates social capital personally owned in hotel firms. *International Journal of Contemporary Hospitality Management*, *31*(8), 3192–3211. https://doi.org/10.1108/IJCHM-09-2018-0748

3 The conceptual model of organizational resilience in hospitality and tourism

Models of organizational resilience

There are many approaches to conceptualizing organizational resilience (see Chapter 1), and, therefore, different models and tools for the measurement thereof. This subchapter offers a critical overview of selected models and measures in the literature on organizational studies. It needs to be stressed, however, that a quantitative measurement of organizational resilience in the hospitality and tourism (H&T) sector is relatively rare, as it is in business and management research as a whole (Hillmann & Guenther, 2021), but necessary due to the role of this sector in the well-being of local communities and the global economy. Moreover, it needs to emphasize that organizational resilience varies across organizations and the industries in which they operate because it is specific to them and depends on their resources and capabilities. Various authors caution against the temptation to propose a one-size-fits-all tool because resilience appears to be path-dependent and idiosyncratic, nevertheless, attempts to do just that have been made. Moreover, there is an agreement that the construct is multidimensional (Hillmann & Guenther, 2021; Lee et al., 2013; Ortiz-de-Mandojana & Bansal, 2016).

Regarding models of organizational resilience, we begin our discussion with *the relative overall resilience model (ROR)* developed by McManus (2008), as it has been operationalized and applied by other authors in their empirical studies. It also formed a basis for the benchmark resilience scale, which, after adaptation, has been used in studies on the H&T sector, as we explain later in this chapter. Based on a qualitative study of ten organizations from different sectors[1] in New Zealand, McManus (2008) proposed a process model of organizational resilience[2] composed of three elements: "situation awareness", "management of keystone vulnerabilities", and "adaptive capacity", as well as five indicators for each factor (15 indicators in total). *Situation awareness* refers to an ability to notice changes and to understand their meaning for an organization. For example, it includes an analysis of a hazard and its consequences or identifying recovery priorities. *Key vulnerabilities* are "aspects of an organization,

DOI: 10.4324/9781003291350-4

The conceptual model of organizational resilience in H&T   73

operational and managerial, that have the potential to have significant negative impacts in a crisis situation" (McManus et al., 2008, p. 83), and managing them encompasses indicators such as planning strategies or participation in exercises. Finally, *adaptive capacity* reflects that an organization can adjust when changes in its surroundings emerge. McManus et al. (2008) imply that such an ability is a measure of an organizational culture, structures, knowledge management and leadership, the communication system, etc., that facilitate decision making. Based on this model, they indicate what can be done to improve organizational resilience. For example, they suggest using a consequences scenario to boost situational awareness or assessing the criticality of organizational components to continue operations. The ROR model is designed to assess and strengthen organizational resilience and is framed on a quantifiable scale. Still, it aspires to be a universal model so that it may omit some crucial context-specific resilience factors. Furthermore, it was built on a small sample of companies from a single economy and qualitative methodology.

Likewise, other authors have proposed their conceptualization of organizational resilience either as integrative models based on literature reviews or frameworks tested on real-world samples (see Table 3.1). An obvious drawback of the literature-based models is their lack of empirical validation. They represent an attempt to integrate different views and clarify the ambiguity and complexity of the issue, but they often combine contrasting approaches to organizational resilience and make a subjective judgment about the elements that should be included or excluded from the model. Furthermore, the authors do not explain which measures to use for each component in the empirical study. They are built as universal approaches that ignore the contexts of organizational resilience, such as industry or culture. On the other hand, the reviewed empirical models by Gracey (2020) and Tasic et al. (2020) were constructed on small, nonrepresentative samples from a single industry (military and security, respectively). The former offers a benchmark tool for improvements, while the latter attempts to grasp a multilevel aspect of organizational resilience.

Concerning measurement tools, one of the first attempts to assess organizational resilience quantitatively was a measure developed by Mallak (1998) for healthcare organizations. Despite several other authors' efforts to operationalize the concept, Hillmann and Guenther (2021) point out that empirical research still struggles to propose a valid measure of organizational resilience. In their systematic review, they identified 14 different scales of the construct. They found that researchers usually treat resilience as a latent variable and a multidimensional, higher-order construct. There are also the modification of a scale developed by Mallack (1998), scales that derive from a qualitative study by McManus (2008), as well as other scales omitted by Hillmann and Guenther (2021) (see Table 3.2). The measures presented have been used to assess the organizational resilience of different types of organizations by industry, size, or other characteristics (innovativeness, social practices, technology-based),

74   *The conceptual model of organizational resilience in H&T*

Table 3.1 Models of organizational resilience

Model name, authors, year	Organizational resilience conceptualization	Brief description
Models embedded in literature reviews		
A conceptual integrative model, Hillmann and Guenther, 2021	An outcome The defensive perspective	The authors propose a formative model, where cause indicators, such as resilient behaviors (e.g., embracing paradoxes), resources (e.g., relational), and capabilities (e.g., sensemaking) affect organizational resilience which, in turn, contributes to organizational growth, measured as renewal, adaptation, and learning. Organizational resilience is operationalized in the model through maintaining functions, time of recovery, and access to resources.
A capability-based conceptualization, Duchek, 2020	A process and meta-capability The adaptation and anticipation perspectives	The author describes organizational resilience as a process consisted of the anticipation, coping, and adaptation stages. For each of them, she defines critical facilitating capabilities that should be developed by organizations to enhance their resilience. Capabilities that trigger a successful completion of the anticipation stage are the observation and identification of critical events (e.g., environmental scanning, scenario planning) and preparation (e.g., emergency planning, business continuity management); for the coping stage, these are accepting problems, developing solutions, and implementing them (e.g., crisis management), whereas the adaptation stage requires reflection and learning (e.g., review sessions, informal discussions) and organizational change (e.g., change management). Additionally, the model includes three antecedents related to each stage, i.e., "resource availability", "social resources", and "power and responsibility", respectively.

Table 3.1 (Continued)

Model name, authors, year	Organizational resilience conceptualization	Brief description
A four-pillar framework, Koronis and Ponis, 2018	An outcome The adaptation and anticipation perspectives	This model defines four factors that influence the capacity for organizational resilience: preparedness (risk mitigation and crisis preparation), responsiveness (timely and constructive responses), adaptability, and learning, which are shaped by a resilient culture and social capital that support trust, employee engagement and identification with the organization, open communication, and allow for mistakes.
Empirical models		
An organizational resilience maturity framework, Gracey, 2020	A capability The adaptation and anticipation perspectives	The major focus of the model is people as a crucial determinant of resilience. It is built on the British Standard BS 65000 Organizational Resilience and other models, e.g., ROR, and, according to the author, can be used as an audit and assessment tool. The framework includes five areas of assessment with five components for each. These are "business assurance", "business agility", "business planning", "business governance and structures", and "business development". It also enables the evaluation of three strategic core elements: "corporate culture maturity", "strategic vision", and "adaptive leadership". Based on the model, organizations can identify gaps and design plans to close the gaps.
A multilevel framework for enhancing organizational resilience, Tasic et al., 2020	A process and capability The anticipation perspective	The model describes four stages that build organizational resilience: reviewing and monitoring context (evaluating capabilities and the external environment), testing preparedness (simulation scenarios), analyzing and assessing responses (lessons learned), and strengthening capabilities (multilevel learning); and three levels (individual, organizational, and environmental level). It shows how learning the multilevel lessons can enforce organizational capabilities, and, in turn, organizational resilience.

Sources: Based on Duchek (2020); Gracey (2020); Hillmann and Guenther (2021); Koronis and Ponis (2018); Tasic et al. (2020).

76 *The conceptual model of organizational resilience in H&T*

Table 3.2 An overview of organizational resilience scales

Authors and year of publication	Sample	Dimensions
Mallack, 1998	U.S. health care organizations	Goal-directed solution-seeking Avoidance Critical understanding Role dependence Source reliance Resource access
Gittell et al., 2006	The airline industry	Time of recovery
Danes et al., 2009	U.S. small family businesses	Role clarity Decision authority Ownership equality Fairness of compensation Failure to resolve firm conflicts Unfair workloads and competition for resources between family and firm
Somers, 2009 (based on Mallack, 1998)	U.S. municipal public works departments	Goal-directed solution-seeking Risk avoidance Critical situation understanding Ability to fill multiple roles Reliance on information sources Access to resources
McCann et al., 2009	A North American sample of domestic and global firms	Resiliency Agility
Stephenson, 2010 (based on McManus et al., 2008)	Various organizations from the Auckland region, New Zealand	Adaptive capacity Planning strategies
Ray et al., 2011	U.S. business schools	Commitment to resilience scale
Mafabi et al., 2012	Parastatal organizations in Uganda	Organizational adaptation Organizational competitiveness Organizational value
Lee et al., 2013 (based on McManus, 2008)	Various organizations from the Auckland region, New Zealand	Planning capacity Adaptive capacity
Richtnér and Löfsten, 2014	Medium-sized Swedish technology-based firms	Emotional resources Cognitive resources Structural resources
Akgün and Keskin, 2014	Turkish innovative firms	Competence orientation Deep social capital Original/unscripted agility Practical habits Behavioral preparedness Broad resource network

The conceptual model of organizational resilience in H&T 77

Table 3.2 (Continued)

Authors and year of publication	Sample	Dimensions
Whitman et al., 2014 (a shortened version of the benchmark resilience tool)	Organizations from various sectors in Canterbury, New Zealand	Planning Adaptive capacity
Moran, 2016 (based on Mallack, 1998)	Smaller, private, nonprofit U.S. higher education institutions	Goal-directed solution-seeking Avoidance Role dependency
Ortiz-de-Mandojana and Bansal, 2016	U.S. companies with social and environmental practices	Survival
Orchiston et al., 2016	Tourism organizations from the Auckland region, New Zealand	Planning and culture Collaboration and innovation
DesJardine et al., 2019	U.S.-based publicly listed firms	Stability Flexibility
Parker and Ameen, 2018	Small South African firms	Firm resilience

Sources: Adapted from Danes et al. (2009); DesJardine et al. (2019); Hillmann and Guenther (2021); Lee et al. (2013); McCann et al. (2009); Orchiston et al. (2016); Ortiz-de-Mandojana and Bansal (2016); Ray et al. (2011); Whitman et al. (2013).

ownership (state, family), and capital origin, with a predominance of samples collected in the United States.

For the H&T sector, various authors used the scale developed by Lee et al. (2013) and adapted by Orchiston et al. (2016) in their research on tourism organizations (Brown et al., 2019; Chowdhury et al., 2019; Filimonau et al., 2020; Jalil et al., 2021; Pathak & Joshi, 2021; Prayag et al., 2020).[3] Lee et al. (2013) propose a benchmark resilience tool that facilitates the comparison of organizations in terms of strengths and weaknesses with respect to resilience, to build resilience strategies. According to those authors, it enables assessing how resilient organizations are and the design of actions to enhance organizational resilience. It measures planned and adaptive resilience (see Chapter 1) using 13 indicators and 53 items. This tool was adapted in a study by Orchiston et al. (2016) to compare tourism organizations to other types of organizations in respect to their resilience factors. These authors applied 13 items and 13 original indicators proposed by Lee et al. (2013).[4] The scale by Orchiston et al. (2016) is also used in the research conducted for this monograph.

In summary, as we noted in Chapter 1, there is a lack of consistency in how organizational resilience, its antecedents and outcomes are defined and conceptualized, and similar concerns can be raised about models and measures

78 *The conceptual model of organizational resilience in H&T*

of this issue. However, the ROR model, with its subsequent operationalization, has attracted broader interest among resilience researchers. It also forms the basis of a measure used in empirical research on the H&T sector. The review reveals that empirical quantitative research on organizational resilience is sparse, concentrated mainly in the United States and New Zealand, and the sector in question needs to be more represented therein.

Theoretical substantiation of the model

Several conceptualizations of organizational resilience have been made, and a few empirical attempts to measure it in the H&T organizations. They reflect different perspectives on the issue and exhibit either a more comprehensive (e.g., Brown et al., 2018, 2019; Jiang et al., 2019) or focused approach (e.g., Chowdhury et al., 2019; Jalil et al., 2021; Prayag et al., 2020). For instance, Jiang et al. (2019) propose a disaster resilience framework that incorporates a processual view of organizational resilience, defined as a capability. Their model shows how dynamic organizational capabilities and slack resources enable the transformation of existing operational routines into new ones needed to achieve resilience. On the other hand, Brown et al. (2018) constructed a multi-capital model of hotel disaster resilience, which is treated as a process of building various capitals (human, economic, physical, natural, social, and cultural) available to hotels. To measure these capitals, they proposed 18 predictors. The model enables the evaluation of organizational strengths and weaknesses regarding the capital predictors of resilience; this information can then be used to address the identified gaps. The authors tested the model in exploratory research in hotels in New Zealand (Brown et al., 2019). They also showed that employees are a vital capital resource for building organizational resilience. There are also other models of organizational resilience in the sector with a narrower scope. For example, Chowdhury et al. (2019) focused on adaptive resilience and, similarly to Brown et al. (2019), applied a capital-based view to their research, albeit they merely analyzed interfirm social capital as a predictor of resilience. They found that of the three components of social capital, only relational capital positively affects adaptive resilience, improving performance. A human capital-based view on organizational resilience is captured in a study by Prayag et al. (2020), who studied the relationship between three levels of resilience, i.e., psychological, employee, and organizational resilience, in tourism organizations in New Zealand. They proved a strong correlation between the psychological resilience of business owners and managers and employee resilience as well as employee and organizational resilience. Likewise, Jalil et al. (2021) focused on the drivers of organizational resilience embedded in human capital, such as psychological capital and coping mechanisms of owners/managers of small tourism firms in Malaysia. They confirmed that psychological capital is positively linked to organizational resilience. Moreover, psychological capital was significantly associated with problem-focused and emotion-focused strategies, which, in turn, improved organizational resilience.

In our conceptual model of organizational resilience (see Introduction), we build upon the existing concepts and the findings from previous studies. In particular, we share with Prayag et al. (2020) and Brown et al. (2018, 2019) the notion that organizational resilience requires the accumulation of different kinds of capital over time. Similarly to Jalil et al. (2021) and Prayag et al. (2020), our focus is on human capital, reflected in psychological capital and personal social capital, and different levels of resilience (i.e., employee and organizational resilience), respectively. The H&T sector is a service industry that relies heavily on people. Thus, human capital appears critical to developing organizational resilience. We agree with Prayag et al. (2020) that improved employee resilience can enhance organizational resilience. Yet, we also keep in mind that "too many strong resilient individuals can even be a barrier to the development of the shared vision that is needed for resilience" (Hillmann & Guenther, 2021, p. 8). Prior research has not investigated the role of personal social capital for the development of employee resilience. In our model, in contrast to that of Chowdhury et al. (2019) who studied interfirm social capital, we intend to test this relationship. For instance, Tasic et al. (2020) imply that "individuals can develop (…) relational capabilities to better anticipate and respond to adverse events" (p. 716). They also indicate the role of culture and organizational learning in supporting organizational resilience. Thus, our model includes these factors under the construct of organizational learning culture. We predict that the relationship between organizational learning culture and employee resilience can be mediated through employee goal orientation. Specifically, learning-oriented individuals may present a greater ability to learn and grow from adversity as well as to adapt (Brykman & King, 2021; Peng et al., 2022). In addition, they are potentially better able to cope with stress associated with challenging work conditions (van Dam et al., 2021). Furthermore, based on prior research, we hypothesize that learning culture may enhance learning goal orientation, since "in a rich learning climate, employees are more likely to develop a goal orientation toward mastering knowledge and skills and improve their abilities through hard work" (Peng et al., 2022).

We substantiate our conceptual model by means of two theories: *conservation of resources theory* (Hobfoll et al., 2018) in organizational psychology and the *capital-based view* in management theory (Lewin, 2012; Lewin & Baetjer, 2011; Lewin & Cachanosky, 2018). The former is a key concept in understanding how people respond to traumatic events. It allows one to assume that employee resilience develops in environments rich in resources, secure against their loss and support their growth (Hobfoll et al., 2015, 2018). In our model, organizational learning culture is an organizational resource that can activate employees' resilience directly or through their goal orientation (Malik & Garg, 2020; Peng et al., 2022). Additionally, the theory states that resources

80   *The conceptual model of organizational resilience in H&T*

in hand can trigger a gain spiral, which augments other resources. Therefore, in our model, we include personal resources (psychological and social capital) that may initiate a resource spiral, fuel employee resilience and, in turn, organizational resilience (Douglas, 2020; Luthans & Broad, 2020). Furthermore, in the view of conservation of resources theory, various resources interact to create more resources; thus, organizational resilience as a resource can also improve employee resilience. Our model includes psychological capital, which – in the context of resilience in the H&T sector – has been insufficiently addressed but should be addressed because, as a vital characteristic of the individuals who make up the human capital of an organization, it can help them recover in crises and is an essential resource for functioning in a VUCA environment (Fang et al., 2020; Jalil et al., 2021; Luthans & Broad, 2020; Pathak & Joshi, 2021). In addition, the model includes personal social capital, since the ability to form and use social connections can help mobilize resources needed for dealing with hazards. Prior research provides evidence that a high level of personal social capital improves mental health, which is necessary to combat strain (Ruiz-Palomino et al., 2022). Our model also builds on the capital-based view in management theory (Lewin, 2012; Lewin & Baetjer, 2011; Lewin & Cachanosky, 2018) and refers to human capital as a critical factor for developing organizational resilience, as when an organization lacks the proper qualities, other capitals are also unable to drive resilience, as it is humans who activate them (Barasa et al., 2018; Douglas, 2020; Fang et al., 2020; Shela et al., 2023). Therefore, we focus on two components of human capital, i.e., personal capitals relevant in the VUCA era, i.e., psychological and social capital (Fang et al., 2020; Luthans & Broad, 2020). The capital-based view sees an organization as a combination of productive capitals, i.e., organizational resources that add value to the productive process over time or, in other words, create additional resources (Brown et al., 2018; Lewin, 2012). A proper capital combination, which is an outcome of organizing, enables organizations to reach their goals and be resilient. Therefore, resilient organizations can generate an adequate combination of capitals to cope with disruptions. We focus on certain attributes of human capital, which, like any other kind of capital, embodies knowledge but, unlike other forms, is not alienable, creating specific challenges for management (Lewin, 2012).[5] Moreover, the value of human capital in the context of organizational resilience reflects the actual and potential extent to which employees and managers exhibit the ability to anticipate problems, properly address them and adapt. The model identifies antecedents associated with human capital that may play a key role in employee and organizational resilience.

To sum up, based on other conceptualizations of organizational resilience in H&T, we constructed a model for empirical validation that reflects a capital-based view of organizations and concentrates on human capital as a core factor that activates other capitals for resilience in the studied sector. In addition, we assume that employee resilience supports organizational resilience. By referring to conservation of resources theory, the model predicts that resource-rich environments contribute better to organizational resilience than those in which resources are scarce. Therefore, it includes personal and organizational resources that can potentially act as a caravan in building resilience. The model stresses the internal structure of human capital based on psychological and social capital.

Hypotheses, variables, and applied measures

In this part we formulate hypotheses that are tested in the subsequent empirical chapters of the monograph. These hypotheses comprise a comprehensive model showing the direct and indirect components of organizational resilience. We also present the variables, measures, and instrument that we used in the empirical study. Our conceptual model includes three types of variables, i.e., predictors (organizational learning culture, social and psychological capital), mediators (learning goal orientation and employee resilience), and outcome (organizational resilience) that are located on the individual and organizational levels. We will also examine an alternative model in which organizational resilience has a mediating function and employee resilience is the outcome.

The comprehensive model combining individual and organizational antecedents of organizational resilience portrays components of organizational resilience (Figure 3.1).

According to the conservation of resources theory (Hobfoll, 2011; Hobfoll et al., 2018) and the multi-capital model (Brown et al., 2018), we assume

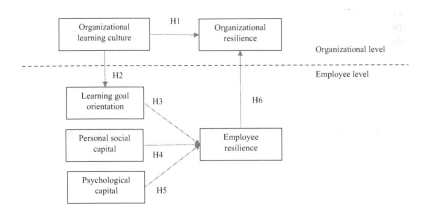

Figure 3.1 Comprehensive conceptual model.

Notes: Direct model: Organizational learning culture → Organizational resilience. Sequential mediation model: Organizational learning culture → Learning goal orientation → Employee resilience → Organizational resilience. Mediation model: Capital (social and psychological) → Employee resilience → Organizational resilience. H = hypothesis.

82 *The conceptual model of organizational resilience in H&T*

conditions for organizational resilience that are located on the organization and employee levels. From an organizational perspective, organizational learning culture is prominent in organizational resilience (Tasic et al., 2020). Therefore, we state that:

Organizational learning culture enhances organizational resilience (**hypothesis H1**) (see direct model).

Moreover, organization and employee levels are closely related. Therefore, organizational learning culture can encourage certain individual resources such as learning goal orientation (Peng et al, 2022), subsequently shaping employee resilience. In line with the multilevel framework for enhancing organizational resilience (Tasic et al., 2020), employee resilience is a core factor for resilience at the organizational level (see the sequential mediation model). Thus, we state that:

Organizational learning culture amplifies individual learning goal orientation (**hypothesis H2**) *and further boosts employee resilience* (**hypothesis H3**) *and, in turn, builds organizational resilience* (**hypothesis H6**).

Regarding the employee level, psychological capital and personal social capital enhance organizational resilience (Brown et al., 2019; Jalil et al., 2021). However, organizational resilience is embedded in employee resilience (Prayag et al., 2020; Tasic et al., 2020). In this regard, we assume that the relationship between both capitals, i.e., psychological capital and personal social capital, and organizational resilience is mediated via employee resilience (see mediation model). Specifically, we argue that:

Personal social capital strengthens employee resilience (**hypothesis H4**) *and further supports organizational resilience* (**hypothesis H6**).

Likewise:

Psychological capital reinforces employee resilience (**hypothesis H5**) *and further increases organizational resilience* (**hypothesis H6**).

We also propose an alternative comprehensive model of employee and organizational resilience (Figure 3.2).

In the conceptual model, the employee-level components (both capitals, learning goal orientation, and employee resilience) drive organizational resilience. There is also exchange between levels, creating a loop from the organizational level to the employee level and back to the organizational level. In the alternative model, organizational resilience stimulates employee resilience. The components of the organizational level drive (feed) the components of the employee level. Thus, the model explores a new mediation model in which an organizational learning culture strengthens organizational resilience (hypothesis H1) and further strengthens employee resilience (*hypothesis H7*). Similar to the conceptual model, there is a multiple predictor model in which social capital and psychological capital stimulate employee resilience (hypotheses H4 and H5, respectively), and a mediation model in which organizational learning culture

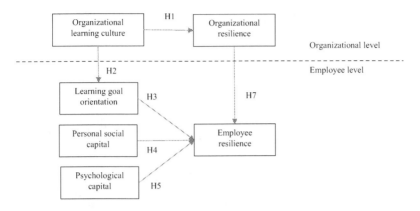

Figure 3.2 The alternative comprehensive model.

Notes: New mediation model: Organizational learning culture → organizational resilience → Employee resilience. Multiple predictors model: Capital (social and psychological) → Employee resilience. Mediation model: Organizational learning culture → Learning goal orientation → Employee resilience.

strengthens learning goal orientation (hypothesis H2) and further reinforces employee resilience (hypothesis H3).

In the following part, we present the variables used in the study and how they were measured.

The outcome variable in the conceptual model is *organizational resilience*, conceptualized in tourism organizations as "the perceived capacity of organizations to adapt to disturbances and seize opportunities emerging from the changed environment" (Prayag et al., 2020, p. 1219). It refers to an organization's adaptive capability and grasp of opportunities in response to the VUCA environment (McManus, 2008). Therefore, in a crisis situation, organizations need both planning and adaptive strategy. As such, planned and adaptive resilience can be built. Planned resilience integrates existing capabilities, i.e., "business continuity" and "precrisis risk management", and prepares the organization for survival. Adaptive resilience is activated during a crisis and is associated with strong organizational culture and innovation (Lee et al., 2013; Orchiston et al., 2016). To measure organizational resilience, we adapted the resilience benchmark tool (Lee et al., 2013) used in a tourism context (e.g., Orchiston et al., 2016; Prayag et al., 2020), consisting of 13 indicators, which assesses both planned resilience (e.g., "We focus on being able to respond to the unexpected") and adaptive resilience based on the features of culture, innovation, and collaboration (e.g., "There would be good leadership from within our organization if

84 *The conceptual model of organizational resilience in H&T*

we were struck by a crisis"). Responses were collected on a 5-point Likert scale (1 = strongly disagree to 5 = strongly agree), where higher scores imply higher level of organizational resilience.

The predictor variables in the model are organizational learning culture, psychological capital, and personal social capital.

Organizational learning culture is conceptualized through the features of a learning organization, as such an organization exhibits a continuous effort toward organizational learning. Organizational learning is the process of collective learning activities and involves shared thoughts and actions, determined by the culture of the organization (Ali et al., 2003; Argyris, 1976; Kim, 1993). In brief, organizational learning is the process of collaborative learning that converts individual knowledge into collective knowledge. In contrast, a learning organization comprises features that promote organizational learning, leading to improved organizational performance (Kim, 1993). In this study, organizational learning culture was evaluated by employing the shortened 21-item Dimensions of Learning Organizations Questionnaire (DLOQ) (Yang et al., 2004). This scale contains seven dimensions that create a culture that supports organizational learning at the organizational level (e.g., "My organization makes its lessons learned available to all employees") and at the level of individual and team learning (e.g., "In my organization, people help each other learn"). According to the theoretical framework, the DLOQ combines both concepts, i.e., learning organization and organizational learning. The learning organization (contextual mechanism) is expressed by "continuous learning", "system connection", and "embedded systems", whereas the organizational learning process is represented by "dialogue and inquiry", "team learning", "empowerment", and "strategic leadership". However, these dimensions are highly correlated and may show the latent trait of learning organization culture (Song et al., 2009). We collected responses on a 5-point Likert scale (1 = strongly disagree to 5 = strongly agree) where higher scores indicate higher organizational learning culture.

Psychological capital is defined as a positive state of development of an individual regarding four personal resources, i.e., hope, self-efficacy, resilience, and optimism (Luthans et al., 2007; Luthans & Youssef, 2004). Hope is a characteristic of a person who strives toward goals and, when needed, changes his/her path to goals. Self-efficacy indicates that an individual believes that s/he can mobilize the necessary motivation, mental resources, or actions to accomplish goals successfully. Personal resilience shows a person's ability to sustain, cope, and adapt in the face of drastic challenges. Moreover, optimistic people view problems as challenges during a crisis (Luthans & Broad, 2020). In view of COR theory, these four personal resources act like a caravan, following and supporting each other (Hobfoll et al., 2018). They also represent the "HERO within" because each of these resources has unique capabilities, but their effectiveness results from collaboration (Youssef-Morgan & Luthans, 2015). Therefore, positive psychological capital is represented as a latent trait including four personal resources. We measure psychological capital with the full version of the PsyCap questionnaire (Luthans et al., 2007), which consists of 24 items combining four components assessing hope resources (e.g., "I can think of many ways to reach my current work goals"), self-efficacy (e.g., "I feel confident contributing to discussions about organizational strategy"), personal resilience (e.g., "I can get through difficult times at work because I've experienced adversity before"), and optimism (e.g., "I'm optimistic about what will happen to me in the future as it pertains to work"). The response options range from 1 (strongly disagree) to 6 (strongly agree), where higher scores show a higher level of psychological capital.

The *personal social capital* of employees can build up the organization's social capital. It can be divided into three types, i.e., "bonding", "bridging", and "linking". Bonding social capital refers to networks connecting employees in the same group or teams, while bridging social capital engages networks that link employees with individuals from other groups, clients, or organizations. Linking social capital includes connections between individuals at different organizational levels and is similar to bridging capital. All types of capitals encompass the size of networks, routine contact, reciprocity, and trustworthiness (Zoghbi-Manrique-de-Lara & Ruiz-Palomino, 2019). Personal social capital was measured by means of an eight-item scale by Wang et al. (2014) adapted to the tourism context by Zoghbi-Manrique-de-Lara and Ruiz-Palomino (2019). Four sentences on bonding refer to personal social capital with peers inside the same group (e.g., "Among the peers in your group, how many can you trust?"). Furthermore, four items on bridging reflect personal social capital with people outside the group (e.g., "Among other entities outside your group [peers from other groups, suppliers, clients, companies, government, associations, NGOs], how do you rate the number of people with whom you have routine contact?"). The response format ranged from 1 (none) to 7 (a lot). The higher the scores, the higher the level of personal social capital.

The mediators in the comprehensive conceptual model (Figure 3.1) are employee resilience and learning goal orientation.

Employee resilience is an emerging individual resource (Näswall et al., 2019). This construct is defined as "an employee's ability, facilitated and supported by the organization, to utilize resources to continually adapt and flourish at work, even if/when faced with challenging circumstances" (Näswall et al., 2015, p. 5). In contrast to resilience as a stable disposition of the individual, this type of resilience reflects the behavior of employees and their adaptive capacity to gather, integrate, and use organizational resources. It is the result of the interaction of individual and external factors. Therefore, employees can use adverse past experiences to behave more flexibly and adaptively in the future (Näswall et al., 2019). Employee resilience was assessed using a nine-item Employee Resilience Scale (Näswall et al., 2015; Näswall et al., 2019), which is unidimensional in nature and reflects the extent to which employees engage in specific

86 *The conceptual model of organizational resilience in H&T*

resilient behavior (e.g., "I learn from mistakes and improve the way I do my job"). The response format ranges from 1 (almost never) to 5 (almost always). The higher the scores, the higher the level of employee resilience.

Learning goal orientation represents employees' mindset when situation requires goal achievement. This individual resource enables employees to develop their skills through self-regulated learning to improve and enjoy working to complete complex tasks (Brykman & King, 2021; Kumar et al., 2022; Warhurst & Black, 2015). Moreover, learning goal orientation cooperates with relational and psychological capital and work engagement (Rozkwitalska et al., 2022). We assessed learning goal orientation using six items derived from the Learning and Performance Goal Orientation Scale (Vandewalle, 1997). For instance, it includes the statement: "At work, I take challenging jobs in order to learn new things". The respondents evaluated each sentence with a 6-point Likert scale ranging from 1 (strongly disagree) to 6 (strongly agree); here higher scores indicated higher level of learning goal orientation.

In summary, based on the conceptual model of organizational resilience we inferred from the literature review, we propose to test two models in our empirical study, both combining individual and organizational components of the phenomenon. In the comprehensive model of organizational resilience, organizational learning culture, social capital, and psychological capital serve as predictors, and learning goal orientation and employee resilience are mediators of organizational resilience. The alternative model predicts that employee resilience is mediated by organizational resilience and shaped by organizational learning culture, learning goal orientation, and both types of capital.

Notes

1 The subsequent subchapter presents selected models of organizational resilience in the H&T sector.
2 Chapter 1 described various approaches to conceptualizing organizational resilience, including viewing it as a process.
3 Njuguna et al. (2021) evaluated the organizational resilience of Kenyan hotels on the basis of a single indicator, namely situational awareness, using seven items obtained from McManus' model.
4 Whitman et al. (2013) also created a shortened version of the benchmark resilience tool based on 13 indicators and 13 items inferred from the scale by Lee et al. (2013) and tested it on a sample of Auckland-based organizations from various sectors. However, some items differ from those included by Orchiston et al. (2016).
5 A capital-based view shares commonalities with the resource-based view or the knowledge-based view and can be regarded as an extension thereof. It expands the former through the notion that the value of productive resources changes over time. It also alters the understanding of knowledge, which in the capital-based view is embedded in all resources and not just in human resources as those views claim (Lewin & Baetjer, 2011).

References

Ali E., Akgün & Keskin, H. (2014). Organisational resilience capacity and firm product innovativeness and performance. *International Journal of Production Research, 52*(23), 6918–6937, DOI: 10.1080/00207543.2014.910624

Ali, E., Gary, S., & John, C. (2003). Organizational learning: A socio-cognitive framework. *Human Relations, 56*(7), 839–868.

Argyris, C. (1976). Single-loop and double-loop models in research on decision making. *Administrative Science Quarterly, 21*(3), 363. https://doi.org/10.2307/2391848

Barasa, E., Mbau, R., & Gilson, L. (2018). What is resilience and how can it be nurtured? A systematic review of empirical literature on organizational resilience. *International Journal of Health Policy and Management, 7*(6), 491–503. https://doi.org/10.15171/ijhpm.2018.06

Brown, N. A., Orchiston, C., Rovins, J. E., Feldmann-Jensen, S., & Johnston, D. (2018). An integrative framework for investigating disaster resilience within the hotel sector. *Journal of Hospitality and Tourism Management, 36*(July), 67–75. https://doi.org/10.1016/j.jhtm.2018.07.004

Brown, N. A., Rovins, J. E., Feldmann-Jensen, S., Orchiston, C., & Johnston, D. (2019). Measuring disaster resilience within the hotel sector: An exploratory survey of Wellington and Hawke's Bay, New Zealand hotel staff and managers. *International Journal of Disaster Risk Reduction, 33*, 108–121. https://doi.org/10.1016/j.ijdrr.2018.09.014

Brykman, K. M., & King, D. D. (2021). A resource model of team resilience capacity and learning. *Group and Organization Management, 46*(4). https://doi.org/10.1177/10596011211018008

Chowdhury, M., Prayag, G., Orchiston, C., & Spector, S. (2019). Postdisaster social capital, adaptive resilience and business performance of tourism organizations in Christchurch, New Zealand. *Journal of Travel Research, 58*(7), 1209–1226. https://doi.org/10.1177/0047287518794319

Danes, S. M., Lee, J., Amarapurkar, S., Stafford, K., Haynes, G., & Brewton, K. E. (2009). Determinants of family business resilience after a natural disaster by gender of business owner. *Journal of Developmental Entrepreneurship, 14*(4), 333–354. https://doi.org/10.1142/S1084946709001351

DesJardine, M., Bansal, P., & Yang, Y. (2019). Bouncing back: Building resilience through social and environmental practices in the context of the 2008 global financial crisis. *Journal of Management, 45*(4), 1434–1460. https://doi.org/10.1177/0149206317708854

Douglas, S. (2020). Building organizational resilience through human capital management strategy. *Development and Learning in Organizations, 35*(5), 19–21. https://doi.org/10.1108/DLO-08-2020-0180

Duchek, S. (2020). Organizational resilience: A capability-based conceptualization. *Business Research, 13*(1), 215–246. https://doi.org/10.1007/s40685-019-0085-7

Fang, S. (Echo), Prayag, G., Ozanne, L. K., & de Vries, H. (2020). Psychological capital, coping mechanisms and organizational resilience: Insights from the 2016 Kaikoura earthquake, New Zealand. *Tourism Management Perspectives, 34*(March 2019), 100637. https://doi.org/10.1016/j.tmp.2020.100637

Filimonau, V., Derqui, B., & Matute, J. (2020). The COVID-19 pandemic and organisational commitment of senior hotel managers. *International Journal of Hospitality Management, 91*(July), 102659. https://doi.org/10.1016/j.ijhm.2020.102659

Gittell, J. H., Cameron, K., Lim, S., & Rivas, V. (2006) Relationships, layoffs, and organizational resilience: Airline industry responses to September 11. *The Journal of Applied Behavioral Science, 42*(3), 300–329.

Gracey, A. (2020). Building an organisational resilience maturity framework. *Journal of Business Continuity & Emergency Planning, 13*(4), 313–327.

Hillmann, J., & Guenther, E. (2021). Organizational resilience: A valuable construct for management research? *International Journal of Management Reviews, 23*(1), 7–44. https://doi.org/10.1111/ijmr.12239

Hobfoll, S. E. (2011). Conservation of resources theory: Its implication for stress, health, and resilience. In S. Folkman (Ed.), *The Oxford handbook of stress, health, and coping* (pp. 127–147). Oxford University Press.

Hobfoll, S. E., Halbesleben, J., Neveu, J.-P., & Westman, M. (2018). Conservation of resources in the organizational context: The reality of resources and their consequences. *Annual Review of Organizational Psychology and Organizational Behavior, 5*, 103–128. https://doi.org/10.1146/annurev-orgpsych-

Hobfoll, S. E., Stevens, N. R., & Zalta, A. K. (2015). Expanding the science of resilience: Conserving resources in the aid of adaptation. *Psychological Inquiry, 26*(2), 174–180. https://doi.org/10.1080/1047840X.2015.1002377

Jalil, M. F., Ali, A., Ahmed, Z., & Kamarulzaman, R. (2021). The mediating effect of coping strategies between psychological capital and small tourism organization resilience: Insights from the COVID-19 pandemic, Malaysia. *Frontiers in Psychology, 12*(December), 1–15. https://doi.org/10.3389/fpsyg.2021.766528

Jiang, Y., Ritchie, B. W., & Verreynne, M. L. (2019). Building tourism organizational resilience to crises and disasters: A dynamic capabilities view. *International Journal of Tourism Research, 21*(6), 882–900. https://doi.org/10.1002/jtr.2312

Kim, D. H. (1993). The link between individual and organizational learning. *The Strategic Management of Intellectual Capital, Sloan Management Review, 35*(1), 37–50. https://doi.org/10.1016/b978-0-7506-9850-4.50006-3

Koronis, E., & Ponis, S. (2018). Better than before: The resilient organization in crisis mode. *Journal of Business Strategy, 39*(1), 32–42. https://doi.org/10.1108/JBS-10-2016-0124

Kumar, D., Upadhyay, Y., Yadav, R., & Goyal, A. K. (2022). Psychological capital and innovative work behaviour: The role of mastery orientation and creative self-efficacy. *International Journal of Hospitality Management, 102*(December 2021), 103157. https://doi.org/10.1016/j.ijhm.2022.103157

Lee, A. V., Vargo, J., & Seville, E. (2013). Developing a tool to measure and compare organizations' resilience. *Natural Hazards Review, 14*(1), 29–41. https://doi.org/10.1061/(asce)nh.1527-6996.0000075

Lewin, P. (2012). A capital-based approach to the firm: Reflections on the nature and scope of the concept of capital and its extension to intangibles. In A. Burton-Jones & J. -C. Spender (Eds.), *The Oxford handbook of human capital* (pp. 146–162). Oxford University Press. https://doi.org/10.1093/oxfordhb/9780199532162.003.0006

Lewin, P., & Baetjer, H. (2011). The capital-based view of the firm. *Review of Austrian Economics, 24*(4), 335–354. https://doi.org/10.1007/s11138-011-0149-1

The conceptual model of organizational resilience in H&T 89

Lewin, P., & Cachanosky, N. (2018). Substance and semantics: The question of capital. *Journal of Economic Behavior and Organization, 150*, 423–431. https://doi.org/10.1016/j.jebo.2018.01.024

Luthans, F., Avolio, B. J., Avey, J. B., & Norman, S. M. (2007). Positive psychological capital: Measurement and relationship with performance and satisfaction. *Personnel Psychology, 60*(3), 541–572. https://doi.org/10.1111/j.1744-6570.2007.00083.x

Luthans, F., & Broad, J. D. (2020). Positive psychological capital to help combat the mental health fallout from the pandemic and VUCA environment. *Organizational Dynamics, 2019*, 100817. https://doi.org/10.1016/j.orgdyn.2020.100817

Luthans, F., & Youssef, C. M. (2004). Human, social, and now positive psychological capital management: Investing in people for competitive advantage. *Organizational Dynamics, 33*(2), 143–160. https://doi.org/10.1016/j.orgdyn.2004.01.003

Mafabi, S., Munene, J., & Ntayi, J. (2012). Knowledge management and organisational resilience: Organisational innovation as a mediator in Uganda parastatals. *Journal of Strategy and Management, 5*(1), 57–80. https://doi.org/10.1108/17554251211200455

Malik, P., & Garg, P. (2020). Learning organization and work engagement: The mediating role of employee resilience. *International Journal of Human Resource Management, 31*(8), 1071–1094. https://doi.org/10.1080/09585192.2017.1396549

Mallak, L. A. (1998). Measuring resilience in health care provider organizations. *Health Manpower Management, 24*(4–5), 148–152. https://doi.org/10.1108/0955206981 0215755

McCann, J., Selsky, J., & Lee, J. (2009). Building agility, resilience and performance in turbulent environments. *People and Strategy, 32*(3), 44.

McManus, S. (2008). *Organisational resilience in New Zealand* [University of Canterbury]. https://ir.canterbury.ac.nz/handle/10092/1574

McManus, S., Seville, E., Vargo, J., & Brunsdon, D. (2008). Facilitated process for improving organizational resilience. *Natural Hazards Review, 9*(2), 81–90. https://doi.org/10.1061/(asce)1527-6988(2008)9:2(81)

Moran, K. A. (2016). Organizational resilience: Sustained institutional effectiveness among smaller, private, non-profit US higher education institutions experiencing organizational decline. *Work, 54*(2), 267–281. https://doi.org/10.3233/WOR-162299

Näswall, K., Kuntz, J., & Malinen, S. (2015). Employee Resilience Scale (EmpRes) measurement properties. *Resilient Organisations Research Report* (Issue August).

Näswall, K., Malinen, S., Kuntz, J., & Hodliffe, M. (2019). Employee resilience: Development and validation of a measure. *Journal of Managerial Psychology, 34*(5), 353–367. https://doi.org/10.1108/JMP-02-2018-0102

Njuguna, P. K., Maingi, S., & Kiria, S. (2021). Recruitment and employee training and organisational resilience in Kenyan hotels. *African Journal of Hospitality, Tourism and Leisure, 10*(3), 999–1012. https://doi.org/10.46222/ajhtl.19770720-145

Orchiston, C., Prayag, G., & Brown, C. (2016). Organizational resilience in the tourism sector. *Annals of Tourism Research, 56*, 145–148. https://doi.org/10.1016/j.annals.2015.11.002

Ortiz-de-Mandojana, N., & Bansal, P. (2016). The long-term benefits of organizational resilience through sustainable business practices. *Strategic Management Journal, 37*(8), 1615–1631. https://doi.org/10.1002/smj

Parker, H. & Khadija, A., (2018). The role of resilience capabilities in shaping how firms respond to disruptions. *Journal of Business Research*, Elsevier, 88(C), 535–541.

90 *The conceptual model of organizational resilience in H&T*

Pathak, D., & Joshi, G. (2021). Impact of psychological capital and life satisfaction on organizational resilience during COVID-19: Indian tourism insights. *Current Issues in Tourism*, *24*(17), 2398–2415. https://doi.org/10.1080/13683500.2020.1844643

Peng, J., Xie, L., Zhou, L., & Huan, T. C. (TC). (2022). Linking team learning climate to service performance: The role of individual- and team-level adaptive behaviors in travel services. *Tourism Management*, *91*(February), 104481. https://doi.org/10.1016/j.tourman.2021.104481

Prayag, G., Spector, S., Orchiston, C., & Chowdhury, M. (2020). Psychological resilience, organizational resilience and life satisfaction in tourism firms: Insights from the Canterbury earthquakes. *Current Issues in Tourism*, *23*(10), 1216–1233. https://doi.org/10.1080/13683500.2019.1607832

Ray, J. L., Baker, L. T., & Plowman, D. A. (2011). Organizational mindfulness in business schools. *Academy of Management Learning and Education*, *10*(2), 188–203. https://doi.org/10.5465/AMLE.2011.62798929

Richtnér, A., & Löfsten, H. (2014). How the capacity for resilience influence creativity. *R&D Manage*, *44*, 137–151. https://doi.org/10.1111/radm.12050

Rozkwitalska, M., Basinska, B. A., Okumus, F., & Karatepe, O. M. (2022). The effects of relational and psychological capital on work engagement: The mediation of learning goal orientation. *Journal of Organizational Change Management*, 35(3), 616–629. https://doi.org/10.1108/jocm-07-2021-0222

Ruiz-Palomino, P., Yáñez-Araque, B., Jiménez-Estévez, P., & Gutiérrez-Broncano, S. (2022). Can servant leadership prevent hotel employee depression during the COVID-19 pandemic? A mediating and multigroup analysis. *Technological Forecasting and Social Change*, *174*. https://doi.org/10.1016/j.techfore.2021.121192

Shela, V., Ramayah, T., & Noor Hazlina, A. (2023). Human capital and organisational resilience in the context of manufacturing: a systematic literature review. *Journal of Intellectual Capital*. 24(2), 535–559. https://doi.org/10.1108/JIC-09-2021-0234

Somers, S. (2009). Measuring resilience potential: An adaptive strategy for organizational crisis planning. *Journal of Contingencies and Crisis Management*, 17, 12–23. https://doi.org/10.1111/j.1468-5973.2009.00558.x

Song, J. H., Joo, B. K., & Chermack, T. J. (2009). The dimensions of learning organization questionnaire (DLOQ): A validation study in a Korean context. *Human Resource Development Quarterly*, *20*(1), 43–64. https://doi.org/10.1002/hrdq.20007

Tasic, J., Amir, S., Tan, J., & Khader, M. (2020). A multilevel framework to enhance organizational resilience. *Journal of Risk Research*, *23*(6), 713–738. https://doi.org/10.1080/13669877.2019.1617340

van Dam, A., Noordzij, G., & Born, M. (2021). Social workers and recovery from stress. *Journal of Social Work*, *21*(5), 999–1018. https://doi.org/10.1177/1468017320911350

Vandewalle, D. (1997). Development and validation of a Work Domain Goal Orientation Instrument. *Educational and Psychological Measurement*, *57*(6), 995–1015. https://doi.org/0803973233

Wang, P., Chen, X., Gong, J., & Jacques-Tiura, A. J. (2014). Reliability and validity of the Personal Social Capital Scale 16 and Personal Social Capital Scale 8: Two short instruments for survey studies. *Social Indicators Research*, *119*(2), 1133–1148. https://doi.org/10.1007/s11205-013-0540-3

Warhurst, R. P., & Black, K. E. (2015). It's never too late to learn. *Journal of Workplace Learning*, *27*(6), 457–472. https://doi.org/10.1108/JWL-07-2014-0050

Whitman, Z. R., Kachali, H., Roger, D., Vargo, J., & Seville, E. (2013). Short-form version of the Benchmark Resilience Tool (BRT-53). *Measuring Business Excellence, 17*(3), 3–14. https://doi.org/10.1108/MBE-05-2012-0030

Whitman, Z. R., Tevenson, J., Kachali, H., Seville, E., Vargo, J., & Wilson, T. (2014). Organisational resilience following the Darfield earthquake of 2010. *Disasters, 38*(1), 148–177. https://doi.org/10.1111/disa.12036

Yang, B., Watkins, K. E., & Marsick, V. J. (2004). The construct of the learning organization: Dimensions, measurement, and validation. *Human Resource Development Quarterly, 15*(1), 31–55. https://doi.org/10.1002/hrdq.1086

Youssef-Morgan, C. M., & Luthans, F. (2015). Psychological capital and well-being. *Stress Health, 31,* 180–188. doi: 10.1002/smi.2623

Zoghbi-Manrique-de-Lara, P., & Ruiz-Palomino, P. (2019). How servant leadership creates and accumulates social capital personally owned in hotel firms. *International Journal of Contemporary Hospitality Management, 31*(8), 3192–3211. https://doi.org/10.1108/IJCHM-09-2018-0748

4 Organizational resilience in Polish hospitality and tourism organizations

The Polish hospitality and tourism sector – environmental analysis

All business entities operate in a specific environment to which they are closely connected with and are part of. Any market entity can only be considered with the environment, as it largely determines the entity's place, decisions, and potential success (Panasiuk, 2019). The factors of the environment condition include both the activities of hotel and tourism (H&T) enterprises and other entities of the tourism economy, as well as tourism destinations (i.e., tourist destinations and regions and entire countries). These are cultural, social, political-legal, natural-ecological, mega-economic, macroeconomic, and technological, in the structure of supply, in the structure of demand, and related to crisis phenomena (Panasiuk, 2019). Panasiuk (2019) conducted a study aiming to evaluate the influence of macro-environmental factors on the operations of a comprehensive tourism business (tourism enterprises) across three-time horizons: short-term (operational), medium-term (tactical), and long-term (strategic). Subjectively adopted rank sizes allowed for the estimation of the impact of individual factors on Polish enterprises. The analysis shows that three groups of factors have by far the greatest impact, namely:

- political-legal factors – general and specific legal regulations on tourism business, internal passport policy and visa policy of other countries, the internal political situation in the country and the European Union and in relations with other countries, especially destinations, but also emission countries,
- macroeconomic factors – economic growth, real incomes, consumption levels, unemployment levels, inflation levels, trade balance, budget deficit, tax regimes, exchange rates, industrialization and post-industrialization,
- crisis factors – sudden economic downturns, natural disasters in reception areas, terrorist activities, military conflicts, local and supra-local social-political crises, environmental and industrial disasters, prolonged adverse weather conditions in reception areas, epidemics and pandemics.

(Panasiuk, 2019)

DOI: 10.4324/9781003291350-5

First, we looked at legal and organizational regulations regarding the tourism business, including the hotel and tourism organization and management system. Such a system significantly affects the manner and scope of the entire hotel and tourism industry. The organization and management system of tourism in Poland in its current form was developed in 2000 and is similar to solutions found in many other European countries (Borzyszkowski, 2005). In 2000, by virtue of the Act on the Polish Tourist Organization (Ustawa, 1999), the Polish Tourist Organization (POT), which is a typical national tourist organization (NTO) and is responsible for operational objectives mainly related to tourism promotion at home and abroad, was established. The specific tasks of the POT include:

- promoting Poland as a country that is attractive to tourists,
- ensuring the functioning and development of the Polish tourist information system in the country and abroad,
- initiating, giving opinions and supporting plans for the development and modernization of tourist infrastructure,
- inspiring the creation of regional tourism organizations, covering the area of one or more provinces, and local tourism organizations, covering the area of one or more local government units, and cooperating with them.

(Ustawa, 1999)

In turn, the functions of the National Tourism Administration (NTA) are currently performed by the Ministry of Sports and Tourism. Its primary tourism-related tasks include:

- the formation of policies on tourism development and matters related to the country's tourism development and mechanisms regulating the tourism market,
- programming development and shaping the legal and economic mechanisms of tourism,
- coordinating work on the development, implementation and monitoring of strategic documents for the development of the tourism sector,
- conducting matters related to international cooperation in tourism,
- coordinating matters related to the education and professional development of tourism personnel and in the field of recognition of qualifications acquired in the Member States of the European Union to perform professions and activities in the field of tourism,
- coordinating the implementation of the minister responsible for tourism tasks, as specified in relevant legal acts.

(Zarządzanie nr 21..., 2019)

94 *Organizational resilience in Polish H&T organizations*

The above structures are supplemented by other entities operating at lower levels of administrative division, e.g., regional tourist organizations (RTOs). There are 16 such organizations, one in each of the provinces (regions). On the other hand, at the local level, there are local tourist organizations (LTOs), of which there are currently approximately 130 (Polska Organizacja Turystyczna, 2022). It is important to note that the Act on the Polish Tourism Organization (Ustawa, 1999) does not specify separate tasks for RTOs and LTOs. All three entities (POT, RTOs, and LTOs) are responsible for operational activities, primarily focused on promoting tourism within a specific region. Additionally, their key tasks may involve supporting the operation and growth of tourist information services and providing input and assistance in creating plans to enhance and modernize tourist infrastructure. In Poland, the consequence of the lack of separation of roles and responsibilities between RTOs and LTOs, as well as the preservation of voluntary membership of local government units and businesses in these organizations, is the constant search for the most effective solutions that would constitute an appropriate framework for tourism management (Zmyślony, 2018). Regardless, the system of tourism organizations (POT-RTOs-LTOs) thus developed has a supervisory and supportive function with regard to hotel and tourism entities and enterprises operating throughout the country.

In the opinion of many experts, the aforementioned Act on the Polish Tourist Organization (Ustawa, 1999) should be subject to significant modifications and changes. This is due, among other things, to the fact that the solutions proposed more than 20 years ago now do not fully correspond to the rules of the modern tourism market. Hence, work is underway to amend this law. New solutions are also being prepared, which will significantly affect the operation of Poland's hotel and tourism market. These solutions include, among others, the obligation to keep records of all accommodation facilities (and thus regulate the principles of short-term accommodation), the need to adjust regulations for tour guides, reform of the tourism promotion system, or the introduction of a tourism fee (Ministerstwo Rozwoju, 2021). To an important extent, changes should affect the abovementioned promotion system (POT-RTOs-LTOs), mainly including local tourist organizations, which in many cases do not fulfill their designated role (Stefanowska & Lipko-Kowalska, 2017). Increased discussion is also being devoted to the introduction of a tourist (residence) fee, which would replace the existing local fee. It would be introduced along the lines of solutions in force in other countries, where it is an important instrument for financing tourism (Borzyszkowski, 2018). It is intended to be universal in nature (to be in force throughout the country and apply to all accommodation facilities), and its implementation would support several entities involved in the process of tourism development in the country, such as LTOs (Gonera & Zmyślony, 2017).

In Poland, as in many other countries, the basic regulations related to the functioning of the tourism market take place through certain law provisions. The most important legislation is the Act of November 24, 2017, on Tourist Events and Related Travel Services (Ustawa, 2017), which replaced the previous Travel Services Act (Ustawa, 1997). Referred to as the "new tourism constitution", the new law has become the most important piece of legislation regulating the activities of tour operators, travel agents, and travel intermediaries. It is worth noting that significant changes have been introduced, including measures to protect travelers from the repercussions of tour operators' insolvency and to facilitate the purchase of tourist services (Maciąg, 2018). As a member of the European Union, Poland is subject to EU regulations in many areas of the tourism market functioning. The legal instruments used by the European Union are mainly legal norms regulating the principles of operation of tourism market entities (Bosiacki & Panasiuk, 2017). The most important areas of tourism market regulation, according to the regulations of European law, are the protection of the competitive market, together with the promotion of competition mechanisms in the tourism market, as well as the protection of the consumer in this market. This follows directly from the regulations of two consecutive EU directives (Council Directive, 1990, Dyrektywa Parlamentu, 2015). In general, in areas where the European Union has exclusive competence, only the Union has the authority to legislate and adopt legally binding acts. At the same time, member states can do so only under the authorization of the Union or to implement regulations issued by it. Slightly greater possibilities of issuing national regulations apply to areas where the European Union shares competence with member states (shared competence) (Cybula & Zawistowska, 2017).

On the other hand, membership in the European Union has created many opportunities to support the Polish hotel and tourism sector. Since 2004, EU funds have been an important means of financial resources in the tourism economy in Poland. In subsequent financial plans, the funds were directed to activities carried out by local government units and tourism organizations. Tourism entrepreneurs could obtain these funds much less (Panasiuk, 2014). From the financial perspective for 2007–2013, tourism and culture were among the main priority axes in the regional operational programs (ROPs) managed through provincial governments. The prioritization of tourism in the analyzed documents indicated its importance to the main developmental determinants of the various regions of Poland. The main activities included in the priority axes related to the development of tourism in the regions were, e.g., the construction, expansion, and modernization of the tourist base; the construction, expansion, and modernization of public tourist and recreational infrastructure; the creation of regional and supra-regional tourist products; the creation of regional tourist information systems; and the promotion of tourism (nationally and internationally; Bosiacki & Panasiuk, 2017).

Macroeconomic factors play an essential role in shaping the size and structure of the hotel and tourism sector. For many years, Poland was a country with relatively good macroeconomic indicators. From 1994, the Polish economy experienced a period of recovery, brought about by the pro-supply reforms

96 *Organizational resilience in Polish H&T organizations*

introduced in 1992–1993 and the slow recovery of the economy from the transformation crisis, among other things. This positive developmental trend lasted until the August 1998 financial crisis in Russia. The absorption of external financial shocks and the policy of economic cooling meant that Poland's economy was characterized by slowing economic growth from the end of 1998 to the end of 2003. Apparent economic growth occurred in 2004 due to Poland's accession to the European Union, access to European funds, and putting public finances in order (Nazarczuk & Marks-Bielska, 2009). Generally, it can be assumed that the driving force behind Poland's economic growth in 1989–2017 was primarily rising labor productivity, a consequence of technological innovation and imitation, and the stock of highly skilled workers. In contrast, it was not due to low labor force wages (Malaga, 2018).

One of the most important macroeconomic factors is the level of unemployment. In the case of Poland, it began to increase markedly during the period of economic transition (after 1989). Significant changes were noted in 2004 when Poland's entry into the European Union resulted in a decrease in the level of unemployment. The opening of the European labor market additionally created the possibility of seeking employment outside the country. A period of large labor emigration began. Departures of Poles abroad intensified in 2006–2007 when it is widely estimated that approximately 2 million people left Poland (Bobrowska, 2013). From the beginning of 2004 to March 2008, there was a decline in unemployment. This positive trend in the labor market was not solely due to emigration but also resulted from high economic growth, increased spending on labor market programs to activate the unemployed, and the utilization of European Union funds. The number of unemployed decreased by more than 2 million during this period. However, in 2008, the number of unemployed increased again, as the international financial crisis triggered changes in the labor market. In the subsequent years, unemployment remained high. Only in 2014, with a slight improvement in the European economy, Poland experienced a higher economic growth rate than in the previous two years. Thanks to this, unemployment rapidly declined in the following years (Jarosz-Nojszewska, 2018). The year 2020 brought many changes not only in Poland but also globally. The events associated with the COVID-19 pandemic undoubtedly also left their mark on global, national, and local labor markets. Today, job insecurity has become a permanent feature of the labor market. In July 2021, there were 974,900 people unemployed in Poland (an overall unemployment rate of 5.8%), compared to 1,029,500 people (6.1%) a year earlier, with the number of jobless at 868,400 (5.2%) as recently as July 2019 (Czapski, 2021).

The rate of inflation is also an important macroeconomic factor. During the period of economic transition, it was the highest, reaching up to several hundred percent per year (1989–1990). In subsequent years, a marked decline was noticeable. Even the period of economic crisis did not noticeably affect the level of inflation (e.g., in 2008 it was 4.2%, and in 2009 it was 3.5%), and in 2015–2016 there was even deflation (0.9% and 0.6%, respectively). Recent years have been a period of first slow and then marked inflation growth: as of July 2022, year-on-year inflation was 15.6% (Główny Urząd Statystyczny, 2022a).

As mentioned, the so-called crisis factors are also important from the point of view of the operation of the tourism sector in Poland. Like any field of the economy, tourism is exposed to various risks. On the one hand, these risks relate to the possible behavior of consumers (demand) in certain conditions, and on the other hand, they relate to the very functioning of tourism enterprises (Gabryjończyk & Gabryjończyk, 2021). For many years, Polish tourism was relatively immune to crisis. On the other hand, the actions of state, regional, and local authorities had not adapted to such situations. The global economic crisis of 2008 is certainly a good example. In the Polish reality, strategic documents did not address the issue of the global economic crisis and its impact on the tourism economy. In a way, this was due to the fact that they were created during the precrisis period and were adopted in the early stages of the crisis, when these phenomena only affected Poland to a small extent. Moreover, the problem of the economic crisis was overlooked in Polish tourism policy. The state did not take specific actions either in the area of influencing supply (tourism entrepreneurs coped with the situation on the market and there were no bankruptcies of enterprises due to too low demand), or in influencing demand, especially to shape the intensity thereof (Panasiuk, 2010).

The COVID-19 pandemic greatly impacted the size and structure of Poland's hotel and tourism sector. Even in the first months of the pandemic, it was estimated that the economic and social consequences caused tens of billions of PLN in losses per month (Jarynowski et al., 2020). The emergence of the pandemic and the associated risk of high levels of the disease triggered reactions from public authorities, leading to the closure of borders, restrictions on the mobility of residents, and freezing the operations of many industries, especially those where there are frequent and massive contacts in the process of production and provision of services, both between workers themselves and between workers and consumers (Panasiuk, 2020). Overall, the pandemic has significantly affected the domestic tourism market in Poland, as in other countries. However, it is difficult to estimate how much of this impact resulted from top-down regulations and how much was due to consumers' fear and self-restraint in terms of engaging in activities that could expose them to infection. At the same time, the Polish tourism sector experienced unfavorable change, i.e., an incomparably greater decline in the number of foreign tourists than domestic ones (Gabryjończyk & Gabryjończyk, 2021).

In the wake of the COVID-19 pandemic, the country has taken numerous measures to limit its impact on industry and the public's tourism activities. One such tourism policy tool was the Polish Tourist Voucher (Polski Bon Turystyczny), introduced in Poland in 2020. The tourist voucher was implemented to support the tourism industry and Polish families during the

98   *Organizational resilience in Polish H&T organizations*

challenging economic situation caused by the COVID-19 pandemic. This voucher could be utilized to cover expenses for hotel services or tourism-related services within Poland. A tourist voucher was available for each of 6.5 million Polish children in the amount of 500 PLN (or 1000 PLN for children with a disability certificate) (Widomski, 2020). Despite the social nature of the tourism voucher, its second purpose was to provide financial assistance to entities affected by the pandemic. This assistance was provided through the ability to accept voucher payments when tourism activities were being "unfrozen" (Borek & Wyrwicz, 2021). Another instrument of support during the pandemic crisis was the so-called crisis shields. The package of laws that made up the crisis shields proposed a number of horizontal solutions, such as the Tourism Shield (Tarcza Turystyczna), aimed directly at the tourism industry. The provisions of these regulations envisaged the provision of preferential loans for refunds of customer deposits of tour operators, a special fund in which money was collected for tourists and tour operators for canceled tourist events, stopovers, and the suspension of social insurance premiums for the entire tourism industry (Niemczyk & Zamora, 2021).

Another current crisis is the war in Ukraine, which broke out in February 2022. As early as April of this year, there were signs of weakening in the Polish hotel and tourism market. This is largely due to foreign tourists' fear of coming to Poland, which directly borders Ukraine. Notable signs include mass cancellations of arrivals to Poland (Forsal.pl, 2022) or increased tourist service prices (Newseria.pl, 2022). The war in Ukraine is also causing other problems, such as the increased number of refugees from that country. It is estimated that a total of 4.45 million refugees from Ukraine arrived in Poland between February and the end of June 2022 (300gospodarka.pl, 2022).

In summary, the environmental environment of the Polish H&T sector is characterized by considerable dynamism. Poland has undergone a number of transformations over the past three decades, mainly of a political and economic nature. Of particular importance for the country was its accession to the European Union in 2004, which provided an opportunity for a marked improvement in many economic indicators. The emergence of crisis situations (especially the COVID-19 pandemic and the war in Ukraine) resulted in a deterioration of the economic situation in the country, which directly affected the H&T industry. Poland is at the stage of preparing and implementing a number of changes in the system of organization and management of tourism.

The structure of Polish hospitality and tourism organizations

It is generally accepted that the situation of the Polish H&T sector up until the outbreak of the COVID-19 pandemic was relatively stable and, in many cases, was characterized by considerable resilience. For example, during the global economic crisis, the tourism industry in Poland reacted much better than most

European countries. There were no such significant declines in tourist arrivals as in many European markets (Bąk-Filipek et al., 2019). On the other hand, Poland's share in the global or European tourism economy has not been substantial so far. For example, the added value generated by the tourism sector in 2018 amounted to 1.3% of Polish GDP. This means a much lower share in relation to the value of the entire economy than the average of OECD countries, which stood at 4.4%. By contrast, the total contribution of tourism to the Polish GDP in 2018 was 4.0% (Polski Instytut Ekonomiczny, 2020). According to the Travel & Tourism Competitiveness Index, Poland's tourism in 2018 was rated at 4.2 on a seven-point scale, leaving it in 42nd place out of 140 countries assessed (19th place among 27 European Union countries) (Juszczak, 2020). Additionally, calculations by the Polish Economic Institute show that in 2018 the tourism industry generated a total of PLN 140.92 billion in added value. Of the total added value generated, 19% was direct impact (PLN 26.65 billion), 61% was indirect impact (PLN 86.02 billion), and 20% was induced impact (PLN 28.24 billion). The multiplier effect was 5.3, which means that every PLN generated by tourism contributes to an additional PLN 4.30 in added value in the economy as a whole. Tourism plays a somewhat important role in creating the domestic labor market. In 2018, the tourism industry contributed to maintaining a total of nearly 1.36 million jobs, of which 32% were a direct impact (433,700), 52% were an indirect impact (700,550), and 16% were an induced impact (221,370). The multiplier effect was 3.1, indicating that each job held by individuals working in the tourism industry contributed to the creation of an additional 2.1 jobs in the overall Polish economy (Polski Instytut Ekonomiczny, 2020).

Depicting the exact size and structure of the H&T sector in Poland is difficult due to the need for complete and reliable statistical data, including imperfections in public statistics. One way to present such information is to analyze the so-called Polish Classification of Activities (Polska Klasyfikacja Działalności – PKD), which classifies individual businesses based on their activities (or declares as such). These activities are classified into divisions and then into groups, classes, and subclasses. Divisions directly or indirectly related to tourism include:

- Division 55 – Accommodation,
- Division 56 – Food service activities,
- Division 49 – Land transport and pipeline transport,
- Division 79 – Activities of tour operators, travel agents and brokers and other reservation services and related activities,
- Division 90 – Creative activities related to culture and entertainment,
- Division 91 – Activities of libraries, archives, museums and other cultural activities,
- Division 93 – Sports, entertainment and recreational activities.

(Główny Urząd Statystyczny, 2022b)

100 *Organizational resilience in Polish H&T organizations*

Table 4.1 shows the number of Polish entities classified in divisions and subclasses that are directly or indirectly related to H&T activities.

The most important enterprises, from the point of view of the operation of the H&T sector, are certainly those classified in divisions 55, 56, 79, and partly in division 49. In turn, several others are only indirectly related to the tourism sector, such as the operation of physical fitness facilities. At the same time, it is worth noting the variety of entities highlighted. Accommodation and catering enterprises alone number more than 126,000. A significant part is also made up of those in the transport sector, but in this case, out of their total number of more than 208,000, only slightly more than 62,000 are at least tangentially related to tourism (of which as many as 46,000 are passenger cab operations). An essential role in creating the tourism economy is also played by the activities of travel agencies, which in Poland are classified as tour operators, tour agents, and travel agents (more than 7800). There are also other entities whose activities are focused not only on tourists (visitors) but, to a large extent, on the residents of a given locality. These are entrepreneurs classified in divisions 90, 91, and 93.

The above data are based on statistics generated from the Polish Classification of Activities (PKD), i.e., companies' declarations regarding the scope of their activities. At this point, it is worth looking at specific subsectors of the Polish H&T industry and, in particular, the changes that have occurred in recent years. First of all, such an analysis was made on the example of hotels as one of the primary and most important accommodation facilities. Table 4.2 illustrates the changes in the hotel market from 2010 to 2020.[1] This period covers the first year of the COVID-19 pandemic. The table presents both data showing changes on the supply side of the market (i.e., the number of hotels and the number of beds) and on the demand side (i.e., the number of overnight stays and the number of nights provided).

The data presented in Table 4.2 illustrate the evident dynamics of changes in the hotel market during the period under review, notably until 2019. In the period 2010–2019, changes on the demand side (users of accommodation and nights provided) were more significant than on the supply side (number of hotels, number of beds): values on the demand side increased by a factor of two or even more, while those on the supply side increased by 50%–60% on average. Nonetheless, all categories clearly showed quite intense growth in all core values. The partial collapse of the hotel market occurred in 2020, the first year of the pandemic. While relatively few changes occurred on the supply side (the number of facilities decreased by 5% and the number of beds by 3%), drastic declines were recorded on the demand side. On average, the number of visitors and the number of nights provided decreased by half. To clarify, both values were more or less at the level of 2010. The effect of these changes was a marked decline in hotel beds use (occupancy). In 2010, it was 33.8%; in 2015, 39%; in 2019, 44.1%; and in 2020, only 26% (Główny Urząd Statystyczny, 2021a).

Table 4.1 Number of Polish hotel and tourism enterprises by PKD classification (data for 2021)

No. of division/subclass	Name of division/subclass	Number of entities
Division 55	**Accommodation**	**31,731**
55.10.Z	Hotels and similar accommodation	9349
55.20.Z	Tourist accommodations and short-stay accommodation	20,650
55.30.Z	Camping grounds (including RV sites) and campsites	375
55.90.Z	Other accommodation	1357
Division 56	**Food service activities**	**94,950**
56.10.A	Restaurants and other fixed catering establishments	61,389
56.10.B	Mobile food establishments	3736
56.21.Z	Preparation and delivery of food for external customers (catering)	8511
56.29.Z	Other food service activities	4215
56.30.Z	Preparing and serving beverages	17,099
Division 49	**Land transport and pipeline transport**	**208,552**
49.31.Z	Passenger land transport, urban and suburban	3560
49.32.Z	Passenger cab business	46,472
49.39.Z	Other passenger land transport, not elsewhere classified	12,823
Division 79	**Activities of tour operators, travel brokers and agents, and other reservation services and related activities**	**11,210**
79.11.A	Activities of travel agents	3187
79.11.B	Activities of travel intermediaries	644
79.12.Z	Activities of tour operators	4000
79.90.A	Activities of tour leaders and tourist guides	2061
79.90.B	Tourist information activities	226
79.90.C	Other reservation service activities, not elsewhere classified	1092
Division 90	**Creative activities related to culture and entertainment**	**21,303**
90.01.Z	Artistic performance exhibition activities	8753
90.02.Z	Activities supporting the exhibition of artistic performances	3385
90.04.Z	Activities of botanical and zoological gardens and nature conservation areas and facilities	2890

(*Continued*)

102 *Organizational resilience in Polish H&T organizations*

Table 4.1 (Continued)

No. of division/subclass	Name of division/subclass	Number of entities
Division 91	**Activities of libraries, archives, museums, and other cultural activities**	**4677**
91.02.Z	Activities of museums	724
91.04.Z	Activities of botanical and zoological gardens and nature conservation areas and facilities	131
Division 93	**Sports, entertainment, and recreational activities**	**50,665**
93.13.Z	Activities of physical fitness facilities	3336
93.21.Z	Activities of amusement parks and theme parks	1440
93.29.A	Activities of escape rooms, haunted houses, dancing venues, and in the field of other forms of entertainment or recreation organized in rooms or other places and enclosed spaces	9850
93.29.B	Other entertainment and recreational activities not elsewhere classified	

Source: Central Statistical Office data.

An interesting phenomenon was also observed in the food service market. The analysis was conducted on restaurants and catering outlets[2] operating between 2010 and 2020 (Table 4.3).

Regarding catering facilities, the situation differed from that of hotels. The food service market did not develop as dynamically as the hotel market. During the period under review, there were both increases and decreases compared to previous years. Decreases were seen three times in the number of restaurants compared to the previous year (2013, 2018, and 2020) and four times for catering outlets (2011, 2013, 2014, and 2020). Other years saw increases ranging from 1% to 8%. Regardless, it can be assumed that until the outbreak of the COVID-19 pandemic, the situation in the food service sector was pretty stable. In 2020, there was a noticeable decline in both the number of restaurants and catering outlets. It is also worth taking a look at the changes in 2019 compared to 2010 and in 2020 compared to 2010, and comparing them with those in the hotel market. Both restaurants and catering outlets experienced aggregate growth. On the other hand, the values were lower than for hotels (Table 4.2).

The above data show that the Polish hotel and tourism market was developing quite dynamically until the pandemic broke out. A certain collapse, characteristic of the industry, occurred in 2020, the first year of the COVID-19 pandemic. In

Organizational resilience in Polish H&T organizations   103

Table 4.2 Basic data illustrating the hotel market in Poland between 2010 and 2020

Year	Number of hotels	Accommodations (in thousands)	Overnight visitors (in thousands)	Overnight stays provided (in thousands)
2010	1796	176.0	11,739.9	21,199.9
2011	1883	187.0	12,721.6	23,096.7
2012	2014	198.1	13,461.3	24,876.8
2013	2107	208.6	14,568.2	26,971.4
2014	2250	227.5	16,138.3	29,900.2
2015	2316	235.6	17,487.1	32,674.8
2016	2463	253.3	19,615.4	37,243.6
2017	2540	261.5	20,916.1	39,461.3
2018	2592	273.8	22,076.5	42,068.0
2019	2635	286.2	23,511.6	44,848.2
2020	2498	276.4	11,131.4	22,973.4
Change 2019 to 2010 (2010 = 100)	147	163	200	212
Change 2020 to 2010 (2010 = 100)	139	157	95	108
Change 2020 to 2019 (2019 = 100)	95	97	47	51

Source: Główny Urząd Statystyczny (2011a, 2012a, 2013a, 2014a, 2015a, 2016a, 2017a, 2018a, 2019a, 2020a, 2021a).

Poland, as in most countries around the world, there was a rather abrupt decline in the number of guests and customers of the H&T industry, which precipitated a number of problems, mainly financial. Preliminary research conducted on a sample of 690 Polish tourism companies in March 2020 showed that as many as 62% of companies are unable to stay in business for more than two months without generating revenue. Minimizing all costs associated with the business was the main measure taken to mitigate the effects of the COVID-19 pandemic (53.9% of indications) (Piwoni-Krzeszowska & Rajchelt-Zublewicz, 2020). One industry that was certainly greatly affected by the pandemic was the hotel sector. To a large extent, this was due to the number of restrictions and strictures imposed by central authorities. Therefore, in 2020, most hotels remained open for only seven or eight months. The best month in 2020 was August, when hotel occupancy was 76% of the August 2019 level. This was a significant improvement over April 2020, when hotel utilization was only 13% of the previous April. Conversely, with the renewed closure of hotels in October and the sealing of that closure in December 2020, the rapid recovery in demand for hotels was again halted (PKO BP, 2021). At the beginning of 2021, it was even believed

104 *Organizational resilience in Polish H&T organizations*

Table 4.3 Basic data showing the market for catering facilities in Poland from 2010 to 2020 (number of facilities)

Year	Restaurants		Catering outlets	
	Number of objects	*Change Previous year = 100*	*Number of objects*	*Change Previous year = 100*
2010	14,937	-	23,892	-
2011	15,287	102	21,932	92
2012	16,478	108	22,120	101
2013	16,202	98	21,761	98
2014	17,414	107	21,493	99
2015	18,789	108	23,080	107
2016	19,648	105	24,484	106
2017	20,127	102	26,350	108
2018	19,675	98	26,663	101
2019	20,015	102	28,167	106
2020	17,676	88	26,086	93
Change 2019 to 2010 (2010 = 100)		134		118
Change 2020 to 2010 (2010 = 100)		118		109

Source: Główny Urząd Statystyczny (2011b, 2012b, 2013b, 2014b, 2015b, 2016b, 2017b, 2018b, 2019b, 2020b, 2021b).

that between 25% and 35% of hotels were at risk of bankruptcy (the lower values referred to resort areas, and the higher ones to city hotels). The result was a significant reduction in employment. By 2020, 38% of those working in the hotel industry had lost their jobs (Szczęsny, 2021). The pandemic also affected the short-term rental market, including a reduction in the number of apartments offered and the number of nights provided. However, the drop in tourist travel was less pronounced in tourist apartments than in registered accommodation. In cities, there were substantial declines in the number of guests in this accommodation type. Outside cities, on the other hand, there was a noticeable growth in the number of overnight stays in tourist apartments in 2021 compared to the pre-pandemic period (Adamiak, 2022).

A dramatic situation was also reported in other sectors of the industry. For example, in 2020, financial results in cultural institutions, such as museums and art galleries, were lower than those compared to the same period last year. There was a 17.4% decrease in total revenues and an 18.2% decrease in total costs. As a result of the COVID-19 pandemic, the value of the hotel food service market declined by 32.1% in 2020 compared to the record-breaking year of 2019. Analysts predict that the industry will fully recover in a few years. Market

Organizational resilience in Polish H&T organizations 105

research and development forecasts for 2021–2026 suggest that a return to 2019 market values will not be possible until around 2024 (Szczęsny, 2021). These phenomena have alarmingly affected the financial condition of the vast majority of hotel and tourism companies. In the first months of the COVID-19 pandemic, the percentage of tourism companies that were struggling financially increased dramatically. Between March and December 2020, the percentage rose from 5.5% to 10.1%, and the total amount of debt from PLN 81.2 million to as much as PLN 171.1 million (Stojczew, 2021). Some recovery, however, took place in 2021 and 2022, when the restrictions and restrictions introduced until that point began to be gradually removed.

In summary, the rather intensive development of the Polish hotel and tourism industry was severely hindered during the COVID-19 pandemic. Most indicators observed apparent declines (including the number of facilities or revenue generated). Meanwhile, the restrictions and strictures introduced translated into low utilization of services offered by hotel and tourism entrepreneurs.

The assessment of organizational resilience in Polish organizations

The Polish survey – sample characteristics and research procedure

In this part, we present empirical validation of the models[3] of organizational resilience in H&T, reflecting a capital-based view of organizations and concentrating on human capital as a core factor in the studied sector. To assess the organizational and employee resilience model in a Polish context, the conceptual model (i.e., the employee-level components drive organizational resilience) and the alternative model (i.e., the components of the organizational level feed the psychological and social capital and employee resilience) are verified.

We conducted an online survey in a cross-sectional design in March 2022. A total of 526 people declared their willingness to participate in the survey; however, only 16% met the criterion of being employed in the H&T industry (n = 830). We also excluded 170 people from the sample who did not confirm their informed consent, 124 respondents who did not complete the survey, and 36 who incorrectly answered the screening question. Finally, 500 completed online protocols were qualified for the study (a response rate of 60%). All respondents participated voluntarily, with anonymity and confidentiality guaranteed.

The H&T sector was represented by companies operating in the following areas: food service activities (division 56; 36%), leisure and entertainment (division 91 and 93; 26%), accommodation (division 55; 17%), land and pipeline transport (division 49; 15%), and activities of tour operators, travel brokers, and agents (division 79; 6%). The structure of the H&T enterprises surveyed is somewhat similar to that found in Poland (see Table 4.1). Taking into account only the subclasses related to tourism (and at the same time assuming that the leisure and entertainment group includes subclasses from the following sections: creative

106 *Organizational resilience in Polish H&T organizations*

activities related to culture and entertainment, activities of libraries, archives, museums, and other cultural activities, and sports, entertainment, and recreation activities), it turns out that the structure of H&T entities in Poland is as follows: accommodation facilities – 13.7%; food and beverage service activities – 41.1%; leisure and entertainment – 13.2%; land and pipeline transportation – 27.2%, and travel agents and brokers – 4.8%. Thus, the most significant differences in relative terms between the structure of the H&T organizations in Poland and that of respondents can be seen in leisure and entertainment and land and pipeline transport (they amounted to several percentage points). The differences in the other three cases do not exceed several percentage points.

The entities surveyed were micro companies (22%), small enterprises (employing 10–49 people; 30%), medium-sized enterprises (with up to 249 employees; 22%), and large organizations (26%). They had been active on the market for more than ten years (28%) or twenty years (43%), mainly with Polish (70%) or mixed, i.e., Polish and foreign capital (22%). Almost one-third of the companies were young and had existed on the market for less than a year (3%), between one and three years (8%), or up to ten years (18%). About 80% of respondents worked on employment contracts (57% for an indefinite period), and only 7% were self-employed. The remaining 13% of respondents combined work with study or retirement. Respondents had been working in these organizations for a relatively short time, with 20% working for less than a year, 43% between one and five years, and 22% between six and ten years. Only 15% of the respondents declared tenure in their current organization of more than ten years. All participants were full-time employees. However, some worked longer, namely more than 50 hours (4%) and more than 60 hours per week (4%). The dominant group worked on-site (84%), and a much smaller percentage worked remotely or in hybrid form (7% and 9%, respectively).

The share of women in the respondents was 54%. The respondents were usually under 48 (39% were between 28 and 37 years old), married or in a partnership (78%). They lived in agglomerations or large cities as well as smaller towns of less than 100,000 inhabitants (49% and 32%, respectively) from all over Poland (most frequently from the Masovian [16%], Silesian [12%], and Lesser Poland [10%] voivodeships). About 48% of respondents had completed secondary education and 42% had completed higher education. Full details of the sample are reported in Table 4.4.

Measurement

We used a set of methods (see Chapter 3 for more details) adapted to the Polish language. In the Polish sample, some retained the original factor structure (PsyCap Questionnaire PCQ-12, Personal Social Capital, Learning Goal Orientation), while some revealed a slightly different factor structure (the Employee Resilience Scale included two instead of three factors). Conversely,

Organizational resilience in Polish H&T organizations 107

Table 4.4 Description of the Polish sample: socio-demographic, employment, and organizations (N = 500)

Set of characteristics		Percentage	N
Socio-demographic			
Age			
	18–27	23.4	117
	28–37	39.2	196
	38–47	23.2	116
	48–57	9.6	48
	Over 57	4.6	23
Gender			
	Male	45.8	229
	Female	54.2	271
Education			
	Primary school	1.8	9
	Vocational school	8.4	42
	Secondary school	40.6	203
	Post-secondary school	7.6	38
	Bachelor's degree	15.0	75
	Master's degree	26.6	133
Marital status			
	Single	22.0	112
	In a partnership	78.0	388
Place of living			
	Agglomeration	10.8	54
	Large city (more than 100,000 inhabitants)	38.6	193
	Small city	32.0	160
	Village	18.6	93
Qualities of employees			
Job tenure			
	Under one year	20.2	101
	1–5 years	43.4	217
	6–10 years	21.6	108
	11–15 years	7.4	37
	16–20 years	3.6	18
	Over 20 years	3.8	19
Employment status			
	Permanent contract (employment contract for an indefinite period)	56.8	284
	Temporary contract (employment contract for a definite period)	23.0	115
	Business activity	7.0	35

(*Continued*)

108   *Organizational resilience in Polish H&T organizations*

Table 4.4 (Continued)

Set of characteristics		Percentage	N
Socio-demographic			
	Combining retirement or pension with work	3.4	17
	Combining study with work	9.8	49
Weekly working time in hours			
	35–39 hours	11.0	55
	40–49 hours	81.0	405
	50–59 hours	4.0	20
	60–69 hours	2.4	12
	70–100 hours	1.6	8
The current form of work			
	Stationary work	83.8	419
	Remote work	6.8	34
	Hybrid work	9.4	47
Company description			
The sector of hospitality and tourism			
	Accommodation facilities	17.0	85
	Food service activities	36.2	181
	Leisure and entertainment	25.8	129
	Land and pipeline transport	15.2	76
	Travel brokers and agents	5.8	29
Size of the company			
	Micro (1–9 employees)	21.8	109
	Small (10–49 employees)	29.6	148
	Medium (50–249 employees)	22.2	111
	Large (250 employees or more)	26.4	132
Age of the company			
	Under 1 year	3.2	16
	1–3 years	8.0	40
	4–9 years	18.0	90
	10–19 years	28.0	140
	20 years or more	42.8	214
Capital of the company			
	Domestic capital	70.2	351
	Foreign capital	7.8	39
	Mixed capital (domestic and foreign capital)	22.0	110

Organizational resilience in Polish H&T organizations 109

the instruments that measure organizational learning culture and organizational resilience were somewhat modified. Three items that focus on embedded systems were removed from the Dimension of Learning Organizations Questionnaire. In line with Yang et al. (2004), 18 items constituted two factors, i.e., organizational learning condition and individual and team learning. The Organization Resilience Scale was cleared of two items and finally constituted two factors: "planning and culture" and "collaboration and innovation". This structure was coherent with prior studies conducted in the H&T sector (Orchiston et al., 2016). The validity of these instruments (model fit indices, average variance extracted, composite reliability, and Cronbach's alpha coefficients) are reported in Table 4.5.

Descriptive statistics

Table 4.6 shows summary statistics and correlations of observed variables.[4]

Organizational and employee resilience were evaluated at a similar level ($t = -0.01$, $p > 0.05$). More specifically, "planning and culture of organization" was assessed higher than "collaboration and innovation" ($t = 4.11$, $p < 0.001$). A higher level of employee adaptive and planned resilience than network leveraging was also reported ($t = 4.42$, $p < 0.001$).

All study constructs were moderately correlated with each other (0.45–0.67, $p < 0.001$), except for personal social capital, which was weakly correlated (0.29–0.39, $p < 0.001$).

Job tenure significantly, albeit trivially, correlated with social and psychological capital (0.10–0.13, $p < 0.05$, respectively). Gender and age were not substantially correlated with the research constructs (−0.07–0.05 and −0.04–0.09, respectively), excluding the significant but weak relationship between gender and learning goal orientation (−0.09, $p < 0.05$). Thus, personal characteristics were not introduced to the structural model.

Analysis of the measurement model

Before testing the relationships, we used Harman's single-factor test as a statistical remedy to control common method variance. The unrotated factor analysis demonstrated that the first factor explained 29.56% of the total variance. Thus, the single factor did not account for most of the measures' variance; it is assumed that common method variance was not an issue in this empirical investigation (Fuller et al., 2016).

To evaluate the measurement model, we performed a series of confirmatory factor analyses using AMOS 25.0. The hypothesized six-factor model fit the data satisfactorily: $\chi^2 (104) = 221.84$, $p < 0.001$; $\chi^2/df = 2.13$; Tucker-Lewis index (TLI) = 0.97; comparative fit index (CFI) = 0.97; standardized root mean square

Table 4.5 Study instruments: item number and validation

Constructs	Methods	Item	Model fit indices	Factor structure	AVE: average variance extraction	CR: composite reliability	α: Cronbach's alpha coefficient5
Organizational level							
OLC	Dimensions of Learning Organizations Questionnaire (Yang et al., 2004)	18	$\chi^2/df = 3.42$ TLI = 0.92 CFI = 0.93 RMSEA = 0.07 SRMR = 0.05	Organizational learning conditions (strategic leadership, system connection, empowerment)	0.50	0.90	0.90
				Individual and team learning (continuous learning, inquiry and dialogue, team learning)	0.47	0.89	0.89
OR	Organization Resilience Scale (Orchiston et al., 2016)	11	$\chi^2/df = 2.34$ TLI = 0.96 CFI = 0.97 RMSEA = 0.05 SRMR = 0.03	Planning and culture (item 1–5)	0.45	0.81	0.80
				Collaboration and innovation (item 8–13)	0.41	0.80	0.80
Employee level							
ER	Employee Resilience Scale (Näshwall et al., 2019)	9	$\chi^2/df = 3.00$ TLI = 0.95 CFI = 0.97 RMSEA = 0.06 SRMR = 0.04	Adaptive and planned resilience	0.45	0.82	0.83
				Networking leveraging	0.47	0.72	0.73

		No. of items	Fit indices				
SocCap	Personal Social Capital (Zoghbi-Manrique-de-Lara and Ruiz-Palomino, 2019)	8	$\chi^2/df = 2.69$ TLI = 0.98 CFI = 0.99 RMSEA = 0.06 SRMR = 0.03	Personal social capital with peers inside the team	0.55	0.83	0.85
				Personal social capital with people outside the team	0.58	0.85	0.86
PsyCap	PsyCap Questionnaire PCQ-12 (Luthans et al., 2007)	12	$\chi^2/df = 3.25$ TLI = 0.94 CFI = 0.96 RMSEA = 0.07 SRMR = 0.04	Self-efficacy	0.54	0.78	0.78
				Hope	0.54	0.82	0.82
				Personal resilience	0.48	0.73	0.72
				optimism	0.55	0.71	0.71
LGO	Learning and Performance Goal Orientation (Vandewalle, 1997)	5	$\chi^2/df = 2.08$ TLI = 0.98 CFI = 0.99 RMSEA = 0.05 SRMR = 0.03	Learning goal orientation	0.57	0.87	0.85

Notes: OLC = organizational learning culture; OR = organizational resilience; ER = employee resilience; LGO = learning goal orientation; PsyCap = psychological capital; SocCap = personal social capital.

112 *Organizational resilience in Polish H&T organizations*

Table 4.6 Means, standard deviations, and correlations of study variables

Variables	M	SD	Sk	K	1	2	3	4	5	6
1. OLC	3.39	0.63	−0.33	0.60						
2. OR	3.62	0.59	−0.13	0.24	0.64					
3. ER	3.62	0.63	−0.17	0.28	0.45	0.47				
4. LGO	4.21	0.88	−0.15	−0.09	0.50	0.46	0.59			
5. PsyCap	4.30	0.75	−0.26	0.21	0.52	0.57	0.67	0.64		
6. SocCap	3.40	1.03	−0.01	−0.34	0.39	0.29	0.36	0.31	0.31	

Notes: OLC = organizational learning culture; OR = organizational resilience; ER = employee resilience; LGO = learning goal orientation; PsyCap = psychological capital; SocCap = personal social capital; M = mean; SD = standard deviation; Sk = skewness; K = kurtosis. All correlation coefficients are statistically significant at $p < 0.001$.

residual (SRMR) = 0.03; root mean error approximation (RMSEA) = 0.05 (90% confidence interval [CI] [0.04; 0.06]).

Conceptual and alternative structural models

The results revealed that the conceptual model was not well fit to the data: χ^2 (5) = 49.03, p < 0.001; χ^2/df = 9.81; TLI = 0.89; CFI = 0.96; SRMR = 0.05; RMSEA = 0.13 (90% CI [0.10; 0.17]), even though the predictors, namely personal social capital, psychological capital, and organizational learning culture, as well as psychological capital and learning goal orientation, were correlated.

Next, we assessed the alternative structural model. In contrast to the conceptual model, the alternative path runs from organizational resilience to employee resilience, which means that the constructs at the organizational level are more likely to stimulate variables at the employee level. However, as with the conceptual model, the results demonstrated a poor fit of the model to the data: χ^2 (5) = 81.38, p < 0.001; χ^2/df = 16.28 TLI = 0.81; CFI = 0.94; SRMR = 0.07; RMSEA = 0.18 (90% CI [0.14; 0.21]).

The in-depth analysis and inspection of modification indices suggested two more paths, i.e., from psychological capital to learning goal orientation and from psychological capital to organizational resilience. These proposals also have theoretical and empirical justification. In line with conservation of resources theory (Hobfoll, 2011; Hobfoll et al., 2018), learning goal orientation can be fostered by personal and organizational resources (Dutton et al., 2007; Niessen et al., 2017). Regarding personal resources, in view of previous research, psychological capital strengthens learning goal orientation because employees gain a sense of developing and self-actualizing (Basinska & Rozkwitalska, 2022; Nawaz et al., 2020; Spreitzer & Hwang, 2019). Moreover, psychological capital affects individual organizational functioning, making it more optimal (Avey et al., 2011; Paterson et al., 2014; Walumbwa et al., 2018). Thus, psychological capital can help employees learn and facilitate the development of organizations. In view of the above, we introduced new paths to the conceptual model.

Structural modified conceptual model

The modified conceptual model showed a good fit to the data: χ^2 (4) = 4.594, p = 0.332; χ^2/df = 1.15; TLI = 0.99; CFI = 1.00; SRMR = 0.01; RMSEA = 0.02 (90% CI [0.00; 0.0.07], BIC = 110.24). The standardized parameter estimates and explained variance (R^2) are given in Figure 4.1. The findings indicated that organizational learning culture and organizational resilience were significantly related (β = 0.46 p < 0.001). This led to the conclusion that H1 was confirmed. Moreover, organizational culture was also in a relationship with learning goal orientation (β = 0.23, p < 0.001), thus, H2 was confirmed. Further, learning goal orientation (β = 0.25, p < 0.001), personal social capital (β = 0.14, p < 0.001), and

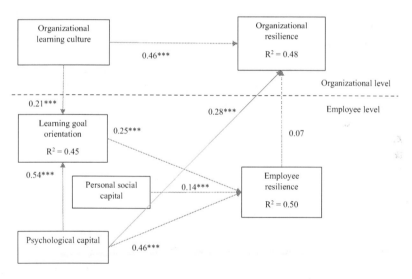

Figure 4.1 Structural equation model on the antecedents of organizational resilience with learning goal orientation as mediator.

Notes: Direct model: Organizational learning culture → Organizational resilience. Sequential mediation model no. 1: Organizational learning culture → Learning Goal orientation → Employee resilience → Organizational resilience. Sequential mediation model no. 2: Psychological Capital → Learning Goal orientation → Employee resilience → Organizational resilience. Mediation model no. 3: Psychological Capital → Employee resilience → Organizational resilience. Mediation model no. 4: Social Capital → Employee resilience → Organizational resilience. Dashed line: the path is statistically insignificant. * $p < 0.05$. ** $p < 0.01$. *** $p < 0.001$.

114   *Organizational resilience in Polish H&T organizations*

psychological capital (β = 0.46, p < 0.001) were positively linked to employee resilience. Hence, H3–H5 were supported. However, there was no empirical support for H6, as employee resilience implied a positive link with organizational resilience (β = 0.07, p > 0.05). It means that we could not examine either the sequential mediation model or a mediation model in which a path from employee resilience to organizational resilience was planned. In simple terms, the components of the organizational level and the employee level of resilience were linked via organizational learning culture but not via employee resilience.

Since we introduced two additional paths to the structural modified model, two hypotheses were added, namely, that psychological capital supports learning goal orientation (H7) as well as organizational resilience (H8). In line with these hypotheses, the findings revealed that psychological capital was positively linked to learning goal orientation (β = 0.52, p < 0.001) and organizational resilience (β = 0.28, p < 0.001). Finally, the results were able to explain 50% of the variance in employee resilience and 48% in organizational resilience.

The results related to mediation effects were obtained from a bootstrapped sample size of 500 using a 90% CI and are included in Table 4.7. The findings indicated that the indirect effect of organizational learning culture on employee resilience through learning goal orientation was statistically significant. Additionally, we observed mediation, where psychological capital positively influenced employee resilience through learning goal orientation. Moreover, the evaluation of the direct effect was also significant. Thus, learning goal orientation partially mediated the relationship between psychological capital and employee resilience. To sum up, we identified two indirect effects in which learning goal orientation served as mediators between organizational and employee levels as well as within the employee level.

Structural modified competitive model

Next, we examined the structural modified alternative model. The findings showed that this model is well fit to the data: χ^2 (4) = 3.48, p = 0.48; χ^2/df = 0.87; TLI = 1.00 CFI = 1.00; SRMR = 0.01; RMSEA = 0.00 (90% CI [0.00; 0.06], BIC = 109.13). The standardized parameter estimates and explained variance are presented in Figure 4.2.

In line with H1, the results confirmed that organizational learning culture was associated with organizational resilience (β = 0.47 p < 0.001). Furthermore, in line with H2, organizational learning culture was also linked to learning goal orientation (β = 0.23, p < 0.001). In addition, organizational resilience was related to employee resilience (β = 0.08, p < 0.05). Hence, H6b was supported. Further, according to H3–H5, learning goal orientation (β = 0.24, p < 0.001), personal social capital (β = 0.13, p < 0.001), and psychological capital (β = 0.43, p < 0.001) were positively associated with employee resilience. The results proved that psychological capital was positively linked to learning goal

Table 4.7 Results of bootstrapping in the direct and mediated models: unstandardized coefficients (B)

Hypotheses	Indirect effect	LLCI	ULCI	p-level	Mediation effect
Conceptual model					
OLC (.32)[a] → LGO (.18)[b] → ER (.07)[d] → OR	0.00	0.00	0.01	0.057	No mediation
PsyCap (.61)[c] → LGO (.18)[b] → ER (.07)[d] → OR	0.04	0.00	0.07	0.091	No mediation
SocCap (.09)[c] → ER (.07)[d] → OR	0.01	0.00	0.01	0.063	No mediation
PsyCap (.39)[c] → ER (.07)[d] → OR	0.04	0.00	0.07	0.091	No mediation
PsyCap (.61)[c] → LGO (.18)[b] → ER	0.11	0.08	0.15	< 0.001	Partial mediation
OLC (.32)[a] → LGO (.18)[b] → ER	0.06	0.03	0.09	< 0.001	Mediation
Competitive model					
OLC (.44)[g] → OR (.08)[h] → ER	0.09	0.05	0.13	< 0.001	Mediation
OLC (.32)[a] → LGO (.17)[f] → ER	0.09	0.05	0.13	< 0.001	Mediation
PsyCap (.26)[f] → OR (.08)[h] → ER	0.13	0.09	0.17	< 0.001	Partial mediation

Notes: OLC = organizational learning culture; OR = organizational resilience; ER = employee resilience; LGO = learning goal orientation; PsyCap = psychological capital; SocCap = personal social capital; LLCI = lower limit confidence interval; ULCI = upper limit confidence interval.
[a] The direct impact of OLC on LGO.
[b] The direct impact of LGO on ER.
[c] The direct impact of PsyCap/SocCap on ER.
[d] The direct impact of ER on OR.
[e] The direct impact of PsyCap on LGO.
[f] The direct impact of PsyCap on OR.
[g] The direct impact of OLC on OR.
[h] The direct impact of OR on ER.

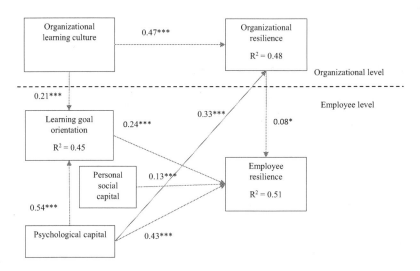

Figure 4.2 Structural equation model on the antecedents of employee resilience and organizational resilience and learning goal orientation as mediators.

Notes: Direct model: Organizational learning culture → Organizational resilience. Sequential mediation model: Organizational learning culture → Learning Goal orientation → Employee resilience → Organizational resilience. Mediation model: Social and Psychological Capital → Employee resilience → Organizational resilience. * $p < 0.05$. ** $p < 0.01$. *** $p < 0.001$.

orientation ($\beta = 0.52$, $p < 0.001$) as well as organizational resilience ($\beta = 0.33$, $p < 0.001$). This led to the conclusion that H7 and H8 were confirmed. Finally, the findings described 51% of the variance in employee resilience and 48% in organizational resilience.

In view of the above, we could examine two new mediation models in which the organizational level stimulated the employee level of resilience via both organizational learning culture and organizational resilience. We could also assess a mediation model in which psychological capital strengthens organizational resilience and further increases employee resilience. This alternative structural model presented more interactions between the organizational and employee levels.

The results concerning the mediation effects are reported in Table 4.7. Within the employee level, we confirmed the direct effect of both psychological and personal social capital. We also proved the indirect effect in which psychological capital built employee resilience via learning goal orientation. In fact, psychological capital strengthens employee resilience via organizational resilience. Due to the direct effect of psychological capital on employee resilience, the abovementioned mediations were partial. Indeed, this means that psychological capital can reinforce employee resilience both directly and indirectly via learning goal orientation. However, the role of psychological capital extends beyond the employee level. At the organizational level, it stimulates organizational resilience and, in return, intensifies employee resilience.

From the point of view of the organizational level, the assessment of the indirect effect of organizational learning culture on employee resilience via organizational resilience was substantial. The CIs did not include zero. Moreover, we confirmed that the organizational learning culture's indirect effect on employee resilience via learning goal orientation was also significant. It means that constructs at the organizational level fulfill an essential function at the employee level, namely for learning goal orientation and employee resilience.

The summary of the Polish survey

To recap, in line with the comprehensive conceptual model, organizational learning culture enhances organizational resilience (H1). Organizational learning culture also amplifies individual learning goal orientation (H2) and further boosts employee resilience (H3). Personal social capital strengthens employee resilience (H4) and psychological capital reinforces employee resilience (H5). Moreover, psychological capital enhances individual learning goal orientation (H7) and further intensifies employee resilience (H4). However, employee resilience does not increase organizational resilience (H6a). Thus, the comprehensive conceptual model, which assumed that employee capitals and resilience stimulate organizational resilience, is not supported. In fact, organizational learning culture promotes employee resilience via learning goal orientation, but organizational resilience does not benefit from employee resilience.

By contrast, the alternative model is more informative for organizational studies and practices. It indicates that organizational learning culture enhances organizational resilience (H1) and further supports employee resilience (H6b). Moreover, psychological capital reinforces organizational resilience (H8) and again builds employee resilience. As in the comprehensive conceptual model, personal social and psychological capital as well as learning goal orientation build employee resilience that is also powered by organizational resilience. Thus, both organizational and employee levels work together, i.e., the more resilient the organization, the more resilient the employees.

In regard to the components of the organizational level, organizational resilience is rooted in an organizational learning culture. Organizational learning culture aims at a progressive effort to create conditions and structures that promote individual and team learning (Kim, 2009; Yang et al., 2004). More specifically, learning organization in terms of contextual mechanism intertwines with the organizational learning process in order to improve organizational resilience. Thus, detailed planning practices and strong organizational culture before and during a crisis are preceded by a robust organizational learning culture.

118 *Organizational resilience in Polish H&T organizations*

Moreover, organizational learning culture reinforces new innovative solutions and stimulates collaboration between employees as well as companies.

In view of the components of the employee level, two individual resources are notably promising, namely learning goal orientation and psychological capital. Learning goal orientation as a personal resource is a vital mediator between organizational learning culture, psychological capital, and employee resilience. Learning-oriented employees can have greater opportunities to reap the benefits of adversity (Brykman & King, 2021; Peng et al., 2022). However, a rich organizational learning culture and employee psychological capital facilitate this. In fact, organizational learning culture reinforces organizational resilience, and both are beneficial to employee resilience, especially in the volatile, uncertain, complex, and ambiguous (VUCA) environment. Thus, practices focused on the creation of a more robust organizational learning culture facilitate the utilization of personal resources and develop them.

According to the multi-capital model (Brown et al., 2018), psychological capital and personal social capital directly enhance employee resilience. Similarly, as Chowdhury et al. (2019) pointed out, social capital makes a certain contribution mainly to adaptive resilience. In line with conservation of resources theory (Hobfoll, 2011), psychological capital can synergistically affect outcomes. Personal resilience is a vital psychological basis for employee resilience. Furthermore, Jalil et al. (2021) and Prayag et al. (2020) indicated that psychological capital supports both employee and organizational resilience. Our most prominent finding indicates that, in the Polish sample, psychological capital also initiates the complex indirect process of employee resilience, first by strengthening employee learning goal orientation and second by fostering organizational resilience. Thus, psychological capital is critical for both employee and organizational resilience (Fang et al., 2020; Luthans & Broad, 2020). These direct and indirect relationships show how organizations can absorb added value from human capital and strengthen employee resilience. As Näshwall et al. (2019) pointed out, an employee's ability is supported by the organization even if aversive circumstances occur. Thus, the more resilient the organization, the more resilient the employees.

Notes

1 No data was available for 2021.
2 According to the nomenclature of the Central Statistical Office: restaurants – catering establishments open to the general public, with full waiter service, offering a wide and varied assortment of food and beverages, served to consumers according to a menu card; catering outlets – catering establishments engaged in limited catering activities, such as fryers, pump houses, ice cream parlors, buffets in cinemas, stadiums, catering activities, etc. (Główny Urząd Statystyczny, 2021b).
3 See Chapter 3.

Organizational resilience in Polish H&T organizations 119

4 The skewness and kurtosis values for each study variable were below 1.0. Therefore, the data's normality has not been compromised (Kline, 2011).

5 Most constructs' AVE was higher than 0.5; however, organizational and employee resilience was higher than 0.40. Though some AVE was below 0.50, we can accept it because composite reliability (CR) for each latent variable was higher than 0.70; thus, the convergent validity of the construct was still proper (Fornell & Larcker, 1981). Moreover, the shared variance between pairs of constructs was below the AVE for each variable. Cronbach's α coefficients for all constructs were also above 0.70. Overall, convergent and discriminant validity was verified.

References

300gospodarka.pl (2022). Ilu uchodźców z Ukrainy jest w Polsce? Retrieved 26 July 2022, from https://300gospodarka.pl/news/uchodzcy-z-ukrainy-w-polsce-liczba

Adamiak, C. (2022). Najem krótkoterminowy w Polsce w czasie pandemii COVID-19. *Czasopismo Geograficzne, 93*(1), 9–32, https://doi.org/10.12657/czageo-93-01

Avey, J. B., Reichard, R. J., Luthans, F., & Mhatre, K. H. (2011). Metaanalysis of the impact of positive psychological capital on employee attitudes, behaviors, and performance. *Human Resource Development Quarterly, 22*(2), 127–152.

Bąk-Filipek, E., Cobb, S.C., & Podhorodecka, K. (2019). The development of the tourism economy in Poland compared to Europe in 2010–2018. *Acta Scientiarum Polonorum, 18*(3), 13–20, DOI: 10.22630/ASPE.2019.18.3.27

Basinska, B. A., & Rozkwitalska, M. (2022). Psychological capital and happiness at work: The mediating role of employee thriving in multinational corporations. *Current Psychology, 41*, 549–562. https://doi.org/10.1007/s12144-019-00598-y

Bobrowska, A. (2013). Migracje Polaków po przystąpieniu do Unii Europejskiej. *Coloquium Wydziału Nauk Humanistycznych i Społecznych, 2*, 49–64.

Borek, D., & Wyrwicz, E. (2021). Agroturystyka jako miejsce realizacji Polskiego Bonu Turystycznego – aspekty prawne. *Zagadnienia Doradztwa Rozlicznego, 2*(104), 70–81.

Borzyszkowski, J. (2005). *Polityka turystyczna państwa*. Wydawnictwo Uczelniane Politechniki Koszalińskiej.

Borzyszkowski, J. (2018). Problem finansowania organizacji zarządzających obszarami recepcji turystycznej – przykład struktur lokalnych. *Ekonomiczne Problemy Turystyki, 1*(41), 23–30, DOI: 10.18276/ept.2018.1.41-02

Bosiacki, S., & Panasiuk, A. (2017). Planowanie rozwoju turystyki – regulacja czy deregulacja. *Studia Oeconomica Posnaniensia, 5*(4), 7–28, DOI: 10.18559/SOEP.2017.4.1

Brown, N. A., Orchiston, C., Rovins, J. E., Feldmann-Jensen, S., & Johnston, D. (2018). An integrative framework for investigating disaster resilience within the hotel sector. *Journal of Hospitality and Tourism Management, 36*(July), 67–75. https://doi.org/10.1016/j.jhtm.2018.07.004

Brykman, K. M., & King, D. D. (2021). A resource model of team resilience capacity and learning. *Group and Organization Management, 46*(4). https://doi.org/10.1177/10596011211018008

Chowdhury, M., Prayag, G., Orchiston, C., & Spector, S. (2019). Postdisaster social capital, adaptive resilience and business performance of tourism organizations in

120 *Organizational resilience in Polish H&T organizations*

Christchurch, New Zealand. *Journal of Travel Research, 58*(7), 1209–1226. https://doi.org/10.1177/0047287518794319

Council Directive 90/314/EEC of 13 June 1990 on package travel, package holidays and package tours, Official Journal of the European Communities L 158/59.

Cybula, P., & Zawistowska, H. (2017). Ocena funkcjonowania Ustawy i o usługach turystycznych i pytania o kierunki przyszłej regulacji. *Studia Oeconomica Posnaniensia, 5*(4), 29–49, DOI: 10.18559/SOEP.2017.4.2

Czapski, G. (2021). Rynek pracy wobec pandemii COVID-19 w województwie lubelskim i mazowieckim. In M. Stradomska (Ed.), *Wymiar współczesnych zagrożeń człowieka w teorii i zagadnieniach praktycznych – ujęcie interdyscyplinarne* (pp. 41–52). ArchaeGraph Wydawnictwo Naukowe.

Dutton, J. E., Glynn, M. A., & Spreitzer, G. (2007). Positive organizational scholarship. In S. Lopez & A. Beauchamps (Eds.), *Encyclopedia of positive psychology*. Blackwell Publishing. Retrieved from http://webuser.bus.umich.edu/janedut/POS/Dutton&Son enshein.pdf

Dyrektywa Parlamentu Europejskiego i Rady (UE) 2015/2302 z dnia 25 listopada 2015 r. w sprawie imprez turystycznych i powiązanych usług turystycznych, zmieniająca rozporządzenie (WE) nr 2006/2004 i dyrektywę Parlamentu Europejskiego i Rady 2011/83/UE oraz uchylająca dyrektywę Rady 90/314/EWG, Dz. Urz. UE L 326/1.

Fang, S. (Echo), Prayag, G., Ozanne, L. K., & de Vries, H. (2020). Psychological capital, coping mechanisms and organizational resilience: Insights from the 2016 Kaikoura earthquake, New Zealand. *Tourism Management Perspectives, 34*(March 2019), 100637. https://doi.org/10.1016/j.tmp.2020.100637

Fornell, C. & Larcker, D. F. (1981). Evaluating structural equation models with unobservable variables and measurement error. *Journal of Marketing Research, 18*(1), 39–50.

Forsal.pl (2022). Zagraniczni turyści boją się przyjeżdżać do Polski. "Ponad 90 proc. Anulacji", Retrieved 15 July 2022, from https://forsal.pl/lifestyle/turystyka/artykuly/8396879,turystyka-w-polsce-anulacje-zagraniczni-turysci-wojna-ukraina.html

Fuller, C. M., Simmering, M. J., Atinc, G., Atinc, Y. & Babin, B. J. (2016). Common method variance detection in business research. *Journal of Business Research, 69*(8), 3192–3198.

Gabryjończyk, K., & Gabryjończyk, P. (2021). Zmiany stopnia wykorzystania turystycznych obiektów noclegowych w okresie zwalczania pandemii COVID-19 w Polsce. *Turystyka i Rozwój Regionalny, 15*, 43–58. DOI 10.22630/TIRR.2021.15.5

Główny Urząd Statystyczny (2011a). *Rocznik statystyczny Rzeczypospolitej Polskiej 2011.* Warszawa.

Główny Urząd Statystyczny (2011b). *Rynek wewnętrzny w 2010 r.* Warszawa.

Główny Urząd Statystyczny (2012a). *Rocznik statystyczny Rzeczypospolitej Polskiej 2012.* Warszawa.

Główny Urząd Statystyczny (2012b). *Rynek wewnętrzny w 2011 r.* Warszawa.

Główny Urząd Statystyczny (2013a). *Rocznik statystyczny Rzeczypospolitej Polskiej 2013.* Warszawa.

Główny Urząd Statystyczny (2013b). *Rynek wewnętrzny w 2012 r.* Warszawa.

Główny Urząd Statystyczny (2014a). *Rocznik statystyczny Rzeczypospolitej Polskiej 2014.* Warszawa.

Główny Urząd Statystyczny (2014b). *Rynek wewnętrzny w 2013 r.* Warszawa.

Organizational resilience in Polish H&T organizations   121

Główny Urząd Statystyczny (2015a). *Rocznik statystyczny Rzeczypospolitej Polskiej 2015*. Warszawa.

Główny Urząd Statystyczny (2015b). *Rynek wewnętrzny w 2014 r.* Warszawa.

Główny Urząd Statystyczny (2016a). *Rocznik statystyczny Rzeczypospolitej Polskiej 2016*. Warszawa.

Główny Urząd Statystyczny (2016b). *Rynek wewnętrzny w 2015 r.* Warszawa.

Główny Urząd Statystyczny (2017a). *Rocznik statystyczny Rzeczypospolitej Polskiej 2017*. Warszawa.

Główny Urząd Statystyczny (2017b). *Rynek wewnętrzny w 2016 r.* Warszawa.

Główny Urząd Statystyczny (2018a). *Rocznik statystyczny Rzeczypospolitej Polskiej 2018*. Warszawa.

Główny Urząd Statystyczny (2018b). *Rynek wewnętrzny w 2017 r.* Warszawa.

Główny Urząd Statystyczny (2019a). *Rocznik statystyczny Rzeczypospolitej Polskiej 2019*. Warszawa.

Główny Urząd Statystyczny (2019b). *Rynek wewnętrzny w 2018 r.* Warszawa.

Główny Urząd Statystyczny (2020a). *Rocznik statystyczny Rzeczypospolitej Polskiej 2020*. Warszawa.

Główny Urząd Statystyczny (2020b). *Rynek wewnętrzny w 2019 r.* Warszawa.

Główny Urząd Statystyczny (2021a). *Rocznik statystyczny Rzeczypospolitej Polskiej 2021*. Warszawa.

Główny Urząd Statystyczny (2021b). *Rynek wewnętrzny w 2020 r.* Warszawa.

Główny Urząd Statystyczny (2022a). *Roczne wskaźniki cen towarów i usług konsumpcyjnych od 1950 roku*. Retrieved 10 July 2022, from https://stat.gov.pl/obsz ary-tematyczne/ceny-handel/wskazniki-cen/wskazniki-cen-towarow-i-uslug-kon sumpcyjnych-pot-inflacja-/roczne-wskazniki-cen-towarow-i-uslug-konsumpcyjnych/

Główny Urząd Statystyczny (2022b). *Polska Klasyfikacja Działalności (PKD 2007)*. Retrieved 10 July 2022, from https://stat.gov.pl/Klasyfikacje/doc/pkd_07/pkd_07.htm

Gonera, H., & Zmyślony, P. (2017). *Produkt – wiedza – współpraca*. Poznań: Uniwersytet Ekonomiczny w Poznaniu.

Hobfoll, S. E. (2011). Conservation of resource caravans and engaged settings. *Journal of Occupational and Organizational Psychology, 84*(1), 116–122.

Hobfoll, S. E., Halbesleben, J., Neveu, J.-P., & Westman, M. (2018). Conservation of resources in the organizational context: The reality of resources and their consequences. *Annual Review of Organizational Psychology and Organizational Behavior, 5*, 103–128.

Jalil, M. F., Ali, A., Ahmed, Z., & Kamarulzaman, R. (2021). The mediating effect of coping strategies between psychological capital and small tourism organization resilience: Insights from the COVID-19 pandemic, Malaysia. *Frontiers in Psychology, 12*(December), 1–15. https://doi.org/10.3389/fpsyg.2021.766528

Jarosz-Nojszewska, A. (2018). Bezrobocie w Polsce w latach 1918–2018. *Kwartalnik Kolegium Ekonomiczno-Społecznego Studia i Prace, 3*, 101–119.

Jarynkowski, A., Wójta-Kempa, M., Płatek, D., & Czopek, K. (2020). Attempt to understand public health relevant social dimensions of COVID-19 outbreak in Poland. *Society Register, 4*(3), 7–44.

Juszczak, A. (2020). *Trendy rozwojowe turystyki w Polsce przed i w trakcie pandemii COVID-19*. Instytut Turystyki w Krakowie sp. z o.o., Kraków.

122   *Organizational resilience in Polish H&T organizations*

Kim, D. H. (2009). The link between individual and organizational learning. *The Strategic Management of Intellectual Capital*, 41–62. https://doi.org/10.1016/b978-0-7506-9850-4.50006-3

Kline, R. B. (2011). *Principles and practice of structural equation modeling (3rd ed.)*. The Guilford Press.

Luthans, F., Avolio, B. J., Avey, J. B. & Norman, S. M. (2007). Positive psychological capital: Measurement and relationship with performance and satisfaction. *Personnel Psychology, 60*(3), 541–572.

Luthans, F., & Broad, J. D. (2020). Positive psychological capital to help combat the mental health fallout from the pandemic and VUCA environment. *Organizational Dynamics, 2019*, 100817. https://doi.org/10.1016/j.orgdyn.2020.100817

Maciąg, K. (2018). Ochrona podróżnego na tle Ustawy o imprezach turystycznych i powiązanych usługach turystycznych oraz Ustawy o usługach turystycznych – analiza porównawcza. *Internetowy Kwartalnik Antymonopolowy i Regulacyjny, 4*(7), 46–59.

Malaga, K. (2018). Bilans przemian w Polsce w latach 1989–2017 w kategoriach transformacji, wolności gospodarczej i wzrostu gospodarczego. *Zeszyty Naukowe Małopolskiej Wyższej Szkoły Ekonomicznej w Tarnowie, 1*(37), 19–34.

Ministerstwo rozwoju (2021). *We wrześniu opłata turystyczna*, Retrieved 15 July 2022, from https://turystyka.rp.pl/noclegi/art17906511-ministerstwo-rozwoju-we-wrzesniu-oplata-turystyczna

Näswall, K., Malinen, S., Kuntz, J., & Hodliffe, M. (2019). Employee resilience: Development and validation of a measure. *Journal of Managerial Psychology, 34*(5), 353–367. https://doi.org/10.1108/JMP-02-2018-0102

Nawaz, M., Abid, G., Arya, B., Bhatti, G. A., & Farooqi, S. (2020). Understanding employee thriving: The role of workplace context, personality and individual resources. *Total Quality Management & Business Excellence, 31*(11–12), 1345–1362.

Nazarczuk, J., & Marks-Bielska, R. (2009). Czynniki wzrostu gospodarczego Polski w świetle neoklasycznego modelu wzrostu. *Prace Naukowe Uniwersytetu Ekonomicznego we Wrocławiu, 39*, 266–273.

Newseria.pl (2022). Wojna w Ukrainie już wpływa na turystykę. Latem Polacy powinni się spodziewać dużego wzrostu cen w biurach podróży. Retrieved 22 July 2022, from https://biznes.newseria.pl/news/wojna-w-ukrainie-juz,p926301789

Niemczyk, A., & Zamora, P. (2021). Interwencjonizm państwowy na rynku usług turystycznych w warunkach pandemii COVID-19. *Ekonomia – Wroclaw Economic Review, 27*(3), 21–34.

Niessen, C., Mäder, I., Stride, C., & Jimmieson, N. L. (2017). Thriving when exhausted: The role of perceived transformational leadership. *Journal of Vocational Behavior, 103*, 41–51. https://doi.org/10.1016/j.jvb.2017.07.012

Orchiston, C., Prayag, G., & Brown, C. (2016). Organizational resilience in the tourism sector. *Annals of Tourism Research, 56*, 145–148. https://doi.org/10.1016/j.annals.2015.11.002

Panasiuk, A. (2010). Uwarunkowania polityki turystycznej w Polsce w aspekcie globalizacji, kryzysu ekonomicznego oraz prezydencji Polski w Unii Europejskiej. *Oeconomia, 9*(4), 379–388.

Panasiuk, A. (2014). *Fundusze Unii Europejskiej w gospodarce turystycznej*. Difin.

Panasiuk, A. (2019). Ocena zmian w makrootoczeniu funkcjonowania współczesnego biznesu turystycznego. *Rozprawy Naukowe AWF we Wrocławiu, 64*, 11–22.

Organizational resilience in Polish H&T organizations   123

Panasiuk, A. (2020). Przyczynek do badań nad wpływem pandemii na stan gospodarki turystycznej. In K. Nessel (Ed.), *Turystyka w naukach społecznych* (pp. 56–70). Uniwersytet Jagielloński, Kraków.

Paterson, T. A., Luthans, F., & Jeung, W. (2014). Thriving at work: Impact of psychological capital and supervisor support. *Journal of Organizational Behavior, 35*(3), 434–446.

Peng, J., Xie, L., Zhou, L., & Huan, T. C. (2022). Linking team learning climate to service performance: The role of individual- and team-level adaptive behaviors in travel services. *Tourism Management, 91*(February), 104481. https://doi.org/10.1016/j.tourman.2021.104481

Piwoni-Krzeszowska, E., & Rajchelt-Zublewicz, M. (2020). The situation of enterprises operating in Poland during the SARS-Cov-2 pandemic. In S. Soliman Khalid (Ed.), *Education excellence and innovation management: A 2025 vision to sustain economic development during global challenges* (pp. 14384–14398). International Business Information Management Association (IBIMA).

PKO BP (2021). *Rynek Hotelowy. Analizy nieruchomości.* Warszawa.

Polska Organizacja Turystyczna (2022). Lokalne Organizacje Turystyczne. Retrieved 14 July 2022, from www.pot.gov.pl/pl/o-pot/wspolpraca-z-regionami/lokalne-organiza cje-turystyczne

Polski Instytut Ekonomiczny (2020). *Branża turystyczna w Polsce. Obraz sprzed pandemii.* Warszawa.

Prayag, G., Spector, S., Orchiston, C., & Chowdhury, M. (2020). Psychological resilience, organizational resilience and life satisfaction in tourism firms: Insights from the Canterbury earthquakes. *Current Issues in Tourism, 23*(10), 1216–1233. https://doi.org/10.1080/13683500.2019.1607832

Spreitzer, G., & Hwang, E. B. (2019). How thriving at work matters for creating psychologically healthy workplaces: Current perspectives and implications for the new world of work. In R. J. Burke & A.M. Richardsen (Eds.), *Creating psychologically healthy workplaces* (pp. 293–310). Edward Elgar Publishing.

Stefanowska, A., & Lipko-Kowalska, M. (2017). Lokalne organizacje turystyczna jako czynnik rozwoju regionalnego – ocena funkcjonowania. *Prace Geograficzne, 149*, 101–121. doi: 10.4467/20833113PG.17.012.6928

Stojczew, K. (2021). Ocena wpływu pandemii koronawirusa na branżę turystyczną w Polsce. *Prace Naukowe Uniwersytetu Ekonomicznego we Wrocławiu, 1*(65), 157–172.

Szczęsny, W. (2021). Turystyka w okresie kryzysu gospodarczego spowodowanego pandemią COVID-19. *Zeszyty Naukowe Turystyka i Rekreacja, 28*(2), 21–32.

Ustawa z dnia 24 listopada 2017 r. o imprezach turystycznych i powiązanych usługach turystycznych, Dzu 2017, poz. 2361.

Ustawa z dnia 25 czerwca 1999 r. o Polskiej Organizacji Turystycznej, DzU 1999, nr 62, poz. 689.

Ustawa z dnia 29 sierpnia 1997 r. o usługach turystycznych, DzU nr 133, poz. 884.

Vandewalle, D. (1997). Development and validation of a Work Domain Goal Orientation Instrument. *Educational and Psychological Measurement, 57*(6), 995–1015.

Walumbwa, F. O., Muchiri, M. K., Misati, E., Wu, C., & Meiliani, M. (2018). Inspired to perform: A multilevel investigation of antecedents and consequences of thriving at work. *Journal of Organizational Behavior, 39*(3), 249–261. https://doi.org/10.1002/job.2216

124 *Organizational resilience in Polish H&T organizations*

Widomski, M. (2020). Turystyka krajowa a pandemia. *Poszerzamy Horyzonty, 21*(1), 771–779.

Yang, B., Watkins, K. E., & Marsick, V. J. (2004). The construct of the learning organization: Dimensions, measurement, and validation. *Human Resource Development Quarterly, 15*(1), 31–55. https://doi.org/10.1002/hrdq.1086

Zarządzenie Nr 21 Ministra Sportu i Turystyki 1 z dnia 1 października 2019 r. w sprawie zakresów czynności Ministra, Sekretarzy Stanu oraz Dyrektora Generalnego w Ministerstwie Sportu i Turystyki, Dz.Urz.MSiT.2019.53.

Zmyślony, P. (2018). O potrzebie utworzenie metropolitalnych organizacji turystycznych. *Studia Periegetica, 1*(21), 13–31.

Zoghbi-Manrique-de-Lara, P., & Ruiz-Palomino, P. (2019). How servant leadership creates and accumulates social capital personally owned in hotel firms. *International Journal of Contemporary Hospitality Management, 31*(8), 3192–3211. https://doi.org/10.1108/IJCHM-09-2018-0748

5 Organizational resilience in hospitality and tourism organizations in Türkiye

An overview of hospitality and tourism in Türkiye

The tourism and hospitality (H&T) sector has been impacted by rapid and unpredictable changes over the years. This volatility is driven by various factors such as economic conditions, political instability, natural disasters, pandemics, and technological innovation. Additionally, shifting consumer preferences, market trends, and government regulations heighten the overall sense of uncertainty in this industry.

The global COVID-19 pandemic affected all businesses, but H&T was among the sectors hardest hit by this crisis, and since then, businesses have struggled to recover (Lubowiecki-Vikuk & Sousa, 2021; Sobaih et al., 2021). This is because (1) both H&T are labor-intensive sectors with millions of employees (Yılancı & Kırca, 2023) and (2) the fundamental nature of these sectors requires intensive or frequent interaction between tourists/customers and service providers (Olorunsola et al., 2023). Therefore, the H&T industry is more sensitive to any crisis that threatens the well-being of humanity. This vulnerability is so evident in a recent report by UNWTO (2022), demonstrating that there was an increase in international tourism by 5% in 2021 when compared to the one in 2020, but international travel remained 71% below 2019 levels before the pandemic. Due to this vulnerability, particularly demonstrated by the COVID-19 pandemic, discussing employee and organizational resilience is a critical issue for the survival and competitiveness of the firms in H&T (Melián-Alzola et al., 2020).

Due to its relatively low indices in human development, Türkiye is categorized as a developing country (UNDP, 2005). Although Türkiye has experienced many positive economic and sociocultural changes and improvements in recent years, the country still struggles with unemployment issues, high inflation rate, and more critically public sector debts. Unfortunately, the existence of these problems has given the country the characteristics of a developing tourist destination despite the fact that its growth performance is even better than in several developed countries.

DOI: 10.4324/9781003291350-6

126 *Organizational resilience in H&T organizations in Türkiye*

Since the early 1980s, H&T has experienced fast growth in Türkiye. The acceleration was even faster after the tourism encouragement law had been enacted in 1982 to regulate and develop the dynamic structure of H&T. Additionally, investors received attractive incentives during that period, which gave rise to a quick increase in the number of beds in the western part of the country over the years. H&T played a crucial role in developing regions suffering from economic disparities. In other words, Türkiye's relatively undeveloped regions introduced new dynamics through improvements in social and physical infrastructure that satisfied tourists and the local community (Goymen, 2000). However, as is the case elsewhere (e.g., Zhang et al., 2023), economic crises, wars, pandemics, environmental disasters, and other unexpected incidents hinder the development of H&T and make it difficult for managers/entrepreneurs/owners to formulate strategies and share knowledge in an unpredictable environment that signifies volatility, uncertainty, complexity, and ambiguity (VUCA; Lubowiecki-Vikuk et al., 2023). Organizations' past experiences with crises such as the COVID-19 pandemic, ongoing economic recession, political conflicts, and energy crises have forced them to continuously deal with the abovementioned four characteristics of the marketplace (Cavusgil et al., 2021).

Türkiye is noted for its natural and historical attractions, including the UNESCO heritage sites and routes (e.g., Göbeklitepe-Şanlıurfa, Mount Nemrut, Mardin Cultural Landscape, and Zeugma). However, the sea, sun, sand tourism, and shopping have been the primary motivation for tourists to visit Türkiye for years (cf. Karagöz et al., 2022; Tosun et al., 2008). Antalya, İstanbul, Muğla, İzmir, Edirne (for Bulgarian tourists), Artvin (for Georgian tourists), and Nevşehir are among the most popular tourist destinations in Türkiye. In 2014, the Turkish Ministry of Culture and Tourism decided to initiate a campaign called "Turkey Home Global Image Campaign" to promote the whole country. Though this standardized international advertising campaign helped the country to attract millions of tourists, recent research demonstrated that the "one-size-fits-all" approach was problematic, and tourists with different nationalities had different expectations (Uner et al., 2023).

Table 5.1 presents an overview of changes in terms of the number of foreign tourists between 2013 and 2022. Türkiye was ranked sixth among the world's most-visited destinations in 2019, with more than 51 million tourists (IIT, 2022). As depicted in Table 5.1, considerable growth is evident in Türkiye's tourism industry during the years, starting with 34,910,098 tourists in 2013 and ending with 51,387,513 tourists in 2022.

Table 5.2 explicitly shows that the number of arriving German, British, Russian, Iranian, Bulgarian, and Georgian tourists between 2013 and 2022 did not fall below 1 million excluding British, Iranian, and Georgian tourists for the years of 2020 and/or 2021. COVID-19 gave rise to such decreases. Among others, the number of arriving American (north), Belgium, Denmark, French,

Organizational resilience in H&T organizations in Türkiye 127

Table 5.1 The number of arriving foreign tourists between 2013 and 2022 in Türkiye

Year	# of foreign tourists
2022	51,387,513
2021	30,038,961
2020	15,971,201
2019	51,747,199
2018	46,112,592
2017	37,969,824
2016	30,906,680
2015	36,244,632
2014	36,837,900
2013	34,910,098

Source: Republic of Türkiye Ministry of Culture and Tourism (2023a).

Table 5.2 The number of arriving German, British, Russian, Iranian, Bulgarian, and Georgian tourists between 2013 and 2022 in Türkiye

Year	Germany	United Kingdom	Russian Federation	Iran	Bulgaria	Georgia
2022	5,679,194	3,370,739	5,232,611	2,331,076	2i882,512	1,514,813
2021	3,085,215	392,746	4,694,422	1,153,092	1,402,795	291,852
2020	1,118,932	820,709	2,128,758	385,762	1,242,961	410,501
2019	5,027,472	2,562,064	7,017,657	2,102,890	2,713,464	1,995,254
2018	4,512,360	2,254,871	5,964,613	2,001,744	2,386,885	2,069,392
2017	3,584,653	1,658,715	4,715,438	2,501,948	1,852,867	2,438,730
2016	3,890,074	1,711,481	866,256	1,665,160	1,690,766	2,206,266
2015	5,580,792	2,512,139	3,649,003	1,700,385	1,821,480	1,911,832
2014	5,250,036	2,600,360	4,479,049	1,590,664	1,693,591	1,755,289
2013	5,041,323	2,509,357	4,269,306	1,196,801	1,582,912	1,769,447

Source: Republic of Türkiye Ministry of Culture and Tourism (2023b).

Italian, and Dutch tourists as well as the ones from the United Arab Emirates was high. The number of arriving Russian tourists in 2016 was below 1 million. This was because of the political tension between Türkiye and the Russian Federation in 2015.

The number of tourists dropped from 51,747,199 in 2019 to 15,971,201 in 2020 due to the COVID-19 pandemic. However, recent research disclosed that the Turkish government supported the H&T sector during periods of instability and promoted the resilience of the sector (Charfeddine & Dawd, 2022). The government's continuous support to H&T sector resulted in an increase in the total number of hotels and beds. Specifically, as of June 2023, the total number of hotels and beds in Türkiye was 20,831 and 1,945,626, respectively (Republic

128 *Organizational resilience in H&T organizations in Türkiye*

Table 5.3 The total number of hotels, rooms, and beds (June 2023)

Accommodation facilities with certificate of tourism establishment			Accommodation facilities with certificate of tourism investment			Accommodation facilities with simple accommodation tourism establishment certificate		
# of hotels	# of rooms	# of beds	# of hotels	# of rooms	# of beds	# of hotels	# of rooms	# of beds
4,969	525,004	1,100,139	715	75,314	168,604	15,147	335,700	676,883

Source: Republic of Türkiye Ministry of Culture and Tourism (2023c).

of Türkiye Ministry of Culture and Tourism, 2023c). The breakdown for hotels and beds was given in Table 5.3.

In the Turkish H&T sector, there are various categories of hotels such as five-, four-, three-, two-, and one-star hotels as well as boutique hotels and special accommodation facility hotels. Holiday villages, (self-contained) apart hotels, bed and breakfast hotels, and thermal hotels are also among these categories (TGA, 2023). Both national (e.g., Limak Hotels, Kaya Hotels, and Elite World Hotels) and international (e.g., Hilton, Marriott, Hyatt, Intercontinental, Wyndham, Accor Group, and Radisson Blu) chain hotels have been welcoming millions of tourists for years in Türkiye.

As is evident in Table 5.1, tourism receipts significantly contribute to the economic growth in Türkiye. Any fluctuation in the industry resulting from internal and/or external factors can affect the destination's economy and its components such as employment. Moreover, tourism is seasonal, and hospitality organizations face many challenges such as reliance on foreign tour operators, low occupancy rate, logistics problems, lack of proper infrastructure, lack of qualified employees in the sector, lack of effective marketing strategies, international conflicts, and terrorism (Köseoglu et al., 2013). These challenges do heighten "environmental uncertainty" in the country. Accordingly, organizations should be resilient enough to overcome every possible challenge in the changing and competitive business environment. This is significant for the sustainable development of tourism in this nation. The following section provides an environmental analysis of the Turkish H&T sector.

The Turkish hospitality and tourism sector environmental analysis

The economic environment

Turkish citizens have suffered from high foreign exchange currencies and high inflation rates for years. Though the inflation rate was below 10% (e.g., between

Organizational resilience in H&T organizations in Türkiye   129

2012 and 2016), it went up to 64.27% in 2022 (Türkiye Cumhuriyet Merkez Bankası, 2023). However, continuous increases in foreign currencies and a high inflation rate reduced consumer purchasing/spending power after the Monetary Policy Committee in the Central Bank of the Republic of Türkiye had started to reduce the interest rate in September 2021. Two devastating earthquakes, which occurred in February 2023, killed thousands of people and collapsed thousands of buildings. These earthquakes caused almost $150 billion in damage, which would also decrease economic growth (Tepav Günlük, 2023). After the Turkish presidential runoff election on May 28, 2023, the Monetary Policy Committee decided to increase the interest rate from 8.5% to 15% in June 2023, followed by an increase from 15% to 17.5% in July 2023. Though these increases are below expectations, it seems that the Monetary Policy Committee will continue to increase the interest rate in the following months in 2023.

Since the inflation rate continues to skyrocket in Türkiye, it is a threat to domestic tourism. Domestic tourists must pay attention to their discretionary spending for vacations and dining out to manage their daily cost of living. Since the Turkish lira (TL) is a poor-performing currency against the U.S. dollar, this can be considered an opportunity for foreign tourism. As of July 14, 1 U.S. dollar is equal to 26.1665 TL (Türkiye Cumhuriyet Merkez Bankası, 2023). The aforesaid claim was supported by a recent study that the depreciation of the TL exerted a positive impact on tourism revenues (Yıldız, 2022). As portrayed in Table 5.4, tourism receipts in 2022 went up to almost $46.5 billion.

Changes in government policies, currency fluctuations, and inflation rates created uncertainty for tourists and businesses alike (Irani et al., 2022). As mentioned above, exchange rates play a crucial role in the tourism industry as they determine the cost of travel for international tourists. When the local currency, such as the Turkish lira, depreciates against major foreign currencies, it becomes more affordable for foreign tourists to visit Türkiye. This can lead to an increase in tourist arrivals and boost the tourism sector. On the other hand,

Table 5.4 Tourism receipts between 2013 and 2022 in Türkiye

Year	Receipts ($, U.S. dollar)
2022	46.477.871
2021	30.173.587
2020	14.817.273
2019	38.930.474
2018	30.545.924
2017	27.044542
2016	22.839.468
2015	32.492.212
2014	35.137.949
2013	33.073.502

Source: Republic of Türkiye Ministry of Culture and Tourism (2023a).

130 *Organizational resilience in H&T organizations in Türkiye*

it becomes more expensive for local tourists to go on vacation. Unfortunately, fluctuating exchange rates can create uncertainty for businesses, challenging planning and managing their operations.

The H&T sector is one of the main contributors to economic growth. For instance, it enables the governmental authorities to find sufficient foreign currencies for the export and import trade, is likely to diminish the income inequality within a nation and can increase the employment rate. However, there are mixed findings across the empirical studies. For example, Katircioglu (2009) reported that "tourism-led growth" hypothesis was not supported for the years between 1960 and 2006 since there was no significant cointegration between international tourism and economic growth in Türkiye. Recent research denoted a positive association between tourism and economic growth for the years between 1996 and 2018 (Aydin, 2022). Eyuboglu and Eyuboglu (2020) demonstrated that the "hidden tourism-led growth" hypothesis was confirmed for countries such as Türkiye and Argentina. Balsalobre-Lorente et al.'s (2023) research also presented evidence for such claim.

Akkemik's (2012) work denoted that the influence of foreign tourist expenditures on "domestic production", "value-added gross domestic product", and "employment" in Türkiye was moderate. In addition, Onder and Durgun (2008) demonstrated a positive association between tourism and employment. H&T can also be a remedy for the reduction in income equality within a nation. This is evident in Uzar and Eyuboglu's (2019) work that the expansion of tourism activities and spread of tourism throughout the whole country would help the governmental authorities to mitigate the income inequality in Türkiye. On the contrary, Raza et al. (2023) found that growth in tourism resulted in an increase in income inequality for countries such as Germany and Türkiye. Worse, in a study conducted between 1990 and 2019 in Türkiye, Köksal (2021) did not find a significant association between tourism development and quality of life. Akkemik and Perlaky's (2022) study illustrated a negative link between COVID-19 and tourism growth and employment in Türkiye. Specifically, they reported that a decrease in international tourism receipts led to a reduction in gross domestic product by 2.6% and engendered a loss of employment by 0.9%. Additionally, Tosun et al. (2023) cogently argue that rapid tourism growth in Türkiye has not become a solution for reducing unemployment and poverty rates to a great extent. Alam and Paramati's (2016) investigation for the years between 1991 and 2012 has shown that if the existing level of tourism becomes double, such an increase will reduce the income inequality in developing countries, including Türkiye.

Several studies explored different factors that could lead to VUCA in the business environment. Demir and Ersan (2018), using the European economic policy uncertainty index, investigated how uncertainty in Europe affected the stock prices of Turkish tourist enterprises. The study found that stock returns in Turkish tourist enterprises appeared to be influenced by both domestic and

Organizational resilience in H&T organizations in Türkiye 131

international economic uncertainties, with the consumer confidence index being the only macroeconomic factor affecting stock returns. This study highlights economic policy uncertainty as a significant determinant of the tourism sector's performance.

The natural environment

According to tourism statistics given by the Republic of Türkiye Ministry of Culture and Tourism (2023d), there are 438 hotels with 133,388 rooms and 285,256 beds that are categorized as "environmentally friendly accommodations facilities". The presence of such hotels signifies that the governmental authorities are now sensitive to the protection of the ecological environment and environmental sustainability. Past and recent writings also stressed the importance of environmental sustainability and indicated that employee engagement in the process was important for the accomplishment of environmental goals (Karatepe et al., 2022; Tabrizi et al., 2023).

On the other hand, Akadiri et al.'s (2019) research done for the years of 1970–2014 in Türkiye disclosed that a 1% increase in international tourists' arrivals gave rise to a 0.129% increase in "metric ton per capita" carbon dioxide emissions. Dogru et al. (2020) reported that tourism development in countries such as Canada and Türkiye depicted a negative linkage with carbon dioxide emission. Raihan and Tuspekova's (2022) research showed that an increase in tourism by 1% in Türkiye would cause carbon dioxide emissions by 0.02%. Pata and Balsalobre-Lorente (2022) analyzed the impact of tourism on the load capacity factor in Türkiye, which "…is a criterion for the sustainability of the current environment" (p. 13493). They found that tourist arrivals exerted a negative long-run influence on the load capacity factor. Another research revealed that tourism, economic growth, and energy consumption in Türkiye were among the causes of carbon dioxide emissions (Eyuboglu & Uzar, 2020). Acaroğlu et al. (2023) illustrated that a decrease in tourist arrivals would be helpful for decreasing temperature and precipitation. These empirical pieces highlight the importance of eco-friendly tourism and environmental sustainability (e.g., investing in energy-saving devices and having close control of reduction in water and electricity) in Türkiye.

It is not possible for a firm to consider long-term or sustainability factors while they want to be resilient. We know that in hotels, unsustainable actions taken during business can ultimately result in unsustainable business operations. For example, hotels that do not consider local reef health when planning tourism activities can damage or degrade reefs, making their facilities unattractive to visitors (Brown et al., 2017). Although there is much in common between sustainability and resilience, it is argued that some goals may contradict each other (Redman, 2014). This conflict holds that the adaptive cycle of resilient systems may adopt a new practice that is unsustainable in the long run but necessary in

132 *Organizational resilience in H&T organizations in Türkiye*

the short term. Specifically, in the hotel context, consider adaptation measures such as gasoline-powered generators to maintain minimal critical functionality, although this is an unsustainable solution, it is also often the case of a short-term necessity to maintain operations (Brown et al., 2017).

Hotel and restaurant firms have also begun to pay attention to the importance of environmental sustainability. Specifically, the 7 Mehmet restaurant that invested in waste management, renewable energies, and energy- and water-saving devices was the first restaurant to receive a green key certification (Rendeiro, 2022). Limak Lara Hotel established the "Zero Waste Management System", obtained the "Zero Waste" certificate, and became the first hotel with such a certificate in Antalya (Limak, 2023).

The political and legal environment

Türkiye's H&T sector contributes to the country's economy, attracting millions of domestic and international visitors annually. The political and legal environment shapes the Turkish H&T sector. Political stability, government policies, regulations, and international relations significantly impact the industry's performance. Periods of political stability have proven favorable for growth, while instability or geopolitical tensions can lead to fluctuations in visitor numbers (Akadiri et al., 2020). The tourism industry in Türkiye has experienced volatility due to geopolitical tensions, regional conflicts, and terrorist attacks in neighboring countries (Groizard et al., 2022). Türkiye's involvement in the Syrian conflict has also created geopolitical tensions. Türkiye has supported certain opposition groups and conducted military operations in northern Syria (Wei, 2019). This has strained relations with regional actors such as Syria, Russia, and the United States, leading to complex regional geopolitical dynamics. Türkiye has been involved in territorial disputes with Greece and Cyprus over maritime boundaries and the rights to explore and exploit offshore energy resources in the Eastern Mediterranean. These disputes have created significant regional geopolitical tensions (Stanič & Karbuz, 2021).

It is well-known that tourism worldwide has been affected by political instability and terrorism. For example, on October 10, 2015, a terrorist attack occurred at the Ankara Train Station. The attack resulted in a devastating incident where multiple explosions occurred during a peace rally, causing a significant loss of life and injuring numerous individuals. The suicide attack, which killed 109 people, has become the deadliest suicide bombing in Türkiye's modern history (Way & Akan, 2017). On November 13, 2022, a terrorist act occurred on Istanbul's Istiklal Street, resulting in a tragic incident, which claimed the lives of 6 individuals and left 81 others injured (CNN, 2022).

Türkiye has faced security concerns due to acts of terrorism. Terrorist attacks, particularly in popular tourist destinations, can significantly negatively impact tourism. These incidents create fear and insecurity among potential visitors,

Organizational resilience in H&T organizations in Türkiye 133

leading to cancellations and decreased tourist numbers (Agarwal et al., 2021). The perception of safety and security plays a crucial role in tourists' decision-making process (Adeloye & Brown, 2018). Despite the aforementioned devastating incidents resulted in unsafe destination image (Ertaş et al., 2021), Türkiye is among the top tourism destinations across the globe.

Another example we have seen recently that has affected Turkish tourism is a war between Russia and Ukraine. Since the beginning of the war, Russia has continued to face heavy sanctions from developed countries. One of the heavy sanctions imposed on Russia is related to payment transactions. Türkiye's tourism businesses could not receive payments from tour operators in Russia due to sanctions on payment transactions. This led to reservation cancellations. Russian Federal Tourism Agency encouraged Russian citizens to participate in domestic tourism activities rather than their participation in tourism activities in another country (Güney et al., 2022). The war between the two countries presents significant challenges for the H&T sector, which is still grappling with the aftermath of the pandemic (Nazli, 2023). While Ukraine and Russia suffer significantly in terms of inbound travel, the poor economic conditions will directly influence other nations. The uncertainties and disruptions caused by the war pose obstacles to the recovery and growth of the hospitality sector, hampering its ability to contribute to the global economy (Balli et al., 2022).

The social environment

Türkiye boosts a rich historical legacy, with a succession of civilizations such as the Hittites, Phrygians, Lycians, Lydians, Ionians, Romans, Byzantines, Seljuks, and Ottomans shaping its past (Tuna, 2016). As a result, the country's diverse population and cultural heritage make it an attractive destination for travelers seeking unique experiences (Alvarez & Korzay, 2011). The nation's cultural and historical treasures, along with its Mediterranean climate, draw visitors from around the world. Additionally, Türkiye's natural landscapes, from the Kaçkar Mountains to the serene shores of the Turkish Riviera, play a significant role in driving tourism (Statista, 2023) and foster the growth tourism and hospitality sector.

The COVID-19 pandemic had a substantial impact on travel and tourism in Türkiye, but the sector has shown signs of recovery since 2021. In 2022, the number of foreign tourists in Türkiye reached 51,387,513 million, nearing the pre-pandemic peak of 51,747,199 million in 2019. In addition, a study by Trading Economics (2023) revealed that international visitor arrivals in Türkiye increased by 16.2% year-on-year, totaling 4.5 million in May 2023, the highest in seven months, following a 29% growth in April. Among the top countries of origin for visitors were Russia with 641,000 visits, Germany with 618,000 visits, the United Kingdom with 453,000 visits, Bulgaria with 259,000 visits, and Iran with 171,000 visits. According to the Turkish Travel Agencies

134 *Organizational resilience in H&T organizations in Türkiye*

Association (TÜRSAB, 2023), Türkiye has gained global recognition as a host for significant meetings and conventions. Notable examples include the 2023 UEFA Champions League final and the 2019 Global Entrepreneurship Congress, among others. TÜRSAB's survey highlights Türkiye's reputation for Turkish cuisine, vibrant nightlife, and cultural events such as the Istanbul Music Festival, Aspendos International Opera and Ballet Festival, and Istanbul Theater Festival, among others. Hassanli et al. (2021) highlighted that showcasing traditional music, cultural events and festivals, dance, and cuisine significantly enhanced the social experience for tourists and locals alike. Such events activate social interaction, cultural exchange, and a sense of belonging.

Despite the high inflation and high foreign currency rates, there is an increase in the number of Turkish residents (having sufficient purchasing power) traveling abroad. Specifically, according to the data from the Turkish Statistical Institute (TUIK, 2023), the number of Turkish residents traveling abroad increased by 137.3% in the third quarter of 2022 compared to the same quarter in the previous year, reaching approximately 3 million people. The average amount spent per person was $534. In this quarter, all categories of spending, except for health and other costs, experienced growth compared to the same quarter in the previous year. Package trip expenditures rose by 110.5% (representing the majority), sports, education, and culture expenditures increased by 81.7%, and foreign transportation expenditures increased by 35.7%. The second most common reason for travel was "visiting relatives and friends", accounting for 17.8%, followed by "shopping" at 2.6%. Furthermore, 64.5% of Turkish residents living abroad traveled to "visiting relatives and friends". These statistics reflect the performance of the H&T sector in Türkiye, both outbound and inbound, and highlight the influence of social elements in driving its growth.

Considering the cultural richness and complexity of Türkiye's social environment, scholarly research explored various aspects of the H&T industry. Zaman and Aktan (2021) conducted a study that revealed the significant impact of residents' perceptions and support toward foreign tourists. The findings underscored the intricate relationship between residents and foreign tourists, emphasizing the importance of understanding cultural intelligence and place perceptions in shaping residents' support for tourism development. Another recent study showed that the positive effect of destination brand personality (i.e., "excitement", "sincerity", "androgyny", and "competence") on postexperience behaviors via destination satisfaction was stronger among British and German tourists than Turkish and Russian tourists who had visited Antalya (Güzel et al., 2022).

A study by Yildirim and Karaca (2022) examined the trend of tea and coffee consumption by studying the habits of individuals in Adana and İzmir. Their research showed that tea was the preferred beverage in Adana (63.3%), whereas coffee was favored by participants in İzmir (53.4%). The ratio of trying international and regional coffees was higher in İzmir than Adana. These differences in beverage preferences can be influenced by various social factors such as personalities, individual tastes, family traditions, and social circles. Such disparities in tourist and local preferences can lead to complexity and uncertainty in the social sphere of the H&T industry.

The technological environment

Technology plays a significant role in the H&T industry in the digital era. With the increasing prevalence of technological advancements and the rise of social media platforms and consumer choices, businesses are leveraging technology to promote their locations, products, and services to visitors (Dedeoğlu et al., 2020). During the global lockdown caused by the COVID-19 pandemic, destinations utilized technology to advertise themselves. Türkiye, for instance, successfully employed a media strategy called the "restorative experience" to attract visitors after the shutdown. Through a video commercial titled "Turkish Colors ReTurkey", beautiful landscapes were showcased, encouraging viewers to explore the refreshing Turkish blues and greens (Ketter & Avraham, 2021).

Studies, like the one conducted by Sanliöz Özgen and Kozak (2015), indicate that platforms such as TripAdvisor are widely utilized as destination marketing tools. The research reveals that hotels in Türkiye pay significant attention to TripAdvisor as an essential tool for various purposes, including marketing and quality management. Turkish hotels are increasingly using social media platforms, search engine optimization techniques, and online advertising to reach their target audience and promote their services, resulting in improved visibility, customer engagement, and revenue generation.

In the Turkish H&T industry, various sectors have been leveraging other technologies to foster growth. Specifically, according to a report by Statista (2021), the revenue of restaurants and mobile food service activities in Türkiye was projected to reach approximately 13.5 billion U.S. dollars by 2023. However, while technology offers numerous opportunities, it also presents challenges for the sector in the country. The existing literature identified issues such as data security, infrastructure limitations, and the digital divide as barriers to technological adoption in the industry (Tlili et al., 2021). Another study by Vatan and Dogan (2021) denoted that the concept "robot" created negative emotions among hotel workers in Türkiye, and such workers stated that service robots would give rise to communication problems with customers and trigger the unemployment rate in the industry. On the other hand, Seyitoğlu et al.'s (2021) research showed that restaurant managers in Türkiye had negative attitudes towards service robots, while restaurant customers supported the use of service robots. Eşitti's (2023) recent work revealed that hotel managers in Türkiye emphasized the role of digital applications (e.g., mobile applications in hotels, automatic travel insurance). These findings explicitly show the need for explicating the positive

136 *Organizational resilience in H&T organizations in Türkiye*

effects of using service robots on the firm's performance and its competitive advantage. Overcoming these challenges requires collaboration among industry stakeholders, policymakers, and technology providers.

The research sample – Türkiye

Sample and procedure

Data were gathered from managerial and supervisory employees in the five-, four-, and three-star hotels in Ankara, the capital city of Türkiye. We used the judgmental sampling procedure to determine the employees, while the convenience sampling technique was used to choose the hotels. This is because of the fact that not all employees would be able to respond to the items in the questionnaire. Therefore, the abovementioned managerial and supervisory employees were selected.

After receiving permission for data collection from the management of each hotel, the questionnaires were distributed to employees in envelopes via the representatives assigned by the management of the hotel. Each employee was requested to seal the questionnaire in the envelope. Each participant was assured of anonymity and confidentiality. The scale items were not grouped under a specific title (i.e., the name of the construct). Participation was voluntary, and each participant gave consent. The questionnaire contained information such as "There were no right or wrong answers to the items". These procedural remedies enabled us to mitigate the risk of common method variance (Podsakoff et al., 2003).

Of the 300 questionnaires distributed, 195 were returned. However, 34 questionnaires were discarded due to missing data. The response rate was 53.7% (161/300). Table 5.5 presents the demographic breakdown of the sample. The size of the hotels was categorized as small (10–49 employees), medium (50–249 employees), and large (more than 249 employees) enterprises. Fifty-one employees worked in the first category, 73 in the second category, and 37 in the third category.

Measurement

All the items used in our research were subjected to the back-translation method. The items were originally prepared in English and then translated into Turkish. The content of the questionnaire was checked by two academicians to confirm the wording. Then, the questionnaire was tested with a pilot sample of ten employees regarding the readability and understandability of the items. As a result of the pilot test, no changes were made in the questionnaire. Sources of the scales were given in Chapter 3.

Organizational resilience in H&T organizations in Türkiye 137

Table 5.5 Participants' profile (n = 161)

Variables	Frequency	%
Age (years)		
18–27	108	67.1
28–37	-	-
38–47	26	16.1
48–57	24	14.9
58 and older	3	1.9
Gender		
Male	107	66.5
Female	54	33.5
Education		
Primary school	7	4.4
Secondary and high school	44	27.3
Two-year college degree	44	27.3
Four-year college degree	53	32.9
Graduate degree	13	8.1
Organizational tenure (years)		
Shorter than 1	61	37.9
1–5	61	37.9
6–10	13	8.0
11–15	17	10.6
16–20	5	3.1
21 and longer	4	2.5
Marital status		
Single or divorced	82	50.9
Married	79	49.1

Data analysis

The proposed and alternative models given in Chapter 3 were tested using structural equation modeling via Partial Least Squares (PLS-SEM) technique. The choice of this technique over other possible ones was motivated by several reasons. First, we intend to test a complex model of mediations and serial mediation from a model formed by first- and second-order constructs. PLS has been shown to be a robust technique when the theorized model is complex (Hair et al., 2017, 2019a). Second, all constructs or latent variables used to represent employee behaviors or perceptions about their organization. Therefore, these latent variables are specified as reflective, where the indicators reflect the construct (Benitez et al., 2020). It has consistently been pointed out that PLS-SEM is able to adequately analyze complex models entirely formed by constructs measured in mode A or reflexive (Hair et al., 2019b; Sarstedt et al., 2016).

138 *Organizational resilience in H&T organizations in Türkiye*

Furthermore, since organizational learning culture, organizational resilience, personal social capital, and psychological capital represent second-order or multidimensional constructs, we assess a reflective–reflective model. Following Sarstedt et al. (2019), we assessed the measurement model in two additional stages by applying the disjoint two-stage approach. In the first step, we analyzed the properties of the measurement model formed from the relationships between the items and the corresponding first-order composites. In the second step, it is possible to gauge the measurement model including the second-order constructs represented by the relationships with their first-order components (Sarstedt et al., 2019). This is: continuous learning, inquiry and dialogue, team learning, embedded system, empowerment, system connection, and strategic leadership for the organizational learning culture second-order composite; adaptive resilience and planned resilience for the organizational resilience second-order composite; social capital-team and social capital-others for personal social capital second-order composite; and finally, self-efficacy, hope, resilience, and optimism for psychological capital second-order composite. To gauge both measurement and structural models, we used SmartPLS v.4 (Ringle et al., 2022).

Results

Measurement model assessment

Confirmatory composite analysis

The most suitable technique to validate the measurement model in a context of PLS-SEM analysis is determined by the use of compounds or latent variables. In this sense, confirmatory composite analysis (CCA) has been pointed out as an adequate method adapted to the characteristics of PLS with which researchers can assess how composites fit the construct they are intended to represent (Henseler & Schuberth, 2020). As stated by Henseler (2017), "confirmatory composite analysis tests whether the discrepancy between the empirical correlation matrix and the correlation matrix implied by the saturated model is so small that the possibility cannot be excluded that this discrepancy is purely attributable to sampling error" (p.184).

We used the bootstrapping test based on 4,999 subsamples and two-tails to construct an empirical distribution of the discrepancies from which to assess the values for the measurement model (saturated model) for both first- and second-order levels. Approximate fit measures such as standardized root mean square residual (SRMR) and exact fit measures such as unweighted least squares distance (d_{ULS}) and geodesic distance (d_G) were gauged. The results were shown in Table 5.6. The values for all the discrepancies were below the threshold set by HI_{99} (99% quantile). Following Henseler (2017), based on an alpha level of 0.05, the model should not be rejected.

Organizational resilience in H&T organizations in Türkiye   139

Table 5.6 Confirmatory composite analysis for the first- and second-order level (saturated model)

Discrepancy	First-order level			Second-order level		
	Value	HI99	Conclusion	Value	HI99	Conclusion
SRMR	0.061	0.053	Supported	0.048	0.053	Supported
d_{ULS}	11.057	11.174	Supported	1.057	1.310	Supported
d_G	7.760	14.895	Supported	0.620	0.893	Supported

Notes: SRMR = standardized root mean square residual; d_{ULS} = unweighted least squares distance; d_G = geodesic distance.

Measurement model

Since all the composites were conceptualized as part of a reflective–reflective high-order model, we must analyze the properties of the measurement model for both first- and second-order components (Hair et al., 2017; Sarstedt et al., 2019). The results were given in Table 5.7.

To test for the reliability of the indicators and dimensions (first-order level), we used factor loadings. We also tested its significance level with a two-tailed bootstrap test. Loadings should generally be larger than 0.707 (Hair et al., 2017, 2020). However, when this value is not met, the recommendation by Hair et al. (2014, 2017) is to keep the information provided by the indicators under two main premises: (1) that the values are always greater than 0.4 and (2) that the item is not problematic to ensure validity and reliability of the construct. Following this recommendation, the loadings in a range of values between 0.458*** and 0.974*** were maintained. Because they did not meet any of the criteria set by Hair et al. (2014, 2017), one indicator of organizational resilience, in addition to three indicators that belonged to psychological capital, were dropped.

To gauge composite reliability, we utilized Cronbach's Alpha, Dijkstra-Henseler's Rho_a, and statistical composite reliability Rho_c. In all cases, both for the first- and second-order level, the values (ranging between 0.766 and 0.972) were above the threshold established for the three statistics used, set at 0.707 (Hair et al., 2019a), illustrating that composite reliability was verified (Benitez et al., 2020).

To assess convergent validity, we resort to the construct's average variance extracted (AVE). The AVEs of our constructs (first- and second order) ranged from 0.557 to 0.945. Since, in all cases, the compounds took values above the threshold of 0.5 (Hair et al., 2019a), convergent validity was verified.

Finally, we measured the discriminant validity of the composites based on a double criterion: Fornell-Larcker criterion and heterotrait-monotrait ratio

140 *Organizational resilience in H&T organizations in Türkiye*

Table 5.7 Assessment of the measurement model for first- and second-order
reflective latent variables

Scales and items	α	ρA	CR	AVE	FL
Organizational learning culture	**0.959**	**0.960**	**0.966**	**0.802**	
Continuous learning	*0.827*	*0.833*	*0.897*	*0.745*	*0.877****
In my organization, people help each other learn					0.871***
In my organization, people are given time to support learning					0.909***
In my organization, people are rewarded for learning					0.805***
Inquiry and dialogue	*0.861*	*0.865*	*0.915*	*0.782*	*0.879****
In my organization, people give open and honest feedback to each other					0.906***
In my organization, whenever people state their view, they also ask what others think					0.873***
In my organization, people spend time building trust with each other					0.874***
Team learning	*0.838*	*0.838*	*0.902*	*0.755*	*0.926****
In my organization, teams/groups have the freedom to adapt their goals as needed					0.876***
In my organization, teams/groups revise their thinking as a result of group discussion or information collected					0.891***
In my organization, teams/groups are confident that the organization will act as their recommendations					0.839***
Embedded system	*0.883*	*0.889*	*0.927*	*0.810*	*0.909****
My organization creates systems to measure gaps between current and expected performance					0.892***
My organization makes its lessons learned available to all employees					0.906***
My organization measures the results of the time and the resources spent on trainings					0.902***
Empowerment	*0.863*	*0.865*	*0.916*	*0.785*	*0.903****
My organization recognizes people for taking initiatives					0.898***
My organization gives people control over the resources their need to accomplish their work					0.882***
My organization supports employees who take calculated risk					0.879***
System connection	*0.884*	*0.885*	*0.928*	*0.812*	*0.885****
My organization encourages people to think from a global perspective					0.885***
My organization works together with the outside community to meet mutual needs					0.918***
My organization encourages people to get answers from across the organization when solving problems					0.900***

Organizational resilience in H&T organizations in Türkiye 141

Table 5.7 (Continued)

Scales and items	α	ρA	CR	AVE	FL
Strategic leadership	*0.863*	*0.864*	*0.916*	*0.785*	*0.887****
In my organization, leaders mentor and coach those they lead					0.877***
In my organization, leaders continually look for opportunities to learn					0.899***
In my organization, leaders ensure that the organization's actions are consistent with its values					0.881***
Organizational resilience	**0.900**	**0.902**	**0.919**	**0.557**	
Adaptative resilience	*0.848*	*0.854*	*0.885*	*0.526*	*0.957****
We proactively monitor our industry to have an early warning of emerging issues					0.660***
People in our organization are committed to working on a problem until it is resolved					0.700***
Our organization maintains sufficient resources to absorb some unexpected change					0.803***
If key people were unavailable, there are always others who could fill their role					0.734***
There would be good leadership from within our organization if we were struck by a crisis					0.775***
We are known for our ability to use knowledge in novel ways					0.739***
We can make tough decisions quickly					0.651***
There are few barriers stopping us from working well with other organizations					Dropped
Planned resilience	*0.827*	*0.838*	*0.879*	*0.594*	*0.950****
Given how others depend on us, the way we plan for the unexpected is appropriate					0.779***
Our organization is committed to practicing and testing its emergency plans to ensure they are effective					0.853***
We have a focus on being able to respond to the unexpected					0.812***
We have clearly defined priorities for what is important during and after a crisis					0.710***
We build relationships with other organizations we might have to work with in a crisis					0.685***
Learning goal orientation	**0.927**	**0.928**	**0.943**	**0.734**	
I often read materials related to my work to improve my ability					0.779***
I am willing to select a challenging work assignment that I can learn a lot from					0.890***
I often look for opportunities to develop new skills and knowledge					0.878***
I enjoy challenging and difficult tasks at work where I will learn new skills					0.851***

(*Continued*)

142 *Organizational resilience in H&T organizations in Türkiye*

Table 5.7 (Continued)

Scales and items	α	ρA	CR	AVE	FL
For me, development of my work ability is important enough to take risk					0.877***
I prefer to work in situations that require a high level of ability and talent					0.859***
Personal social capital	**0.942**	**0.944**	**0.972**	**0.945**	
Social capital – team	*0.849*	*0.867*	*0.896*	*0.684*	*0.971******
How do you rate the number of friends you have?					0.861***
With how many do you have routine contact?					0.830***
How many can you trust?					0.778***
How many will definitely help you if you ask?					0.836***
Social capital – others	*0.886*	*0.898*	*0.921*	*0.744*	*0.974******
How do you rate the number of people you interact with?					0.870***
How do you rate the number of people with whom you have routine contact?					0.916***
How many have great social influence, broad connections, or significant power for decision making?					0.847***
How many of these people will definitely help you if you ask?					0.816***
Psychological capital	**0.911**	**0.912**	**0.938**	**0.790**	
Self-efficacy	*0.909*	*0.913*	*0.930*	*0.689*	*0.876******
I feel confident analyzing a long-term problem to find a solution					0.809***
I feel confident in representing my work area in meetings with management					0.847***
Item3					0.862***
Item4					0.873***
Item5					0.792***
Item6					0.793***
Hope	*0.851*	*0.865*	*0.889*	*0.573*	*0.920******
If I should find myself in a jam at work, I could think of many ways to get out of it					0.704***
At the present time, I am energetically pursuing my work goals					0.793***
Item3					0.730***
Item4					0.821***
Item5					0.747***
Item6					0.741***

Organizational resilience in H&T organizations in Türkiye 143

Table 5.7 (Continued)

Scales and items	α	ρA	CR	AVE	FL
Resilience	*0.892*	*0.897*	*0.921*	*0.699*	*0.912****
When I have a setback at work, I have trouble recovering from it, moving on (R)					Dropped
I usually manage difficulties one way or another at work					0.832***
Item3					0.831***
Item4					0.787***
Item5					0.865***
Item6					0.865***
Optimism	*0.766*	*0.835*	*0.844*	*0.587*	*0.846****
When things are uncertain for me at work, I usually expect the best					0.803***
If something can go wrong for me work wise, it will (R)					Dropped
Item3					0.875***
Item4					0.855***
Item5					Dropped
Item6					0.458***
Employee resilience	**0.900**	**0.904**	**0.952**	**0.909**	
I successfully manage a high workload for long periods of time					0.743***
I resolve crises competently at work					0.778***
I learn from mistakes at work and improve the way I do my job					0.773***
I re-evaluate my performance and continually improve the way I do my work					0.783***
I effectively respond to feedback at work, even criticism					0.754***
I seek assistance to work when I need specific resources					0.745***
I use change at work as an opportunity for growth					0.683***
I effectively collaborate with others to handle unexpected challenges at work					0.762***
I approach managers when I need their support					0.690***

Notes: Italics used for first-order composites (dimensions).
α = Cronbach's Alpha; ρA = Dijkstra-Henseler's Rho_a; CR = composite reliability; AVE = average variance extracted; FL = factor loadings. ***p < 0.001.

144 *Organizational resilience in H&T organizations in Türkiye*

(HTMT). The results are presented in Table 5.8. For the Fornell-Larcker matrix, the square root of the AVE was always higher than the rest of the correlations between variables (Fornell and Larcker, 1981). For the HTMT matrix, the ratio values were below the marked threshold of 0.9 (Hair et al., 2017; Henseler et al., 2015). The combination of these results helped us to verify discriminant validity.

In addition to procedural remedies, Harman's single-factor test was performed to check common method variance. The unrotated exploratory factor analysis demonstrated that the first factor explained only 39.54% of the total variance. The question of "Where do you live" was used as a marker variable. The partial correlation analysis demonstrated that the marker variable did not amend the significance of the correlations among the study variables. Therefore, common method variance was not a problem in this research. Table 5.9 presents the summary statistics and correlations.

The assessment of organizational resilience in hotels in Türkiye

Structural model

As has been recommended by Hair et al. (2014), prior to the assessment of the structural model, tests based on the variance inflation factor (VIF) should be performed to eliminate the possibility of collinearity between the constructs of the model. In our results, the VIF values for all the constructs were in the range between 1,324 and 2,868. From a conservative point of view, it has been considered that values greater than 3 may be a symptom that indicates collinearity problems in the proposed model (Hair et al., 2019a). Our data returned values below this conservative threshold. Therefore, multicollinearity cannot be considered a problem in our data.

The hypothesis test was carried out by the bootstrapping test from 9,999 samples, one-tail since all hypotheses, both direct and mediated, were defined with a positive sign, and percentile bootstrap as the confidence interval calculation method (Hair et al., 2017). In view of this test, we assessed significance, algebraic sign and magnitude of the regression coefficients, the effect size (f^2), and the values of explained variance (R^2) for each endogenous construct.

Our work first proposed a comprehensive conceptual model (Figure 3.1), which included six direct hypotheses (H1–H6) that also gave rise to three mediations considering employee learning goal orientation and employee resilience as mediators and one serial mediation that considered both learning goal orientation and employee resilience (in that order) as mediators. We depicted the results in Table 5.10.

Our results showed that organizational learning culture was positively related to organizational resilience ($\beta = 0.557$, p_{one}-tailed < 0.000). Hence, hypothesis 1 was confirmed. In the same way, we were able to verify that organizational learning culture was positively related to the learning goal orientation of

Table 5.8 Discriminant validity assessment

Construct	Fornell-Larcker criterion						Heterotrait-Monotrait criterion					
	1	*2*	*3*	*4*	*5*	*6*	*1*	*2*	*3*	*4*	*5*	*6*
(1)OLC	0.895											
(2)OR	0.749	0.953					0.804					
(3)LGO	0.629	0.672	0.857				0.665	0.734				
(4)PSC	0.442	0.404	0.489	0.972			0.465	0.439	0.522			
(5)PsyCap	0.571	0.761	0.790	0.432	0.889		0.608	0.838	0.859	0.467		
(5)ER	0.588	0.653	0.787	0.491	0.745	0.747	0.626	0.721	0.858	0.533	0.821	

Notes: OLC = organizational learning culture; OR = organizational resilience; LGO = learning goal orientation; PSC = personal social capital; PsyCap = psychological capital; ER = employee resilience.

Table 5.9 Summary statistics and correlations

Variables	1	2	3	4	5	6	7	8	9
1. Gender									
2. Organizational tenure	−0.166*	-							
3. Size of the hotel	0.066	0.092	-						
4. Learning organizational culture	0.037	0.025	0.134	-					
5. Organizational resilience	−0.001	−0.048	0.130	0.744**	-				
6. Learning goal orientation	−0.029	−0.001	0.183*	0.622**	0.674**	-			
7. Personal social capital	−0.115	−0.025	−0.010	0.479**	0.385**	0.443**	-		
8. Psychological capital	−0.032	−0.097	0.179*	0.565**	0.761**	0.784**	0.411**	-	
9. Employee resilience	−0.036	−0.023	0.214**	0.574**	0.651**	0.785**	0.440**	0.729**	-
Mean	0.34	2.11	2.91	3.75	4.05	4.89	4.25	4.96	4.20
Standard deviation	0.47	1.25	0.74	0.85	0.68	1.00	1.50	0.82	0.73

Notes: Gender was coded as 0 = male and 1 = female. Organizational tenure was measured in six categories. The size of the hotel was measured in three categories.

employees (β = 0.629, p_{one}-tailed < 0.000), supporting hypothesis 2. At the individual or employee level, as expected, both learning goal orientation (β = 0.479, p_{one}-tailed < 0.000), personal social capital (β = 0.121, p_{one}-tailed < 0.020), and psychological capital (β = 0.314, p_{one}-tailed < 0.000) were positively related to employee resilience, confirming hypotheses 3, 4, and 5, respectively. Finally, we were able to verify that the relationship in hypothesis 6 between employee resilience and organizational resilience was positive (β = 0.326, p_{one}-tailed < 0.000).

Though not hypothesized, the analysis of the effects of the mediation and serial mediation was carried out following the guidelines developed by Carrion et al. (2017). Our data confirmed that learning goal orientation positively mediated the relationship between organizational learning culture and employee resilience (β = 0.302, p_{one}-tailed < 0.000). In the same way, we confirmed that employee resilience functioned as a mediator of the relationship between personal social capital and organizational resilience (β = 0.039, p_{one}-tailed < 0.036), and the relationship between psychological capital and organizational resilience (β = 0.102, p_{one}-tailed < 0.008). In addition, learning goal orientation and employee resilience would act as serial mediators between orientational learning culture and organizational resilience. The test results (β = 0.098, p_{one}-tailed < 0.000) offered evidence to confirm the serial mediation.

Finally, R^2 helps us to determine the explanatory power of the model. There is some agreement in considering a threshold around 0.200 as an adequate minimum when analyzing the behaviors or attitudes of employees (Benitez et al., 2020; Hair et al., 2019a). As Table 5.10 showed, the value of R^2 was much higher than this threshold for the endogenous variables of the model, especially for the result variable at the organizational level (organizational resilience) and the result variable at the employee level (employee resilience). To assess the size of the effect (f^2), we followed the criteria indicated by Cohen (1992). In our results, f^2 values generally ranged from 0.033 to 0.656. Although the weak effect found for hypothesis 4 was an exception (0.033), generally prevailing a medium effect of the relationships studied in hypothesis 3 and hypothesis 6 (0.243 and 0.188, respectively) and the strong effect confirmed hypothesis 1 and hypothesis 2 with values for f^2 being 0.549 and 0.656, respectively.

On the other hand, our work proposed the alternative comprehensive model (Figure 3.2), which included six direct hypotheses (H1–H5 and H7) that also gave rise to two mediations considering organizational resilience and learning goal orientation as two independent mediators that could complementarily explain the relationship between organizational learning culture and employee resilience. We showed the results in Table 5.11.

For the analysis of this alternative model, our results showed that organizational learning culture was positively associated with organizational resilience (β = 0.749, p_{one}-tailed < 0.000). Therefore, hypothesis 1 was confirmed. In the same way, we were able to confirm that organizational learning culture was positively related to learning goal orientation (β = 0.629, p_{one}-tailed < 0.000),

148   *Organizational resilience in H&T organizations in Türkiye*

Table 5.10 Assessment of the comprehensive conceptual model

	Path coefficient	*t-value*	*CI*	f^2	*Conclusion*
Direct effects test					
H1: OLC -> OR	0.557(0.000)	9.229	0.455–0.652	0.549	Supported
H2: OLC -> LGO	0.629(0.000)	9.189	0.500–0.726	0.656	Supported
H3: LGO -> ER	0.479(0.000)	5.693	0.327–0.605	0.243	Supported
H4: PSC -> ER	0.121(0.020)	2.051	0.025–0.219	0.033	Supported
H5: PsyCap -> ER	0.314(0.000)	3.507	0.170–0.463	0.112	Supported
H6: ER -> OR	0.326(0.000)	4.875	0.211–0.430	0.188	Supported
Mediating effects test					
OLC -> LGO -> ER	0.302(0.000)	4.832	0.198–0.405		Supported
OLC -> LGO -> ER -> OR	0.098(0.000)	3.957	0.060–0.141		Supported
PSC -> ER -> OR	0.039(0.036)	1.804	0.006–0.077		Supported
PsyCap -> ER -> OR	0.102(0.008)	2.410	0.043–0.182		Supported
Endogenous variable	**R^2**		**Adjusted R^2**		
OR	0.630		0.625		
ER	0.670		0.664		
LGO	0.396		0.392		
Structural model fit	**Value**		**HI_{99}**		
SRMR	0.054		0.055		Supported
d_{ULS}	1.380		1.428		Supported
d_G	0.659		0.901		Supported

Notes: OLC = organizational learning culture; OR = organizational resilience; LGO= learning goal orientation; PSC = personal social capital; PsyCap = psychological capital; ER = employee resilience.; SRMR = standardized root mean square residual; d_{ULS} = unweighted least squares distance; d_G = geodesic distance.
CI = bootstrapping confidence interval based on the [9999] one-tailed test; p-value in parentheses.

supporting hypothesis 2. At the individual or employee level, learning goal orientation ($\beta = 0.587$, p_{one}-tailed < 0.000), personal social capital ($\beta = 0.120$, p_{one}-tailed < 0.027), and psychological capital ($\beta = 0.252$, p_{one}-tailed < 0.005) were positively linked to employee resilience, confirming hypotheses 3, 4, and 5, respectively. Finally, we were able to verify that the relationship hypothesized in H7 between organizational resilience and employee resilience was positive ($\beta = 0.210$, p_{one}-tailed < 0.001).

As was the case in the first model, the analysis of the effects of the mediation and serial mediation was performed in view of the guidelines developed by Carrion et al. (2017). Our data verified that organizational resilience mediated

Organizational resilience in H&T organizations in Türkiye 149

Table 5.11 Test of the alternative comprehensive model

	Path coefficient	t-value	CI	f2	Conclusion
Direct effects test					
H1: OLC -> OR	0.749(0.000)	12.434	0.670–0.811	1.276	Supported
H2: OLC -> LGO	0.629(0.000)	9.188	0.503–0.728	0.656	Supported
H3: LGO -> ER	0.587(0.000)	8.793	0.479–0.698	0.495	Supported
H4: PSC -> ER	0.120(0.027)	1.923	0.067–0.305	0.031	Supported
H5: PsyCap -> ER	0.252(0.005)	2.556	0.091–0.416	0.054	Supported
H7: OR -> ER	0.210(0.001)	3.022	0.019–0.212	0.070	Supported
Mediating effects test					
OLC -> OR -> ER	0.157(0.002)	2.967	0.072–0.245		Supported
OLC -> LGO -> ER	0.369(0.000)	5.948	0.270–0.474		Supported
Endogenous variable	**R²**		**Adjusted R²**		
OR	0.561		0.558		
ER	0.675		0.667		
LGO	0.396		0.392		
Structural model fit	**Value**		**HI₉₉**		
SRMR	0.061		0.065		Supported
d_{ULS}	1.317		1.502		Supported
d_G	0.432		0.598		Supported

Notes: OLC = organizational learning culture; OR = organizational resilience; LGO = learning goal orientation; PSC = personal social capital; PsyCap = psychological capital; ER = employee resilience; SRMR = standardized root mean square residual; d_{ULS} = unweighted least squares distance; d_G = geodesic distance.
CI = bootstrapping confidence interval based on the [9999] one-tailed test; p-value in parentheses.

the relationship between organizational learning culture and employee resilience (β = 0.157, p_{one}-tailed < 0.002). In the same way, we confirmed that learning goal orientation functioned as a mediator between organizational learning culture and employee resilience (β = 0.396, p_{one}-tailed < 0.000).

Regarding the analysis of R^2 and f^2 of the alternative model, as Table 5.11 illustrated, the value of R^2 was much higher than the threshold set at 0.200 (Benitez et al., 2020; Hair et al., 2019a) for the endogenous variables of the model. Especially, the value of R^2 demonstrated great explanatory power of the model on the outcome variable at the employee level (employee resilience). Regarding the effect size (f^2), we followed the criteria indicated by Cohen (1992). That is, f^2 values generally ranged from 0.031 to 0.656. Although the values for hypotheses 4, 5, and 7 should be classified as weak effect (0.031,

150   *Organizational resilience in H&T organizations in Türkiye*

0.054, and 0.070, respectively), the values for hypotheses 1–3 confirmed a strong effect based on Cohen's (1992) classification.

General discussion

The findings reported above delineate support for the study hypotheses. In the comprehensive conceptual model, organizational learning culture and employee resilience are the critical predictors of organizational resilience. The findings illustrate the critical roles of leadership, culture, and learning that would enable hotel firms to acquire, create, and transfer knowledge to strengthen both employee and organizational resilience. This is especially important in highly dynamic VUCA contexts (cf. Zhang-Zhang et al., 2022). Luthans and Broad (2022) assert that employee resilience can be used to recover from global mental health challenges. A number of empirical pieces support the notion that investment in human resources bolsters organizational resilience (Su et al., 2021).

An organizational learning culture is also a foundation for hotel employees' learning goal orientation while learning goal orientation and psychological capital significantly contribute to employee resilience. Among the abovementioned dimensions, learning goal orientation appears to be the most important personal resource/human capital triggering employee resilience. The empirical results suggest that learning goal orientation mediates the link between organizational learning culture and employee resilience, while employee resilience mediates the association between psychological capital or personal social capital and organizational resilience. In addition, learning goal orientation and employee resilience sequentially mediate the link between organizational learning culture and organizational resilience. In the alternative comprehensive model, organizational resilience or learning goal orientation acts as a mediator between organizational learning culture and employee resilience.

In a firm where organizational learning is one of the significant elements of culture, employees would learn from failure practices that strengthen their resilience and therefore support organizational resilience (cf. Yuan et al., 2022). The findings explicitly highlight the critical role of organizational learning culture in the enhancement of personal resources and, therefore, organizational (employee) resilience and employee (organizational) resilience.

References

Acaroğlu, H., Güllü, M., & Seçilmiş, C. (2023). Climate change, the by-product of tourism and energy consumption through a sustainable economic growth: A nonlinear ARDL analysis for Turkey. *Environmental Science and Pollution Research, 30,* 81585–81599.

Adeloye, D., & Brown, L. (2018). Terrorism and domestic tourist risk perceptions. *Journal of Tourism and Cultural Change, 16*(3), 217–233.

Organizational resilience in H&T organizations in Türkiye 151

Agarwal, S., Page, S. J., & Mawby, R. (2021). Tourist security, terrorism risk management and tourist safety. *Annals of Tourism Research, 89*, 103207.

Akadiri, S. S., Alola, A. A., & Akadiri, A. C. (2019). The role of globalization, real income, tourism in environmental sustainability target: Evidence from Turkey. *Science of the Total Environment, 687*, 423–432.

Akadiri, S. S., Eluwole, K. K., Akadiri, A. C., & Avci, T. (2020). Does causality between geopolitical risk, tourism and economic growth matter? Evidence from Turkey. *Journal of Hospitality and Tourism Management, 43*, 273–277.

Akkemik, K. A. (2012). Assessing the importance of international tourism for the Turkish economy: A social accounting matrix analysis. *Tourism Management, 33*(4), 790–801.

Akkemik, K. A., & Perlaky, D. P. (2022). Impact of COVID-19 on tourism: Evidence from SAM assessments of Hungary and Turkey. *Advances in Hospitality and Tourism Research, 11*(1), 146–170.

Alam, Md. S., & Paramati, S. R. (2016). The impact of tourism on income inequality in developing economies: Does Kuznets curve hypothesis exist? *Annals of Tourism Research, 61*, 111–126.

Alvarez, M. D., & Korzay, M. (2011). Turkey as a heritage tourism destination: The role of knowledge. *Journal of Hospitality Marketing and Management, 20*(3–4), 425–440.

Aydin, M. (2022). The impacts of political stability, renewable energy consumption, and economic growth on tourism in Turkey: New evidence from Fourier Bootstrap ARDL approach. *Renewable Energy, 190*, 467–473.

Balli, F., Billah, M., & Chowdhury, I. (in press). Impact of the Russia–Ukraine war on hospitality equity markets. *Tourism Economics*.

Balsalobre-Lorente, D., Luzon, L. I., Usman, M., & Jahanger, A. (2023). The relevance of international tourism and natural resource rents in economic growth: Fresh evidence from MINT countries in the digital era. *Environmental Science and Pollution Research, 30*, 81495–81512.

Benitez, J., Henseler, J., Castillo, A., & Schuberth, F. (2020). How to perform and report an impactful analysis using partial least squares: Guidelines for confirmatory and explanatory IS research. *Information and Management, 57*(2), 103168.

Brown, N. A., Rovins, J. E., Feldmann-Jensen, S., Orchiston, C., & Johnston, D. (2017). Exploring disaster resilience within the hotel sector: A systematic review of literature. *International Journal of Disaster Risk Reduction, 22*, 362–370.

Carrión, G. C., Nitzl, C., & Roldàn, J. L. (2017). Meidation analyses in partial least squares structural equation modeling: Guidelines and empirical examples. In Latan, H., & Noonan, R. (Eds), *Partial least suqares path modeling* (pp. 173–195). Springer.

Cavusgil, S. T., van der Vegt, S., Dakhli, M., De Farias, S., Doria, E., Eroglu, S., & Wang, E. Y. (2021). International business in an accelerated VUCA world: Trends, disruptions, and coping strategies. *Rutgers Business Review, 6*(3), 219–243.

Charfeddine, L., & Dawn, I. (in press). Analysis of the resilience of the Turkey tourism industry to exogenous shocks: New evidence from a NARDL model. *Tourism Recreation Research*.

CNN. (2022). "Suspect in custody in Istanbul blast that killed 6 and injured 81, officials say" https://edition.cnn.com/2022/11/13/europe/istanbul-turkey-explosion-intl/index.html (accessed on 14 July 2023).

Cohen, J. (1992). Statistical power analysis. *Current Directions in Psychological Science, 1*(3), 98–101.

152 *Organizational resilience in H&T organizations in Türkiye*

Dedeoğlu, B. B., Taheri, B., Okumus, F., & Gannon, M. (2020). Understanding the importance that consumers attach to social media sharing (ISMS): Scale development and validation. *Tourism Management, 76*, 103954.

Demir, E., & Ersan, O. (2018). The impact of economic policy uncertainty on stock returns of Turkish tourism companies. *Current Issues in Tourism, 21*(8), 847–855.

Dogru, T., Kocak, E., Isik, C., Suess, C., & Sirakaya-Turk, E. (2020). The nexus between tourism, economic growth, renewable energy consumption, and carbon dioxide emissions: Contemporary evidence from OECD countries. *Environmental Science and Pollution Research, 27*, 40930–40948.

Ertaş, M., Sel, Z. G., Kırlar-Can, B., & Tütüncü, Ö. (2021). Effects of crisis on crisis management practices: A case from Turkish tourism enterprises. *Journal of Sustainable Tourism, 29*(9), 1490–1507.

Eşitti, B. B. (2023). The impact of coronavirus (Covid-19) pandemic: Digital transformation changes in tourism. *Journal of Tourism Theory and Research, 9*(1), 15–23.

Eyuboglu, K., & Uzar, U. (2020). The impact of tourism on CO_2 emission in Turkey. *Current Issues in Tourism, 23*(13), 1631–1645.

Eyuboglu, S., & Eyuboglu, K. (2020). Tourism development and economic growth: An asymmetric panel causality test. *Current Issues in Tourism, 23*(6), 659–665.

Fornell, C., & Larcker, D. F. (1981). Evaluating structural equation models with unobservable variables and measurement error. *Journal of Marketing Research, 18*(1), 39–50.

Goymen, K. (2000). Tourism and governance in Turkey. *Annals of Tourism Research, 27*(4), 1025–1048.

Groizard, J. L., Ismael, M., & Santana-Gallego, M. (2022). Political upheavals, tourism flight, and spillovers: The case of the Arab spring. *Journal of Travel Research, 61*(4), 921–939.

Güney, T., Göktepe, S., & Kokonalıoğlu, H. T. (2022). Rusya-Ukrayna Savaşı'nın Türkiye turizmine olası etkileri. *Batman Üniversitesi Yaşam Bilimleri Dergisi, 12*(1), 92–104.

Güzel, Ö., Ünal, C., & Şahin, İ. (in press). How does the cross-cultural view shape the destination brand personality and brand image? Evidence from the travelers. *Journal of Quality Assurance and in Hospitality and Tourism.*

Hair, J.F., Howard, M. C., & Nitzl, C. (2020). Assessing measurement model quality in PLS-SEM using con fi rmatory composite analysis. *Journal of Business Research, 109*, 101–110.

Hair, J. F., Hult, G. T., Ringle, C. M., & Sarstedt, M. (2014). *A primer on partial least squares structural equation modeling (PLS-SEM).* 2nd ed. Sage Publications.

Hair, J. F., Risher, J., Sarstedt, M., & Ringle, C. M. (2019a). When to use and how to report the results of PLS-SEM. *European Business Review, 31*(1), 2–24.

Hair, J. F., Risher, J. J., Sarstedt, M., & Ringle, C. M. (2019b). When to use and how to report the results of PLS-SEM. *European Business Review, 31*(1), 2–24.

Hair, J. F., Sarstedt, M., Ringle, C. M., & Gudergan, S. P. (2017). *Advanced issues in partial least squares structural equation modeling.* Sage Publications.

Hassanli, N., Walters, T., & Williamson, J. (2021). 'You feel you're not alone': How multicultural festivals foster social sustainability through multiple psychological sense of community. *Journal of Sustainable Tourism, 29*(11–12), 1792–1809.

Henseler, J. (2017). Bridging design and behavioral research with variance-based structural equation modeling. *Journal of Advertising, 46*(1), 178–192.

Organizational resilience in H&T organizations in Türkiye 153

Henseler, J., Ringle, C. M., & Sarstedt, M. (2015). A new criterion for assessing discriminant validity in variance-based structural equation modeling. *Journal of the Academy of Marketing Science*, *43*(1), 115–135.

Henseler, J., & Schuberth, F. (2020). Using confirmatory composite analysis to assess emergent variables in business research. *Journal of Business Research*, *120*, 147–156.

IIT. (2022). Invest in Turkiye. Retrieved (August 17) from www.ceicdata.com/en/indicator/turkey/visitor-arrivals

Irani, F., Athari, S. A., & Hadood, A. A. A. (2022). The impacts of country risk, global economic policy uncertainty, and macroeconomic factors on the Turkish tourism industry. *International Journal of Hospitality and Tourism Administration*, *23*(6), 1242–1265.

Karagöz, D., Aktaş, S. G., & Kantar, Y. M. (2022). Spatial analysis of the relationship between tourist attractions and tourist flows in Turkey. *European Journal of Tourism Research*, *31*, 3102.

Karatepe, T., Ozturen, A., Karatepe, O. M., Uner, M. M., & Kim, T. T. (2022). Management commitment to the ecological environment, green work engagement and their effects on hotel employees' green work outcomes. *International Journal of Contemporary Hospitality Management*, *34*(8), 3084–3112.

Katircioglu, S. T. (2009). Revisiting the tourism-led-growth hypothesis for Turkey using the bounds test and Johansen approach for cointegration. *Tourism Management*, *30*, 17–20.

Ketter, E., & Avraham, E. (2021). # StayHome today so we can# TravelTomorrow: Tourism destinations' digital marketing strategies during the Covid-19 pandemic. *Journal of Travel and Tourism Marketing*, *38*(8), 819–832.

Köksal, C. (2021). The impact of international trade and tourism development on quality of life: Evidence from Turkey. *Journal of Emerging Economies and Policy*, *6*(2), 406–413.

Köseoglu, M. A., Topaloglu, C., Parnell, J. A., & Lester, D. L. (2013). Linkages among business strategy, uncertainty and performance in the hospitality industry: Evidence from an emerging economy. *International Journal of Hospitality Management*, *34*, 81–91.

Limak (2023). News & announcements. Retrieved (July 17) from www.limak.com.tr/news-and-press/news-announcements/limak-lara-hotel-became-the-first-facility-with-zero-waste-certification-in-antalya

Lubowiecki-Vikuk, A., Budzanowska-Drzewiecka, M., Borzyszkowski, J., & Taheri, B. (2023). Critical reflection on VUCA in tourism and hospitality marketing activities. *International Journal of Contemporary Hospitality Management*, *35*(8), 2983–3005.

Lubowiecki-Vikuk, A., & Sousa, B. (2021). Tourism business in a VUCA world: Marketing and management implications. *Journal of Environmental Management and Tourism*, *12*, 867–876.

Luthans, F., & Broad, J. D. (2022). Positive psychological capital to help combat the mental health fallout from the pandemic and VUCA environment. *Organizational Dynamics*, *51*, 1–13.

Melián-Alzola, L., Fernández-Monroy, M., & Hidalgo-Peñate, M. (2020). Hotels in contexts of uncertainty: Measuring organizational resilience. *Tourism Management Perspectives*, *36*, 100747.

154 *Organizational resilience in H&T organizations in Türkiye*

Nazli, M. (in press). Adaptation of local businesses to the new era during the COVID-19 and the Russia-Ukraine war: Case of Çeşme. *Current Issues in Tourism.*

Olorunsola, V. O., Saydam, M. B., Lasisi, T. T., & Eluwole, K. K. (in press). Customer experience management in capsule hotels: A content analysis of guest online review. *Journal of Hospitality and Tourism Insights.*

Onder, K., & Durgun, A. (2008). Effects of tourism sector on the employment in Turkey: An econometric application. *1st International Conference on Management and Economics.* Epoka University, Albania.

Pata, U. K., & Balsalobre-Lorente (2022). Exploring the impact of tourism and energy consumption on the load capacity factor in Turkey: A novel dynamic ARDL approach. *Environmental Science and Pollution Research, 29,* 13491–13503.

Podsakoff, P. M., MacKenzie, S. B., Lee, J-Y., & Podsakoff, N. P. (2003). Common method biases in behavioral research: A critical review of the literature and recommended remedies. *Journal of Applied Psychology, 88*(5), 879–903.

Raihan, A., & Tuspekova, A. (2022). Dynamic impacts of economic growth, renewable energy use, urbanization, industrialization, tourism, agriculture, and forests on carbon emission in Turkey. *Carbon Research, 1*(20), 1–14.

Raza, S. A., Shah, N., Kumar, R. R., & Alam, M. S. (2023). Tourism growth, income inequality and the dependence between their quantiles: Evidence from quantile on quantile approach. In Okumus, F., Rasoolimanesh, S. M., & Jahani, S. (Ed.), *Cutting edge research methods in hospitality and tourism* (pp. 71–93). Emerald Publishing Limited.

Redman, C. L. (2014). Should sustainability and resilience be combined or remain distinct pursuits? *Ecology and Society, 19*(2), 37.

Rendeiro, M. (2022). 7 Mehmet: the first restaurant in Turkey to receive a green key certification. Retrieved (July 17, 2023) from www.greenkey.global/stories-news-1/2022/4/15/wi8cufozga67prmse6fpnbv39m2600

Republic of Türkiye Ministry of Culture and Tourism (2023a). Tourism receipts-expenditures and average expenditure 2004–2023. Retrieved (July 13) from www.ktb.gov.tr/EN-249307/tourism-receipts-and-expenditures.html

Republic of Türkiye Ministry of Culture and Tourism (2023b). Border statistics. Retrieved (July 14) from www.ktb.gov.tr/EN-249298/border-statistics.html

Republic of Türkiye Ministry of Culture and Tourism (2023c). Establishment statistics. Retrieved (July 12) from www.ktb.gov.tr/EN-249283/tourism-statistics.html.

Republic of Türkiye Ministry of Culture and Tourism (2023d). Turizm Yatırım ve İşletme (Bakanlık) Belgeli Tesis İstatistikleri. Retrieved (July 14) from https://yigm.ktb.gov.tr/TR-201136/turizm-yatirim-ve-isletme-bakanlik-belgeli-tesis-istatistikleri.html

Ringle, C. M., Wende, S., & Becker, J. M. (2022). SmartPLS 4. SmartPLS GmbH, available at: www.smartpls.com

Sanliöz Özgen, H. K., & Kozak, M. (2015). Social media practices applied by city hotels: A comparative case study from Turkey. *Worldwide Hospitality and Tourism Themes, 7*(3), 229–241.

Sarstedt, M., Hair, J. F., Cheah, J .H., Becker, J. M., & Ringle, C. M. (2019). How to specify, estimate, and validate higher-order constructs in PLS-SEM. *Australasian Marketing Journal, 27*(3), 197–211.

Organizational resilience in H&T organizations in Türkiye 155

Sarstedt, M., Hair, J. F., Ringle, C. M., Thiele, K. O., & Gudergan, S. P. (2016). Estimation issues with PLS and CBSEM: Where the bias lies! *Journal of Business Research, 69*(10), 3998–4010.

Seyitoğlu, F., Ivanov, S., Atsız, O., & Çiftçi, I. (2021). Robots as restaurant employees: A double-barrelled detective story. *Technology in Society, 67,* 101779.

Sobaih, A. E. E., Elshaer, I., Hasanein, A. M., & Abdelaziz, A. S. (2021). Responses to COVID-19: The role of performance in the relationship between small hospitality enterprises' resilience and sustainable tourism development. *International Journal of Hospitality Management, 94,* 102824.

Stanič, A., & Karbuz, S. (2021). The challenges facing Eastern Mediterranean gas and how international law can help overcome them. *Journal of Energy and Natural Resources Law, 39*(2), 213–247.

Statista (2021). Industry revenue of "restaurants and mobile food service activities" in Turkey from 2011 to 2023. Retrieved (July 17, 2023) from www.statista.com/foreca sts/413934/restaurants-and-mobile-food-service-activities-revenue-in-turkey

Statista (2023). Travel and tourism in Turkey – statistics & facts. Retrieved (July 17) from www.statista.com/topics/9676/travel-and-tourism-in-turkey/#topicOverview

Su, D. N., Tra, D. L., Huynh, H. M. T., Nguyen, H. H. T., & O'Mahony, B. (2021). Enhancing resilience in the Covid-19 crisis: Lessons from human resource management practices in Vietnam. *Current Issues in Tourism, 24*(22), 3189–3205.

Tabrizi, R. S., Karatepe, O. M., Rezapouraghdam, H., Rescalvo-Martin, E., & Enea, C. (2023). Green human resource management, job embeddedness and their effects on restaurant employees' green voice behaviors. *International Journal of Contemporary Hospitality Management, 35*(10), 3453–3480.

Tepav Günlük (2023). Deprem sonrası ihtiyaç analizi, Fatih Özatay. Retrieved (July 14) from www.tepav.org.tr/tr/blog/s/7163/Deprem+sonrasi+ihtiyac+analizi

TGA (2023). Accommodation facilities registered by Ministry of Culture and Tourism. Retrieved (July 13) from https://tga.gov.tr/search-hotel-en/?certificateType=4&certif icateTY=0

Tlili, A., Altinay, F., Altinay, Z., & Zhang, Y. (2021). Envisioning the future of technology integration for accessible hospitality and tourism. *International Journal of Contemporary Hospitality Management, 33*(12), 4460–4482.

Tosun, C., Çalışkan, C., Şahin, S. Z., & Dedeoğlu, B. B. (2023). A critical perspective on tourism employment. *Current Issues in Tourism, 26*(1), 70–90.

Tosun, C., Okumus, F., & Fyall, A. (2008). Marketing philosophies: Evidence from Turkey. *Annals of Tourism Research, 35*(1), 127–147.

Trading Economics (2023). Turkey – tourist arrivals. Retrieved (July 17) from https://tradingeconomics.com/turkey/tourist-arrivals

TUIK (2023). Tourism Statistics Quarter III: July–September 2022. Retrieved (July 17) from https://data.tuik.gov.tr/Bulten/Index?p=Tourism-Statistics-Quarter-III:-July---September,-2022-45788&dil=2

Tuna, F. (2016). The role and potential of Halal tourism in Turkey. In Egresi, I. (Ed.), *Alternative tourism in Turkey: Role, potential development and sustainability* (pp. 259–267), Springer.

Türkiye Cumhuriyet Merkez Bankası (2023). Günlük döviz kurları. Retrieved (July 14) from www.turkiye.gov.tr/doviz-kurlari

156 *Organizational resilience in H&T organizations in Türkiye*

TÜRSAB (2023). Turkish tourism industry today. Retrieved (July 17) from www.tursab. org.tr/statistics-en/turkish-tourism-industry-today

UNDP (2005). Human development report. New York: United Nations Development.

Uner, M. M., Karatepe, O. M., Cavusgil, S. T., & Kucukergin, K. G. (2023). Does a highly standardized international advertising campaign contribute to the enhancement of destination image? Evidence from Turkey. *Journal of Hospitality and Tourism Insights*, *6*(3), 1169–1187.

UNWTO. (2022). Impact assessment of the covid-19 outbreak on international tourism. Retrieved (August 10) from www.unwto.org/impact-assessment-of-the-covid-19-outbreak-on-international-tourism

Uzar, U., & Eyuboglu, K. (2019). Can tourism be a key sector in reducing income inequality? An empirical investigation for Turkey. *Asia Pacific Journal of Tourism Research, 24*(8), 822–838.

Vatan, A., & Dogan, S. (2021). What do hotel employees think about service robots? A qualitative study in Turkey. *Tourism Management Perspectives*, *37*, 100775.

Way, L. C., & Akan, A. (2017). Coverage of bombings for political advantage: Turkish on-line news reporting of the 2016 Ankara attacks. *Social Semiotics*, *27*(5), 545–566.

Wei, M. (2019). Turkish foreign policy towards the Syrian crisis: Dynamics of transformation. *Asian Journal of Middle Eastern and Islamic Studies*, *13*(3), 462–477.

Yılancı, V., & Kırca, M. (in press). Testing the relationship between employment and tourism: A fresh evidence from the ARDL bounds test with sharp and smooth breaks. *Journal of Hospitality and Tourism Insights*.

Yildirim, O., & Karaca, O. B. (2022). The consumption of tea and coffee in Turkey and emerging new trends. *Journal of Ethnic Foods*, *9*(1), 1–11.

Yıldız, S. (2022). Time-based change of tourism revenues and the effects of Turkish Liras values. *International Journal on Social Sciences*, *7*(1), 1–12.

Yuan, R., Luo, J., Liu, M. J., & Yu, J. (2022). Understanding organizational resilience in a platform-based sharing business: The role of absorptive capacity. *Journal of Business Research*, *141*, 85–99.

Zaman, U., & Aktan, M. (2021). Examining residents' cultural intelligence, place image and foreign tourist attractiveness: A mediated-moderation model of support for tourism development in Cappadocia (Turkey). *Journal of Hospitality and Tourism Management*, *46*, 393–404.

Zhang, J., Xie, C., & Huang, S. (S). (in press). Resilient leadership in hospitality and tourism enterprises: Conceptualization and scale development. *International Journal of Contemporary Hospitality Management*.

Zhang-Zhang, Y. Y., Rohlfer, S., & Varma, A. (2022). Strategic people management in contemporary highly dynamic VUCA contexts: A knowledge worker perspective. *Journal of Business Research*, *144*, 587–598.

6 Organizational resilience in hospitality and tourism organizations in the United States[1]

The American hospitality and tourism sector environmental analysis

The political and legal environment

Political turmoil and other international activity influence industry revenues, especially for businesses that serve international tourists (Hiner, 2021). The latest geopolitical turmoil in Ukraine, caused by Russia's invasion in early 2022, is an example of this (Minchin, 2022). This armed conflict is contributing to the inflation and high prices of oil and energy (Kiesnoski, 2022; Minchin, 2022; UNWTO, n.d.) discussed before. Furthermore, it could impact the post-pandemic recovery for U.S. operators that sell Eastern European destinations and cruises with stops in St. Petersburg, Russia (Kelleher, 2022; Kiesnoski, 2022; Minchin, 2022). The effects of this war could as well dampen the recovery of long-haul destinations while the Russian airspace is closed, as this increases the costs and time to travel (Kamal-Chaoui, 2022; Kelleher, 2022; Minchin, 2022). Nevertheless, economic experts and industry practitioners suggest that the effect on U.S. tourism is small (Kiesnoski, 2022) because Russia, Ukraine, and other neighboring destinations are not highly popular among U.S. travelers, nor do the former countries' nationals represent an important international tourist market for U.S. destinations (Kelleher, 2022; Kiesnoski, 2022). The effects of summer travel to other European destinations are also likely to be small as industry operators still report strong bookings. However, the growth rate of new sales of airplane tickets to Europe has slowed down (Economist Intelligence, 2022; Kamal-Chaoui, 2022; Kiesnoski, 2022). This is a sign that Americans, commonly risk-averse travelers, are rethinking making new travel bookings to Europe due to concerns about the conflict extending to the west side of the continent (Kelleher, 2022).

Besides political turmoil, the industry is influenced by a medium level of regulation that is increasing: labor, safety, and health regulations; food safety standards; liquor licensing; franchise regulations; and, gambling regulations (Hiner, 2021). Also, pandemic-related regulations are still affecting international

DOI: 10.4324/9781003291350-7

158 *Organizational resilience in H&T organizations in the U.S.*

travel and its recovery but are expected to continue decreasing as the pandemic evolves into an endemic-like treatment (Mintel, 2022b; U.S. Travel Association, 2022c). Overall, government assistance – e.g., subsidies and/or tax breaks – is limited for the hospitality industry. However, some sectors may enjoy assistance indirectly as state governments impose lodging taxes that "support and encourage the tourism industry within the specified region, indirectly benefiting operators in accommodation industries that provide services to these tourists" (Hiner, 2021, p. 40).

The economic environment

According to IBISWorld (Hiner, 2021), the hospitality and tourism (H&T) industry demand is driven by seven key external drivers: consumer spending, national unemployment rate, number of households, corporate profit, domestic and international trips by U.S. residents, and inbound trips by non-U.S. residents. Moreover, "sector performance is highly dependent on economic cycles" (Hiner, 2021, p. 16). The industry is "sensitive to consumer sentiment and levels of consumer spending based on their discretionary nature" (Hiner, 2021, p. 11). Consumers and households represent 80% of the market for accommodation and food services. Therefore, these sectors benefit from an increased number of households and increased consumer spending. The latter is complemented by increased discretionary spending and low levels of unemployment, which also increases domestic travel. Increasing international tourism to the United States benefits the industry too because their spending is higher than domestic tourists (IBISWorld, 2021). International tourists also "stay five to 10 times longer than domestic travelers" (AHLA & Accenture, 2022, p. 6). However, a strong economy also increases international travel by U.S. residents, which is not favorable for the domestic hospitality industry. Approximately 17% of the market for accommodation and food services comes from businesses. Therefore, increases in corporate profit also benefit the industry (Hiner, 2021).

Before the COVID-19 pandemic, consumer spending was at a high and demand for accommodation and food services increased, which caused the industry to have strong revenue growth. Nevertheless, the industry was severely hit by the pandemic (Hiner, 2021) and not all sectors have had the same recovery. According to the U.S. Travel Association (2022b) "overseas visitation remained 43% below 2019 levels in April" and international visitors' arrivals and spending are not expected to recover until 2024 or 2025 (U.S. Travel Association, 2021, 2022c). The slow recovery of international visitors to the United States is likely to continue until restrictions, such as predeparture COVID testing, ease (U.S. Travel Association, 2022c). However, high performance represents an opportunity for the industry in the following years (Hiner, 2021). In the next five years, improved economic conditions are likely to bring growth in consumer spending, consumer confidence, and corporate profit. Also,

Organizational resilience in H&T organizations in the U.S. 159

"as travel restrictions are eased, domestic trips by U.S. residents and inbound trips by non-US residents are expected to recover, growing at an accelerated pace during the outlook period" (Hiner, 2021, p. 9).

Nevertheless, this positive outlook is threatened by inflation levels in the United States and global supply chain issues (Mintel, 2022b). Considering that 34.7% of the industry's revenue goes into purchase costs (Hiner, 2021), these threats are a key area of concern for hospitality businesses. In a survey conducted by AHLA in late 2021, 86% of hotels reported supply chain disruptions that significantly impact hotel operations, including lack of availability, production backups, and shipping delays. Moreover, approximately 78% of hotels have seen increased costs for cleaning, housekeeping, and food and beverage supplies (AHLA, 2021).

Inflation has reached levels not seen since the early 1980s (Bureau of Labor Statistics, 2022b). Between April 2021 and April 2022, the Consumer Price Index increased by 8.3% (Bureau of Labor Statistics, 2022a). Specifically, the price of groceries and eating out have increased by 10.8% and 7.2%, respectively, while energy prices are up by over 30% (Bureau of Labor Statistics, 2022a, 2022b). This affects both consumers and hospitality businesses. In fact, consumer sentiment is in a downward trend and at its lowest level since 2011 as Americans worry about inflation and increasing borrowing costs (University of Michigan, 2022; Yadoo, 2022). According to the U.S. Travel Association (2022b), nearly 60% of Americans state that the price of gas will affect their decision to travel in the next following months. Interestingly, a strong job market and rising wages have helped keep consumer spending stable (Yadoo, 2022). For example, PGAV Destinations (2022) reports that the "average annual household income of attraction visitors rose to $91,000 in 2021, compared with $85,200 in 2020" (p. 14). This could be one of the reasons why, in early 2022, travel spending was 3% above pre-pandemic levels and the industry's contribution to the U.S. gross domestic product was also 6.2% higher (PGAV Destinations, 2022; U.S. Travel Association, 2022b). Thus, there is a positive outlook for 2022 summer travel (U.S. Travel Association, 2022b).

However, it is important to consider that, when inflation is high, consumers in lower-income brackets are forced to watch their discretionary spending – including holidays – to deal with the increased cost of living (Mintel, 2022a). According to Mintel (2022a), based on other periods of financial hardship, we can expect substitution behaviors (e.g., staycations instead of international trips, value destinations, etc.) from consumers who are most affected by the current inflation levels. During these times, families may sacrifice short vacations and holiday breaks for their annual summer or winter vacation. An opportunity still lies in low-cost outdoor experiences like caravanning and camping, which have experienced increased demand since the start of the pandemic. Nevertheless, high-income households are less affected. This, together with pent-up demand for travel and increased savings during the pandemic for this customer group,

160 *Organizational resilience in H&T organizations in the U.S.*

represents an opportunity for luxury hospitality experiences (Mintel, 2022a). Nonetheless, experts suggest caution as consumer spending is bound to slow down if the current inflation trends continue, especially because pandemic savings – which drove the initial industry recovery – might be starting to run out (PGAV Destinations, 2022) and any pauses in loan payments (e.g., federal student loans) have come to an end (Mintel, 2022b).

The social environment

The silver lining of the pandemic has been the pent-up demand for H&T services, especially among millennials and Gen Z travelers, as travel restrictions lift and more people get vaccinated (AHLA & Accenture, 2022). According to AHLA and Accenture (2022), in the last quarter of 2021, 50% of Americans were expecting to travel for leisure in the next six months. PGAV Destinations (2022) and Mintel (2022b) state in their latest reports that almost 80% of Americans are planning a leisure trip in 2022, among those, 39% say they intend to travel internationally in the same year (PGAV Destinations, 2022). More importantly, almost 50% of those planning to travel are also planning to increase their vacation spending (Mintel, 2022b). For example, in its latest market research study, PGAV Destinations (2022) found that two-thirds of the surveyed attraction visitors intend to continue to indulge in their attraction spending in 2022 as a way to compensate for all the time that they were not able to enjoy attractions.

The above strongly reflects how, in 2022, vacationing and saving for vacations have become top priorities for American consumers (AHLA & Accenture, 2022; Mintel, 2022b). According to Accenture, "44% of U.S. consumers say the pandemic caused them to rethink their personal purpose and re-evaluate what's important in life" (AHLA & Accenture, 2022, p. 11). Moreover, they realized the importance of travel for their social well-being (Mintel, 2022b). Multiple market studies have revealed that relaxation is the number one motivator for purchasing travel and hospitality experiences in 2022, closely followed by safety (Mintel, 2022b; PGAV Destinations, 2022). As PGAV Destinations (2022) states, the post-pandemic consumer environment is characterized by "the push-pull between the need to relax and the need to feel safe" (PGAV Destinations, 2022, p. 12). The latter is even more important for Asian, Black, and Hispanic consumers, which were affected more than White consumers by the pandemic, thus, still display higher concerns about the spread of the virus (Mintel, 2022b). Vacationers are not just looking for an escape but also crave and hope to recover some sense of normalcy in their travels, i.e., while they still appreciate safety measures, they want a vacation experience that comes as close as possible to those pre-pandemic (Mintel, 2022b).

The demand for hospitality services is also influenced by consumer trends that force operators to change to remain relevant (Hiner, 2021). In this new post-COVID environment, two customer segments represent vast opportunities

Organizational resilience in H&T organizations in the U.S. 161

for industry operators. First, bleisure travel, which represents "a profound shift in consumer's attitudes and behaviours related to travel" (AHLA & Accenture, 2022, p. 2). Bleisure travelers are those who make a leisure trip out of a business trip and vice versa. The pandemic has transformed this segment into more mainstream, instead of just observable among the younger generations. Second, the digital nomads' segment, which refers to people who can work from anywhere. The pandemic significantly increased this type of flexible work arrangement, representing "a profound rethinking of the traditional dynamic between work and travel" (AHLA & Accenture, 2022, p. 13). These changes in consumer behavior also represent an opportunity for hotels to revamp their loyalty programs (AHLA & Accenture, 2022). However, Mintel (2022b) suggests caution as only 9% of employed travelers are planning to lengthen their 2022 vacations by working remotely during their trips. This could increase though as industry operators improve their infrastructure to serve this market (Mintel, 2022b).

Other social trends that directly affect food services include health- and fusion-oriented dining (Hiner, 2021). While these might have higher production costs, they can also be sold at a premium, which contributes to growing revenues (Hiner, 2021). However, the combination of increasingly health-conscious diners, pandemic-related stay-at-home restrictions, and increasingly popular grocery delivery services and meal delivery boxes have contributed to the trend of cooking at home (Hiner, 2021), thus, representing a threat to the industry.

In addition, in the current social environment, customers have increased their awareness of inclusion and equality issues and demand companies take a stand on ethical topics, such as rectifying systemic racism (Mintel, 2022b; PGAV Destinations, 2022). Mintel (2022b) suggests that better representation of the Black and LGBTQ+ communities in marketing represents an opportunity for hospitality companies to show that they care and what they are doing. The centrality of this issue is growing rapidly. For example, in recent years, there has been an upward trend regarding the share of racial minorities visiting attractions (PGAV Destinations, 2022). This share has moved from a historic average of 25% to 33% in 2021 (PGAV Destinations, 2022). Considering that 40% of the U.S. population belongs to a racial minority – i.e., other than non-Hispanic Whites – multiple opportunities exist for hospitality businesses to better serve this important market, which is expected to represent 65% of the U.S. population by 2045 (PGAV Destinations, 2022).

Inclusion and equality issues have also been voiced regarding the integration and treatment of people with disabilities, which is a priority for the entire H&T industry (PGAV Destinations, 2022). To illustrate, PGAV Destinations (2022) found in a recent survey that, in 2021, almost one-third of parties visiting an attraction had at least one member with a disability. While multiple hospitality companies offer world-class accommodations for people with disabilities, this is not the case for every business nor necessarily equates to true inclusion where

162 *Organizational resilience in H&T organizations in the U.S.*

everyone can enjoy hospitality experiences fully. PGAV Destinations (2022) states that better serving this market is one of the most important opportunities for the industry moving forward. Services that this market would appreciate the most include readily accessible pre-arrival information to plan their visit, accommodating and trained employees, quiet areas, graphic signage and menus, and special programs.

The technological environment

The pandemic increased customers' desire to be in control of as many aspects as possible of their vacation planning, which is facilitated by technology (Mintel, 2022b). That is, Americans mostly prefer to plan on their own instead of going to professionals. So, they want optimized and convenient websites that help them plan and book their vacations effectively while giving them an enjoyable online experience (Mintel, 2022b). Some noteworthy features include filters to show only relevant options, instalment plans, and integrations with streaming services and home assistants, all accompanied by flexible bookings without cancelation and change fees (Mintel, 2022b). Social media has also become increasingly important for travel planning (Mintel, 2022b).

Moreover, customers of hospitality services look for websites and mobile apps to interact with companies before and during their vacation (Hiner, 2021; IBISWorld, 2021). According to AHLA and Accenture (2022), the role of technology in the hotel sector is increasingly important to respond to guests' needs and wants. Technological tools that further the personalization of the guest experience and simultaneously help businesses acquire customer knowledge will continue to be key. Technology also continues to change the customer journey reducing the stages that depend on customer-staff interactions. This self-service increase should translate into more meaningful customer service initiatives. Therefore, these technologies might also help operators increase revenues and reduce labor costs (IBISWorld, 2021). Similarly, attraction operators who incorporated online reservations and mobile app ordering during the pandemic will continue to experience high adoption among guests not only because of safety but also because of the contribution of these and other technologies that help improve the overall experience, inclusivity, and ease of visiting an attraction (PGAV Destinations, 2022). Nevertheless, there is a technological divide among industry operators and benefits are mostly experienced by those with economies of scale and access to a national customer base, which limits the industry's "overall ability to comply with changing technological trends" (Hiner, 2021, pp. 12–13).

The ecological environment

The World Economic Forum has declared climate change and global failure in taking action as the top global risk (Sustainable Hospitality Alliance, 2021).

Organizational resilience in H&T organizations in the U.S. 163

According to Sustainable Travel International (2020), "tourism is responsible for roughly 8% of the world's carbon emissions" and this is primarily emitted by U.S. travelers. Evidently, transportation is the industry sector that creates the most emissions (Sustainable Travel International, 2020). Climate change directly impacts the hospitality industry via extreme weather, penalties, and other environmental policies (Sustainable Hospitality Alliance, 2021). Furthermore, sustainable travel has become a top priority for consumers, especially among the younger generations (Mintel, 2022b). While the urge to go back to "normal" vacations may temporarily pause making environmentally conscious decisions, sustainability must be a strategic priority for industry operators to protect their own and the country's resources and satisfy a growing traveler segment (Mintel, 2022b).

Therefore, an opportunity lies in including environmentally friendly messaging in marketing as means to promote how companies contribute to offsetting the negative effects of travel (Mintel, 2022b). Innovations to reduce carbon footprint, waste, energy consumption, and greenhouse gas emissions will also continue to grow in importance and occurrence (TEA/AECOM, 2020), e.g., energy-saving appliances, temperature control systems, and solar-powered water heaters (Sustainable Travel International, 2020). Moreover, sustainability efforts should span all areas of operations as travelers' preference for sustainable food and merchandise is expected to continue growing (McDonald, 2018; Sarsfield-Hall, 2020). With that said, industry operators should approach sustainability holistically as travelers are demanding more authentic experiences that are both enriching for them and beneficial to the local economies (Mintel, 2022b).

The structure of American hospitality and tourism organizations

American H&T organizations serve locals, other businesses, and domestic and international tourists alike. Moreover, these belong to several closely related sectors. These include accommodations (lodging), food and beverage, clubs, attractions and recreation, gaming, meetings and conventions, and travel and transportation (Okumus, Altinay, Chathoth, & Köseoğlu, 2020). Considering that the main market for hospitality services consists of individuals and households, "the locations of establishments are primarily distributed in line with US population" with businesses located in key destinations enjoying an increased volume of guests, thanks to tourists (Hiner, 2021, p. 21). Therefore, like the U.S. population, hospitality businesses concentrate in three main regions of the country: Southeast (23.4% of establishments), West (18.3%), and Mid-Atlantic (16.8%). Within these regions, three states are respective leaders: Florida, California, and New York. This is not surprising as these states have vibrant cities and tourist destinations (Hiner, 2021). The main inbound international markets to the United States are Canada, Mexico, Japan, China, and the United Kingdom, which represent 65% of international visitors. Some of the top destinations that international travelers are interested in visiting when vacationing in the United States are Disney theme parks, New York City, and Las Vegas (PGAV Destinations, n.d.).

The H&T industry is characterized by low concentration, globalization, mature life cycle, increasing regulations, technology change at a medium rate, very high revenue volatility, low barriers to entry, low industry assistance, high internal and external competition and substitutes, and medium capital intensity (Hiner, 2021; IBISWorld, 2021). Having low concentration positively impacts the H&T industry as major players control less than 7% of the market share. Major players include American Airlines, Delta Air Lines, The Walt Disney Company, Hilton Worldwide, and Marriott International (IBISWorld, 2021). When exclusively considering the accommodations and food and beverage sectors, the market share of major players increases to approximately 15%. The latter includes large corporations such as McDonald's, Yum! Brands Inc., Marriott International, Hilton Hotels, Starbucks, and Darden Restaurants (Hiner, 2021). These large corporations benefit from economies of scale that enable higher and more stable profit margins (IBISWorld, 2021). In addition, capital costs are not an ongoing feature of the industry. Nevertheless, the initial capital intensity to enter the industry varies dramatically between the industry's sectors (Hiner, 2021). The same can be said about industry revenues. In 2021, the H&T industry had annual revenues of US$772.5 billion: 39.7% transportation, 24.6% accommodations, 22% recreation and entertainment, and 13.6% food service and drinking places (IBISWorld, 2021).

In 2022, the most popular types of travel are expected to be family vacations and visits to friends and family (Mintel, 2022b; PGAV Destinations, 2022). That is, consumers want to "reconnect with their loved ones" (Mintel, 2022b, p. 34). After this, it is clear that the consumer preference for outdoor activities still remains a top priority as the popularity of national parks, beaches, and mountain destinations continues (Mintel, 2022b; PGAV Destinations, 2022). Nevertheless, consumers are ready to return to more crowded activities including theme parks, water parks, zoos, and aquariums (PGAV Destinations, 2022). All in all, consumers lean toward enjoyment and exploration (Mintel, 2022b). The pandemic contributed to a renewed sense of exploration among consumers as they had to be open to alternative vacation experiences and new destinations (Mintel, 2022b). This will force established destinations to offer new products and experiences that allow visitors to explore a well-known destination in an unconventional way, which may attract new traveler segments and off-season travel (Mintel, 2022b). It is important to note that, in 2022, consumers also want familiarity and few will vacation to new destinations or overseas (Mintel, 2022b).

Next, this chapter goes into further detail regarding the impact of the pandemic on key industry sectors and offers evidence of how resilient this industry is.

Organizational resilience in H&T organizations in the U.S. 165

Accommodation and food services sectors

In the United States, the accommodation and food services sectors include one million businesses and growth is modest – only a projected rate of 5.9% between 2021 and 2026 (Hiner, 2021). Over 27% of these represent the accommodation sector (27.8%) and the rest the food services sector. These sectors were hard-hit by the pandemic, thanks to severe revenue loss, government regulations, and an unemployment rate of up to 39.3% (Hiner, 2021). On the one hand, between 2020 and 2021, U.S. hotels lost US$111.8 billion in room revenue. In early 2020, occupancy was only 24.5%, a historic low (AHLA & Accenture, 2022), and 70% of employees were furloughed or laid off (Hiner, 2021). On the other hand, by December 2020, 17% of U.S. restaurants closed permanently and the sector experienced a loss of US$270 billion in revenue (Hiner, 2021; National Restaurant Association, 2021).

According to IBISWorld (Hiner, 2021), the accommodation and food services sectors compete on the basis of six critical success factors: (1) close monitoring of the competition to offer competitive services at a competitive price; (2) maintaining a good reputation that translates into positive customer reviews, which bring new customers; (3) location and proximity to key markets; (4) maintaining inventory at optimal levels; (5) a well-trained, flexible, and multiskilled workforce; and, (6) ability to keep purchase costs stable. From these factors, monitoring competition is key to success because "there is a high level of price-based competition within this sector as many operators offer similar products and services, especially within their respective industries. This forces establishments to match prices of similar services offered by competing operators" (Hiner, 2021, p. 28). Since the hospitality industry depends on discretionary spending, customers are price sensitive. Nevertheless, they also value quality so businesses that offer higher quality and better service than the competition can charge premium prices (Hiner, 2021).

The accommodation and food services sectors generate US$853.1 billion of annual revenue, which is expected to grow 6.9% between 2021 and 2026 (Hiner, 2021). This modest revenue growth represents a threat to the industry (Hiner, 2021). The growth of internal and external competition is what holds back the potential for higher revenue growth rates (Hiner, 2021). In 2021, profit margins were only 6.4% (Hiner, 2021). Nevertheless, this is expected to increase to 7.7% in 2026, thanks to an overall recovery of the U.S. economy after the pandemic and recovered demand for the industry's services (Hiner, 2021). It is important to note that not all sectors of the hospitality industry enjoy the same profit margins. Overall, food services have lower profit margins than accommodation services (Hiner, 2021).

All things considered, the U.S. hospitality industry has demonstrated to be incredibly resilient. In the accommodation sector, the leisure segment is

166 *Organizational resilience in H&T organizations in the U.S.*

expected to fully recover in 2022 and the business segment in 2023 (AHLA & Accenture, 2022; Mintel, 2022b). "In fact, Thanksgiving week 2021 was a record-breaker for U.S. hotels – occupancy rates were at 53%, and RevPAR was 20% higher than during the same period in 2019" (AHLA & Accenture, 2022, p. 5). Furthermore, in both March and April 2022, GOPPAR surpassed pre-pandemic levels and profit margins at over 41% had not been experienced since November 2018 (CoStar Group, 2022b). By May 2022, year-to-date occupancy levels were at 60% – 9 percentual points higher than in 2021 – and ADR has increased by 13% compared to a similar period in 2019. This has led to strong RevPAR, the best since the pandemic started (CoStar Group, 2022a). However, Mintel (2022b) suggests that "ADR recovery is outpacing the occupancy rate" (p. 23). High hotel prices, together with the effects of inflation discussed before and increased RV sales during the pandemic, may drive consumers to favor other accommodation options (Mintel, 2022b).

Unfortunately, because of staffing shortages, the slow recovery in the business segment and non-room revenue, and other financial pressures – including low cash reserves, inflation, loan payments, and delayed improvement projects – true recovery of the hotel sector is projected until 2025 (AHLA & Accenture, 2022). Interestingly, in the post-COVID environment, one of the biggest industry challenges has been to bring the workforce back after layoffs and voluntary transfers to other industries during the pandemic (Mintel, 2022b). For example, by the last quarter of 2021, 94% of hotels were understaffed and 96% were hiring but unable to fill open jobs (AHLA & Accenture, 2022). In April 2022, the hospitality industry had over 1.3 million jobs available (Bureau of Labor Statistics, 2022c). This translates into industry employment levels 8.5% lower than in 2019. The issue may extend to 2023 too. For example, "by the end of 2022, hotels are expected to employ 2.19 million people – 93% of their pre-pandemic levels" (AHLA & Accenture, 2022, p. 9).

The accommodation and food services sectors spend annually US$300.1 billion in wages, representing 35.2% of the industry's revenue, and wages are expected to increase 6.1% between 2021 and 2026 (Hiner, 2021). Considering the importance of labor for the hospitality industry, labor shortages are currently one of the top threats to full industry recovery as it limits the ability of operators to cope with pent-up customer demand (AHLA & Accenture, 2022). Except for mining, no other industry has been this affected in terms of labor since the pandemic started (U.S. Travel Association, 2022a). The latter is driven by intense competition for recruitment in several industries and because the number of unemployed people in the United States is far less than the number of jobs available, thus, opportunities lie in the number of teenagers entering the workforce and access to foreign labor via temporary work visas (AHLA & Accenture, 2022; National Restaurant Association, 2022; U.S. Travel Association, 2022a). Other opportunities for the industry lie in offering career paths – instead of jobs – increasing the flexibility of work arrangements, offering and communicating

Organizational resilience in H&T organizations in the U.S.   167

training and development programs that increase employability, and furthering the diversity of the workforce (AHLA & Accenture, 2022).

Attractions and recreation sectors

Similar to the accommodation and food services sectors of the hospitality industry, the attractions and recreation sectors were also severely hit by the pandemic. For example, in U.S. theme parks, attendance decreased by 72% and revenue by 58.2% (Brocker, 2021; TEA/AECOM, 2020). Nevertheless, the attractions sector of the hospitality industry had a "remarkable rebound" in 2021 and it is expected to fully recover in 2022 (PGAV Destinations, 2022, p. 3). According to the latest results from the Voice of Visitor market study conducted by PGAV Destinations (2022), 2021 was even the best year financially for some attractions operators and loyalty rates were at an all-time high based on recommendation intentions (62%) and ownership of seasonal passes (60%). This positive outlook is driven by a favorable socioeconomic environment (see above discussion) and by the escapist nature of the sector, which places it in top of mind to satisfy travelers' relaxation needs and help them cope with the challenges of the pandemic and post-pandemic world (PGAV Destinations, 2022).

On average, an American consumer visited 3.5 attractions in 2021 – note that the pre-pandemic average was 4.1 but represents an improvement from the 2020 average of 2.5 (PGAV Destinations, 2022). The most visited attractions included, in order of visitation, historic landmarks, national parks, zoos and aquariums, theme parks, and family entertainment centers. In 2022, PGAV Destinations (2022) projects growth beyond recovery with an average of 4.3 visited attractions. Nonetheless, following the accommodations and food services sectors, positive projections for the attractions and recreation sectors are being challenged by labor shortages and supply chain disruptions (PGAV Destinations, 2022). Another sector challenge moving forward is correcting the satisfaction gap between non-Hispanic Whites and racial minorities as the latter report satisfaction rates 0.42 points lower than the former driven by unfriendly and/or differential treatment, limited diversity in attractions' staff, and limited services and food offerings that are familiar and attractive to them (PGAV Destinations, 2022).

The American research sample

Sample characteristics and research procedure

A sample of U.S. H&T employees was recruited with the help of Prolific, an online data collection firm. A total of 322 responses were received between February and April 2023. Responses with missing data (4), failed attention checks (2), conflicting responses to negatively worded items (4), and a clear

168   *Organizational resilience in H&T organizations in the U.S.*

indication of straight-lining (1) were removed to ensure data quality. That is, 309 high-quality complete responses were received.

Preliminary data cleaning and analysis included reversing the negatively worded items and assessing multivariate outliers and common method bias. Multivariate outliers were assessed via standardized residuals, Cook's distance, and Mahalanobis distance (Glen, 2016; Hair, Black, Babin, & Anderson, 2010; Pallant, 2010). Based on the combination of these factors, two cases were deemed problematic, and the researchers decided to exclude these cases for analysis. Thus, 307 responses were retained for analysis. Then, Harman's single-factor test was conducted to determine the presence of common method bias (Podsakoff, MacKenzie, Lee, & Podsakoff, 2003). One factor explained only 31% of the variance; therefore, common method bias is not a threat to this study.

The analysis of the demographic characteristics of the sample revealed that most of the participants were female (56.7%) and between 18 and 37 years old (66.7%), and almost half had a college education (46.9%). Most participants lived in a big city or agglomeration (59.9%) and were currently employed (80.1%); this does not include the 36 participants who were self-employed and/ or entrepreneurs. While the number of hours worked per week ranged from seven to 80 hours – averaging 38.03 hours/week – 34% of participants worked part-time (less than 40 hours/week) and 65.8% worked full time, with almost 25% of participants working overtime.

Different sectors of the H&T industry were represented in the sample, such as accommodation (30.9%), food services (25.7%), and recreation and entertainment (17.6%). Large employers and SMEs are also represented in fairly equal numbers, 42.7% and 47.2%, respectively. Moreover, most organizations in which the participants worked have been in operation for over 20 years (53.1%) and have exclusively domestic capital (70.4%). Table 6.1 shows the complete demographic characteristics of the American research sample.

Measurement model

The measurement instrument included the scales detailed in Chapter 3. First, the researchers evaluated the distribution of the data. All constructs under study approached a normal distribution with skewness and kurtosis values well under ±3 (Kline, 2015). Additionally, all the study constructs were positively correlated. Table 6.2 presents the complete correlation, skewness, and kurtosis values, among others.

Then, the validity, reliability, and fit of the measurement model were assessed following Hair et al. (2010). Overall, the measurement scales were reliable based on Cronbach's alpha (α) and composite reliability (CR) scores above the 0.7 threshold. Most scales also achieved convergent validity with AVE values above 0.5. Except for a few items that will be described next, most standardized items loadings were satisfactory (above 0.5 and most above 0.7). Goodness of fit was

Organizational resilience in H&T organizations in the U.S. 169

Table 6.1 Description of the American sample

Set of characteristics		N	Percentage
Sociodemographic			
Age			
	18–27	99	32.2%
	28–37	106	34.5%
	38–47	61	19.9%
	48–57	27	8.8%
	58 and over	14	4.6%
Gender			
	Male	122	39.7%
	Female	174	56.7%
	3	10	3.3%
	4	1	0.3%
Education			
	Primary school	3	1.0%
	Vocational school	13	4.2%
	Secondary school	79	25.7%
	Post-secondary school	68	22.1%
	Bachelor's degree	129	42.0%
	Master's degree	15	4.9%
Marital status			
	Single	141	45.9%
	In a partnership	166	54.1%
Place of living			
	Agglomeration (a cluster of cities)	48	15.6%
	Big city (above 100,000 inhabitants)	136	44.3%
	Small city	115	37.5%
	Village	8	2.6%
Employment			
Employment status			
	Unemployed	4	1.3%
	Full-time employment	88	28.7%
	Employment for an indefinite period	158	51.5%
	Retired	19	6.2%
	Self-employment or won business	36	11.7%
	Working student	2	0.7%
Weekly working time in hours			
	Less than 20 hours/week	16	5.2%
	20–29 hours/week	35	11.4%
	30–39 hours/week	54	17.6%
	40 hours/week	126	41.0%
	41–49 hours/week	34	11.1%

(Continued)

170 *Organizational resilience in H&T organizations in the U.S.*

Table 6.1 (Continued)

Set of characteristics		N	Percentage
	50–59 hours/week	30	9.8%
	60 or more hours/week	12	3.9%
Sector			
	Accommodation	95	30.9%
	Catering/food services	79	25.7%
	Recreation and entertainment	54	17.6%
	Transport	12	3.9%
	Tour operators and travel agents	10	3.3%
	Other	57	18.6%
Company size			
	Micro (1–9 employees)	31	10.1%
	Small (10–49 employees)	79	25.7%
	Medium (50–249 employees)	66	21.5%
	Large (250 employees and above)	131	42.7%
Company age			
	Less than a year	5	1.6%
	1–3 years	25	8.1%
	4–9 years	47	15.3%
	10–19 years	67	21.8%
	20 years and above	163	53.1%
Company capital			
	Domestic capital exclusively	216	70.4%
	Foreign capital exclusively	3	1.0%
	Both domestic and foreign capital	88	28.7%

Table 6.2 Means, standard deviations, and correlations of study variables

Constructs	M	SD	S	K	1	2	3	4	5	6
1. Organisational resilience	3.61	0.72	−0.49	0.25						
2. Organisational learning culture	3.52	0.80	−0.69	0.50	0.79					
3. Psychological capital	4.51	0.71	−0.65	1.26	0.54	0.54				
4. Personal social capital	3.44	1.11	0.33	−0.36	0.23	0.30	0.31			
5. Employee resilience	3.83	0.56	−0.32	0.66	0.49	0.52	0.71	0.27		
6. Learning goal orientation	4.31	1.00	−0.61	0.57	0.45	0.47	0.64	0.28	0.69	

Notes: M = mean; SD = standard deviation; S = skewness; K = kurtosis. All correlation coefficients are statistically significant at $p < 0.001$.

Organizational resilience in H&T organizations in the U.S. 171

primarily assessed based on standardized root mean residuals (SRMR), Tucker Lewis Index (TLI), and comparative fit index (CFI) values. Fit was deemed satisfactory as most scales resulted in SRMR values below 0.1 and TLI and CFI values of approximately 0.9 or above.

Nevertheless, some modifications were made to the original scales to ensure the above. In the Organisational Resilience scale (Lee et al., 2013), two out of the 13 indicators of the scale were excluded because their standardized factor loadings were below 0.5 and their exclusion ensures the achievement of convergent validity (Hair et al., 2010). Two of the four dimensions of psychological capital (Luthans et al., 2007) included negatively worded items, which were reversed accordingly – as explained before. However, some researchers have identified that these items tend to be problematic (Solís Salazar, 2015). In fact, the three negatively worded items in the study had standardized factor loadings below 0.5 and their removal improved the reliability, validity, and fit of the scales. Thus, the scale capturing the optimism dimension was reduced from six to four items. The scale capturing the personal resilience dimension was reduced from six to three items since, in addition to the negatively worded item, the scale included two other items with standardized factor loadings in the low 0.50s, which become candidates for exclusion if doing so improves other scale qualities (Hair et al., 2010). In this case, the latter was necessary to achieve AVE values above 0.5. Lastly, the employee resilience scale (Näswall et al., 2019) presented measurement challenges. While this is usually believed to be a unidimensional scale, the current study found two factors. Assessing the scale based on these two resulting factors, instead of one, led to satisfactory reliability and goodness of fit. Nevertheless, the convergent validity of the two factors was not ideal since AVE values are 0.42 for both factors. Considering that the reliability of these scales is above 0.7, AVE values between 0.4 and 0.5 are not concerning (Fornell & Larcker, 1981). Table 6.3 presents a complete picture of the measurement model characteristics.

The assessment of organizational resilience in American organizations

Conceptual and alternative structural models

With a valid measurement model, the researchers tested the structural model. The results revealed that the conceptual model did not fit the data well ($\chi2$ (6) = 118.70, p < 0.001; $\chi2/df$ = 19.78; TLI = 0.69; CFI = 0.87; SRMR = 0.100; RMSEA = 0.25 (90% CI [0.21; 0.29])) despite social capital, psychological capital, and organizational learning culture being correlated. Therefore, the alternative structural model was tested only to reveal poor fit as well: fit $\chi2$ (6) = 120.68, p < 0.001; $\chi2/df$ = 20.11; TLI = 0.88; CFI = 0.87; SRMR = 0.102; RMSEA = 0.25 (90% CI [0.21; 0.29]). In this alternative model, social capital, psychological capital, and organizational learning culture were correlated.

172 *Organizational resilience in H&T organizations in the U.S.*

Table 6.3 Measurement model validation

Construct	Factors	Items	SRMR	TLI	CFI	AVE	CR	α
Organizational resilience (Lee et al., 2013)	Organizational resilience	oar_1 opr_2 opr_3 opr_4 opr_5 oar_6 oar_7 oar_9 oar_10 oar_11 opr_12	0.05	0.92	0.94	0.51	0.92	0.92
Organizational learning culture (Yang et al., 2004)	Continuous learning	cl_1 cl_2 cl_3	0.00	1.00	1.00	0.70	0.88	0.87
	Embedded systems	es_10 es_11 es_12	0.00	1.00	1.00	0.62	0.83	0.83
	System connection	syscon_16 syscon_17 syscon_18	0.00	1.00	1.00	0.64	0.84	0.84
	Inquiry and dialogue	id_4 id_5 id_6	0.00	1.00	1.00	0.63	0.84	0.83
	Team learning	tl_7 tl_8 tl_9	0.00	1.00	1.00	0.69	0.87	0.87
	Empowerment	emp_13 emp_14 emp_15	0.00	1.00	1.00	0.65	0.85	0.84
	Strategic leadership	lead_20 lead_21 lead_22	0.00	1.00	1.00	0.73	0.89	0.89
Psychological capital (Luthans et al., 2007)	Self-efficacy	se_1 se_2 se_3 se_4 se_5 se_6	0.03	0.97	0.98	0.64	0.91	0.91
	Hope	h_7 h_8 h_9 h_10 h_11 h_12	0.06	0.90	0.94	0.54	0.87	0.87

Organizational resilience in H&T organizations in the U.S. 173

Table 6.3 (Continued)

Construct	Factors	Items	SRMR	TLI	CFI	AVE	CR	α
	Personal resilience	res_16 res_17 res_18	0.00	1.00	1.00	0.62	0.83	0.83
	Optimism	opt_19 opt_21 opt_22 opt_24	0.01	1.00	1.00	0.63	0.87	0.87
Personal social capital (Zoghbi-Manrique-de-Lara & Ruiz-Palomino, 2019)	Personal social capital with peers inside the team	sct_1 sct_2 sct_3 sct_4	0.08	0.65	0.88	0.59	0.85	0.85
	Personal social capital with people outside the team	sco_5 sco_6 sco_7 sco_8	0.06	0.84	0.95	0.61	0.86	0.86
Learning goal orientation (Vandewalle, 1997)	Learning goal orientation	lgo_1 lgo_2 lgo_3 lgo_4 lgo_5	0.02	0.99	1.00	0.65	0.90	0.91
Employee resilience (Näshwall et al., 2019)	Adaptive and planned resilience	epr_1 epr_2 ear_3 ear_4 epr_5	0.06	0.87	0.93	0.42	0.78	0.78
	Networking leveraging	enl_6 ear_7 enl_8 enl_9	0.02	0.99	1.00	0.43	0.75	0.74

Notes: SRMR = standardized root mean residuals; TLI = Tucker Lewis Index; CFI = comparative fit index; AVE = average variance extraction; CR = composite reliability; α = Cronbach's alpha coefficient.

Structural conceptual modified model

Similar to the Polish sample, the in-depth analysis and inspection of modification indices suggested two new paths, (1) from psychological capital to learning goal orientation and (2) from organizational learning culture to employee resilience. As established in Chapter 4, the relationship between psychological capital and learning goal orientation has theoretical and empirical justification (see Chapter 4). This is the same for the relationship between organizational learning culture and employee resilience. This is because organizational learning culture is an organizational resource that can activate employees' resilience not only through their goal orientation but also directly (Malik & Garg, 2020; Peng et al., 2022).

Study results suggest that this structural conceptual modified model has a good fit: $\chi^2 (5) = 7.54$, p = 0.110; $\chi^2/df = 1.88$; TLI = 0.995; CFI = 0.996; SRMR = 0.017; RMSEA = 0.05 (90% CI [0.00; 0.11]). The standardized parameter estimates and explained variance (R^2) are given in Figure 6.1. Except for H4, all hypotheses were supported. Specifically, the results indicated that organizational learning culture showed a significant relationship with organizational resilience ($\beta = 0.72$, p < 0.001), supporting H1. The results also found support for H2 since there is a significant relationship between organizational learning culture and learning goal orientation ($\beta = 0.14$, p < 0.01). Moreover, learning goal orientation ($\beta = 0.39$, p < 0.001) and psychological capital ($\beta = 0.36$, p < 0.001) were positively linked to employee resilience. Hence, H3 and H5 were supported. However, there was no empirical support for H4, as personal social capital ($\beta = 0.01$, p > 0.05) does not have a significant relationship with employee resilience. H6 was also supported as employee resilience depicted a positive relationship with organizational resilience ($\beta = 0.12$, p < 0.01).

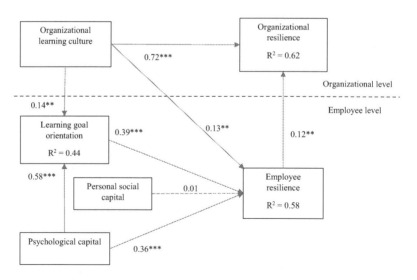

Figure 6.1 Structural equation model on the predictors of organizational resilience.
Notes: Dashed line: the path is statistically insignificant. * $p < 0.05$. ** $p < 0.01$. *** $p < 0.001$.

Organizational resilience in H&T organizations in the U.S. 175

Another two hypotheses were added based on the two additional paths introduced to the structural conceptual modified model. H7 tested the relationship between psychological capital and learning goal orientation, which was supported (β = 0.58, p < 0.001). H8 tested the relationship between organizational learning culture and employee resilience, which was also supported (β = 0.13, p < 0.01). Lastly, the results of this structural conceptual modified model explained 58% of the variance in employee resilience and 62% in organizational resilience.

Figure 6.1 reveals several indirect effects. To analyze their significance, a mediation analysis based on a bootstrapped sample size of 5,000 via the 90% confidence interval (CI) was conducted. The analysis revealed that the relationship between organizational learning culture and organizational resilience is partially mediated via employee resilience, and via both learning goal orientation and employee resilience. The relationship between organizational learning culture and employee resilience is also partially mediated via learning goal orientation. Another partially mediated relationship is that between psychological capital and employee resilience via learning goal orientation. Fully mediated relationships include those between (1) psychological capital and organizational resilience via employee resilience, and via learning goal orientation and employee resilience; and (2) learning goal orientation and organizational resilience via employee resilience. Table 6.4 summarizes these mediated relationships.

Table 6.4 Bootstrapping results for mediated relationships (unstandardized coefficients)

Relationship	Direct effect	Indirect effects	LLCI	ULCI	Mediation effect
Organizational learning culture →organizational resilience	.656***	.020**	.007	.038	Partial mediation
psychological capital →organizational resilience	.121	.071**	.025	.115	Mediation
organizational learning culture →employee resilience	.089**	.038*	.012	.067	Partial mediation
psychological capital →employee resilience	.274***	.173***	.129	.226	Partial mediation
learning goal orientation →organizational resilience	.000	.034**	.011	.057	Mediation

Notes: LLCI = lower limit confidence interval; ULCI = upper limit confidence interval. * p < 0.05. ** p < 0.01. *** p < 0.001.

Structural alternative modified model

The in-depth analysis and inspection of modification indices also suggested two new paths for the structural alternative modified model, (1) from psychological capital to learning goal orientation and (2) from psychological capital to organizational resilience. The theoretical and empirical justifications for these relationships have been addressed previously in this chapter and Chapter 4. The results suggest that this model fits the data well: χ^2 (4) = 5.80, p = 0.214; χ^2/df = 1.45; TLI = 0.992; CFI = 0.998; SRMR = 0.015; RMSEA = 0.04 (90% CI [0.00 0.10]). The standardized parameter estimates and explained variance are presented in Figure 6.2.

The alternative model substituted H6 for H6b addressing the effect of organizational resilience on employee resilience. In addition, this modified model added two new hypotheses to reflect the two additional paths introduced to the alternative modified model. Similar to the conceptual modified model, all the hypotheses in this model were supported, except for H4 since personal social capital (β = 0.02, p > 0.05) does not have a significant relationship to employee resilience. This means that the relationship between organizational learning culture and organizational resilience (H1: β = 0.72, p < 0.001), between organizational learning culture and learning goal orientation (H2: β = 0.14, p < 0.01), between learning goal orientation and employee resilience (H3: β = 0.39, p < 0.001), and between psychological capital and employee resilience (H5: β = 0.36, p < 0.001) remained significant. Moreover, the results support H6b finding a

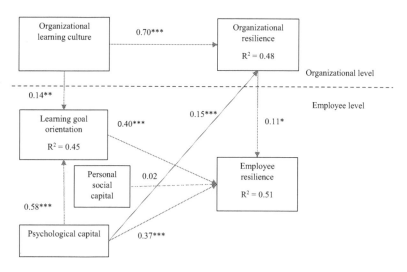

Figure 6.2 Structural equation model on the predictors of employee resilience.

Organizational resilience in H&T organizations in the U.S. 177

Table 6.5 Bootstrapping results for mediated relationships (unstandardized coefficients) – structural alternative modified model

Relationship	Direct effect	Indirect effects	LLCI	ULCI	Mediation effect
Organizational learning culture →employee resilience	.000	.090**	.046	.134	Mediation
psychological capital →employee resilience	.281***	.186***	.141	.240	Partial mediation

Notes: LLCI = lower limit confidence interval; ULCI = upper limit confidence interval. * $p < 0.05$. ** $p < 0.01$. *** $p < 0.001$.

positive significant relationship from organizational resilience to employee resilience ($\beta = 0.11$, $p < 0.05$). Additionally, H7 tested the relationship between psychological capital and learning goal orientation, which was supported ($\beta = 0.58$, $p < 0.001$). H9 tested the relationship between psychological capital and organizational resilience, which was also supported ($\beta = 0.15$, $p < 0.001$). Lastly, the results of this structural conceptual modified model explained 62% of the variance in organizational resilience and 58% in employee resilience.

Figure 6.2 also reveals indirect effects. To analyze their significance, a second mediation analysis based on a bootstrapped sample size of 5,000 via the 90% CI was conducted. The analysis revealed that the relationship between organizational learning culture and employee resilience is mediated via organizational resilience, and via learning goal orientation. The relationship between psychological capital and employee resilience is partially mediated via learning goal orientation, and via organizational resilience. Table 6.5 summarizes these mediated relationships.

Summary of the American survey

In short, an organizational learning culture and employees' psychological capital are foundational resources to boost the resiliency of American organizations. These two resources contribute to a learning goal orientation (H2 and H7, respectively). Interestingly, social capital does not seem to be a significant resilience-building resource for American employees (H4). At the organizational level, the significance of organizational learning culture in building organizational resilience is evident (H1). This means that the more American organizations become learning organizations, the better they would be able to withstand the effects of today's volatile, uncertain, complex, and ambiguous environment. Nonetheless, psychological capital also has an important direct effect on organizational resilience (H9). At the employee level, employee resilience may be

178 *Organizational resilience in H&T organizations in the U.S.*

increased by the employees' learning goal orientation and psychological capital (H3 and H5, respectively). The former effect trickles down from the organizational level, thanks to the mediated effect of organizational learning culture on employee resilience via learning goal orientation. While psychological capital directly contributes to employee resilience, the effect is also partially mediated via organizational resilience. This highlights once again how organizational resilience trickles down to positively impact the resiliency of the employees (H6b). So, like Polish organizations (see Chapter 4), the more resilient American organizations become, the more resilient the American workforce would be.

Note

1 This chapter was coauthored by Dr. Gabriela Lelo de Larrea and Dr. Fevzi Okumus

References

AHLA. (2021). Survey: 86% of hotels say supply chain issues impacting operations. Retrieved from www.ahla.com/press-release/survey-86-hotels-say-supply-chain-iss ues-impacting-operations

AHLA, & Accenture. (2022). *The American Hotel & Lodging Association 2022 State of the Hotel Industry Report.* Retrieved from www.ahla.com/sites/default/files/ AHLA%20SOTI%20Report%202022%201.24.22.pdf

Brocker, M. (2021). *Amusement parks in the US* (Industry Report 71311). Retrieved from ibisworld.com

Bureau of Labor Statistics. (2022a). Consumer Price Index. Retrieved from www.bls. gov/cpi/#:~:text=The%20Consumer%20Price%20Index%20(CPI,U.S.%20and%20 various%20geographic%20areas

Bureau of Labor Statistics. (2022b). Food prices up 10.8 percent for year ended April 2022; largest 12-month increase since November 1980. *The Economics Daily.* Retrieved from www.bls.gov/opub/ted/2022/food-prices-up-10-8-percent-for-year-ended-april-2022-largest-12-month-increase-since-november-1980.htm

Bureau of Labor Statistics. (2022c). Job openings and labor turnover – April 2022 [Press release]. Retrieved from www.bls.gov/news.release/pdf/jolts.pdf

CoStar Group. (2022a). Market recovery monitor – 21 May 2022. Retrieved from https:// str.com/data-insights-blog/market-recovery-monitor-week-ending-21-may

CoStar Group. (2022b). U.S. hotel profitability surpassed 2019 levels for second consecutive month [Press release]. Retrieved from https://str.com/press-release/us-hotel-profitability-surpassed-2019-levels-april

Economist Intelligence. (2022). How the war in Ukraine will affect tourism. Retrieved from eiu.com

Fornell, C., & Larcker, D. F. (1981). Structural equation models with unobservable variables and measurement error: Algebra and statistics. *Journal of Marketing Research, 18*(3), 382–388. https://doi.org/10.2307/3150980

Glen, S. (2016). Cook's distance / Cook's D: Definition, interpretation. *Statistics how to.* Retrieved from www.statisticshowto.com/cooks-distance/

Organizational resilience in H&T organizations in the U.S. 179

Hair, J. F., Black, W. C., Babin, B. J., & Anderson, R. E. (2010). *Multivariate data analysis* (7th ed.). Prentice Hall.

Hiner, J. (2021). Accommodation and food services in the US (Industry Report 72). Retrieved from ibisworld.com

IBISWorld. (2021). Tourism in the US (iExpert Report NN002). Retrieved from ibisworld.com

Kamal-Chaoui, L. (2022). More tough times ahead for the tourism sector – the impacts of the war in Ukraine. Retrieved from https://oecdcogito.blog/2022/04/08/more-tough-times-ahead-for-the-tourism-sector-the-impacts-of-the-war-in-ukraine/

Kelleher, S. R. (2022). War in Ukraine is making Americans rethink trips to Europe. Retrieved from www.forbes.com/sites/suzannerowankelleher/2022/03/04/war-ukraine-travel-americans/?sh=66214d8176b9

Kiesnoski, K. (2022). Russia-Ukraine war is having a limited impact on Europe vacation bookings, experts say. Retrieved from www.cnbc.com/2022/04/10/russia-ukraine-war-has-limited-impact-on-europe-vacation-bookings.html

Kline, R. B. (2015). *Principles and practice of structural equation modeling.* The Guilford Press.

Lee, A. V., Vargo, J., & Seville, E. (2013). Developing a tool to measure and compare organizations' resilience. *Natural Hazards Review, 14*(1), 29–41. https://doi.org/10.1061/(asce)nh.1527-6996.0000075

Luthans, F., Avolio, B. J., Avey, J. B., & Norman, S. M. (2007). Positive psychological capital: Measurement and relationship with performance and satisfaction. *Personnel Psychology, 60*(3), 541–572. https://doi.org/10.1111/j.1744-6570.2007.00083.x

Malik, P., & Garg, P. (2020). Learning organization and work engagement: The mediating role of employee resilience. *International Journal of Human Resource Management, 31*(8), 1071–1094.

McDonald, N. (2018). Name dropping 101: The best logoed merchandise at zoos and aquariums. Retrieved from https://sgnmag.com/name-dropping-101-the-best-logoed-merchandise-at-zoos-and-aquariums/

Minchin, J. (2022). Tourism effects of Russia's war on Ukraine. Retrieved from oxfordeconomics.com

Mintel. (2022a). How inflation will impact the travel industry. Retrieved from mintel.com

Mintel. (2022b). Vacation plans and priorities in 2022. Retrieved from https://store.mintel.com/report/us-vacation-plans-and-priorities-market-report-2022

National Restaurant Association. (2021). Association looks ahead to industry's recovery. Retrieved from https://restaurant.org/education-and-resources/resource-library/association-looks-ahead-to-industry%E2%80%99s-recovery/

National Restaurant Association. (2022). Summer hiring likely to be challenged by a tight labor market. Retrieved from https://restaurant.org/research-and-media/research/economists-notebook/analysis-commentary/summer-hiring-likely-to-be-challenged-by-a-tight-labor-market/

Näswall, K., Malinen, S., Kuntz, J., & Hodliffe, M. (2019). Employee resilience: Development and validation of a measure. *Journal of Managerial Psychology, 34*(5), 353–367. https://doi.org/10.1108/JMP-02-2018-0102

Okumus, F., Altinay, L., Chathoth, P., & Köseoğlu, M. A. (2020). *Strategic management for hospitality and tourism* (2nd ed.). Routledge.

180 *Organizational resilience in H&T organizations in the U.S.*

Pallant, J. (2010). *SPSS survival manual a step by step guide to data analysis using SPSS* (4th ed.). Open University Press/McGraw-Hill.

Peng, J., Xie, L., Zhou, L., & Huan, T. C. (TC). (2022). Linking team learning climate to service performance: The role of individual- and team-level adaptive behaviors in travel services. *Tourism Management, 91*(February), 104481.

PGAV Destinations. (2022). 2022 Voice of the visitor: Annual outlook on the attractions industry. Retrieved from https://pgavdestinations.com/wp-content/uploads/2020/06/VoiceoftheVisitor2020-Final-Online.pdf

PGAV Destinations. (n.d.). Welcome! profile of international visitors to America Retrieved from https://content.yudu.com/web/2r8b9/0A2rlk8/Welcome/html/index.html?page=2&origin=reader

Podsakoff, P. M., MacKenzie, S. B., Lee, J.-Y., & Podsakoff, N. P. (2003). Common method biases in behavioral research: A critical review of the literature and recommended remedies. *Journal of Applied Psychology, 88*(5), 879.

Sarsfield-Hall, A. (2020). The evolution of food and drink in themed experiences and attractions. Retrieved from https://blooloop.com/museum/in-depth/attractions-food-drink-experiences

Solís Salazar, M. (2015). The dilemma of combining positive and negative items in scales. *Psicothema, 27*(2), 192–199.

Sustainable Hospitality Alliance. (2021). Climate action. Retrieved from https://sustainablehospitalityalliance.org/our-work/climate-action/

Sustainable Travel International. (2020). Carbon footprint of tourism. Retrieved from https://sustainabletravel.org/issues/carbon-footprint-tourism/

TEA/AECOM. (2020). 2020 Theme Index and Museum Index: The global attractions attendance report. Retrieved from https://aecom.com/wp-content/uploads/documents/reports/AECOM-Theme-Index-2020.pdf

University of Michigan. (2022). Surveys of consumers. Retrieved from www.sca.isr.umich.edu/

UNWTO. (n.d.). Impact of the Russian offensive in Ukraine on international tourism. *UNWTO Tourism Market Intelligence and Competitiveness.* Retrieved from www.unwto.org/impact-russian-offensive-in-ukraine-on-tourism#:~:text=A%20prolonged%20conflict%20could%20translate,US%24%204.7%20billion%2C%20respectively.

U.S. Travel Association. (2021). Travel forecast. *Forecast.* Retrieved from www.ustravel.org/research/travel-forecasts

U.S. Travel Association. (2022a). Leisure & hospitality employment update. Retrieved from www.ustravel.org/sites/default/files/2022-05/leisure-hospitality-employment_may-2022-update.pdf

U.S. Travel Association. (2022b). Monthly travel data report. *Outlook & Monthly Statistics.* Retrieved from www.ustravel.org/research/monthly-travel-data-report

U.S. Travel Association. (2022c). New survey finds U.S. pre-departure testing is significant barrier to international travel and economic recovery [Press release]. Retrieved from www.ustravel.org/press/new-survey-finds-us-pre-departure-testing-significant-barrier-international-travel-and

Vandewalle, D. (1997). Development and validation of a Work Domain Goal Orientation Instrument. *Educational and Psychological Measurement, 57*(6), 995–1015. https://doi.org/0803973233

Yadoo, J. (2022). US consumer sentiment falls to lowest in more than a decade. Retrieved from www.bloomberg.com/news/articles/2022-05-13/us-consumer-sentiment-falls-to-fresh-decade-low-on-inflation

Yang, B., Watkins, K. E., & Marsick, V. J. (2004). The construct of the learning organization: Dimensions, measurement, and validation. *Human Resource Development Quarterly, 15*(1), 31–55. https://doi.org/10.1002/hrdq.1086

Zoghbi-Manrique-de-Lara, P., & Ruiz-Palomino, P. (2019). How servant leadership creates and accumulates social capital personally owned in hotel firms. *International Journal of Contemporary Hospitality Management, 31*(8), 3192–3211. https://doi.org/10.1108/IJCHM-09-2018-0748

7 Concluding remarks

**Organizational resilience in hospitality and tourism organizations –
a comparative analysis**

It is evident that the management of firms is supposed to handle the four characteristics of the marketplace designated by volatility, uncertainty, complexity, and ambiguity (VUCA) (Cavusgil et al., 2021). Studies show that in such a market environment, both organizational resilience and employee resilience pay off. For example, during the COVID-19 pandemic, it was found that employees' resilience could reduce the adverse effect of job insecurity within hospitality and tourism organizations (Aguiar-Quintana et al., 2021). Melián-Alzola et al. (2020) reported that the strategy (an organization's plan for the future in a challenging marketplace) and change (intention of an organization for transformation) aspects had a positive impact on a hotel's resilience and exerted a positive influence on hotel performance. Lee et al. (2013) underlined that the resilience of a community and an organization were linked to and depended on each other. Colmekcioglu et al. (2022) recommend that resilient firms adopt long-term planning that focuses on human resource management, marketing innovation, and changing consumer behavior. As a dynamic resource (cf. Ho et al., 2023), organizational resilience can be a source of competitive advantage and a driver of cultural adaptability. It can also help a community to recover successfully. Developing organizational resilience has a lot to do with leadership, power, and personal responsibility at the individual level. Ho et al. (2023) pointed out how important it was to create a resilient, firm leadership–followership interplay where leaders could generate a foundation for change and anticipation so that sharp messages could flow from top management to all levels of the firm.

Given that both organizational resilience and employee resilience are critical in the management of firms during complex and challenging times, using conservation of resources theory (Hobfoll, 2011; Hobfoll et al., 2018) and capital-based view (Lewin & Baetjer, 2011), we developed and tested two research models that investigated the factors influencing organizational resilience and employee resilience via data obtained from employees in the hospitality

DOI: 10.4324/9781003291350-8

Concluding remarks   183

industry in Türkiye and hospitality and tourism industry in Poland and the United States. In the comprehensive conceptual model, organizational learning culture predicts learning goal orientation and organizational resilience, while learning goal orientation, personal social capital, and psychological capital (PsyCap) are predictors of employee resilience. In addition, employee resilience positively relates to organizational resilience. In the alternative comprehensive model, organizational learning culture positively relates to learning goal orientation and organizational resilience. In contrast, organizational resilience, learning goal orientation, personal social capital, and PsyCap are the determinants of employee resilience. Several mediating mechanisms were subjected to an empirical test in both the abovementioned models.

The results suggest several *similarities* and *differences*. For instance, in the *comprehensive conceptual model*, the results in the Turkish sample show that organizational learning culture is a strong predictor of organizational resilience and learning goal orientation. This is in congruence with the works of Peng et al. (2022) and Tasic et al. (2020). However, in the Polish and U.S. samples, the effect of organizational learning culture on learning goal orientation is small compared to its effect on organizational resilience. This may be due to the fact that organizational learning culture is an organizational resource that is specifically used to activate the firm resilience, while it is considered less important to foster employee learning goal orientation. In an organization where continuous learning and team learning, empowerment, and/or strategic leadership are promoted, both firms and employees become more resilient in managing complex and challenging situations.

The results of the Polish and Turkish samples further suggest that learning goal orientation, personal social capital, and PsyCap positively related to employee resilience. In the Turkish sample, the positive effect of learning goal orientation on employee resilience was more substantial than those of personal social capital and PsyCap. In contrast, in the Polish sample, the positive impact of PsyCap on employee resilience was more robust than those of learning goal orientation and personal social capital. Employees devote much time and effort to developing their abilities to boost the level of their resilience and become ready to work in situations where ability and talent are the priorities. On the other hand, in the U.S. sample, both learning goal orientation and PsyCap significantly contributed to employee resilience, whereas personal social capital did not. This is surprising because it raises the question of why social capital is not important for enhancing the level of resilience. Strategic leadership promotes camaraderie, teamwork, social interaction, and humility and can help employees to enhance their resilience. A potential reason for this intriguing finding may be the need for more strategic leadership.

Employee resilience predicts organizational resilience for both the Turkish and the U.S. samples. Once employees learn from their mistakes at work, consider change a chance for growth and development, focus on enhancing

184 *Concluding remarks*

their work performance, and handle difficulties associated with excessive job demands, they become more resilient and therefore enable the firm to strengthen its resilience. This is especially important when organizations suffer from volatile, uncertain, complex, and ambiguous conditions. Surprisingly, employee resilience has no bearing on organizational resilience in the Polish sample. This may be due to the fact that employees do not work in an environment that promotes the need for resilience among employees.

Akin to the findings reported in the Polish and the U.S. samples, the results in the Turkish sample suggest that learning goal orientation is a mediator between organizational learning culture and employee resilience. Unlike the findings in the Polish and U.S. samples, the results in the Turkish sample suggest that learning goal orientation and employee resilience sequentially link organizational learning culture to organizational resilience. That is, it is a serial mediating process. This is a significant finding, because in an organization that nurtures a learning culture, employees high on learning goal orientation become more resilient and therefore help the firm to elevate the level of its resilience in a marketplace that consists of the four characteristics of VUCA.

Like the finding reported in the U.S. sample, employee resilience mediates the link between PsyCap and organizational resilience in the Turkish sample. The results signify the influence of employee resilience in the intermediate link between PsyCap and organizational resilience. However, this mediating effect is not supported in the Polish sample. In addition, employee resilience mediates the association between personal social capital and organizational resilience. This mediation is absent in the Polish and the U.S. samples since personal social capital is not a significant predictor of the mediating construct. In consonance with the conservation of resources theory (Hobfoll, 2011; Hobfoll et al., 2018), learning goal orientation, personal social capital, and PsyCap are among the critical personal resources that strengthen employee resilience and therefore augment organizational resilience. Based on the capital-based view (Lewin & Baetjer, 2011), they are the critical human capitals that would enable employees to make the firm magnify its resilience (Fang et al., 2020; Luthans & Broad, 2020).

In the *alternative comprehensive model*, the results in the Turkish, Polish, and U.S. samples delineate support for the direct effects, similar to the ones in the comprehensive conceptual model. The mediating effects were also supported in these three samples. Specifically, organizational resilience or learning goal orientation functioned as a mediator between organizational learning culture and employee resilience. Firms with learning cultures invest in becoming resilient during complex and challenging times. The presence of a learning culture enables the firm to work on complex problems until a resolution is achieved, make difficult decisions for the internal and external environment, and know the organizational priorities. Employees working in these firms learn how to collaborate with others and become resilient.

In the *modified comprehensive conceptual model* in the U.S. sample, organizational learning culture depicts a positive association with employee resilience. In contrast, PsyCap positively affects learning goal orientation in the Polish and U.S. samples. These findings suggest the critical role of learning culture in enhancing employee resilience, where resilient employees can contribute to the firm resilience. These findings also suggest that employees high on PsyCap are learning goal-oriented at high levels. This highlights the issue of whether employees high on PsyCap are learning goal-oriented or vice versa.

The evaluation above of the findings and comparative analysis has been done in light of a limitation that the assessment of the structural models in the Polish and the U.S. samples and the Turkish sample was performed via covariance-based structural equation modeling and variance-based structural equation modeling, respectively.

Organizational resilience model for hospitality and tourism organizations – theoretical and practical contributions

Nowadays, organizations operate in a growingly chaotic business environment (Liu et al., 2019). This is especially true after the emergence of the coronavirus pandemic, which has greatly influenced the way firms and people usually do business and work (Rezapouraghdam & Karatepe, 2020). It is obvious that organizations are now under pressure to find strategies to ensure their survival because the COVID-19 crisis showed how vulnerable businesses were. However, such challenges taught businesses to become more adaptable, innovative, flexible, and resilient (Liu et al., 2019). Resilience makes it possible for organizations to act quickly to develop alternatives, manage the risks, and find potential benefits that may result from unfavorable situations (Ho et al., 2023).

Our research conducted in Poland, Türkiye, and the United States enhances the *current knowledge* in the following ways. First, our research makes a significant contribution to the pertinent literature that personal social capital, learning goal orientation, and PsyCap are the critical human capitals cultivating employee resilience *simultaneously*. Employees can use these capitals to strengthen their resilience in a VUCA environment. Though personal social capital is not significantly linked to employee resilience in the U.S. sample, there is a need to conduct empirical studies with different types of hotels (e.g., luxury and/or international chain hotels in the United States) to ascertain whether personal social capital is promoted among employees whose resilience levels could be heightened.

Second, the findings in the Polish, Turkish, and U.S. samples suggest that learning goal orientation is a mediator of the influence of organizational learning culture on employee resilience. This critical finding underscores the need for the creation and maintenance of an environment that nurtures a learning culture in a VUCA marketplace and the provision of employees with an opportunity to be

186 *Concluding remarks*

learning goal-oriented and therefore fuel their resilience levels. As advanced by the capital-based view (Lewin & Baetjer, 2011), the presence of learning culture amends and improves the understanding of knowledge associated with the VUCA environment and contributes to productive resources (e.g., learning goal orientation).

In the test of the alternative comprehensive model, organizational resilience mediates the link between organizational learning culture and employee resilience. Investment in a learning culture magnifies the firm's planned and adaptive resilience that would, in turn, elevate employee resilience. In a VUCA environment where the value of resources changes over time, the firm's appetite for investment in continuous learning, inquiry and dialogue, team learning, embedded system, empowerment, system connection, and strategic leadership would contribute to its resilience and therefore enhance employee resilience.

Third, learning goal orientation and employee resilience sequentially mediate the association between organizational learning culture and organizational resilience. This is a significant finding reported in the Turkish sample because in a VUCA market environment, having a workplace that promotes a learning culture enables employees to cultivate their knowledge, skills, and abilities and therefore strengthen their resilience. These employees, in turn, help the firm to establish its planned and adaptive resilience and make it stronger.

Fourth, the findings in the Turkish and U.S. samples further support the premise that employee resilience acts as a mediator between PsyCap and organizational resilience. However, employee resilience was reported as a mediator between personal social capital and organizational resilience only in the Turkish sample, and no mediating effects were found in the Polish sample. PsyCap is an essential personal resource (Luthans & Broad, 2020) that would enable employees to build up their resilience. For example, employees high on PsyCap would be able to handle problems emanating from crises at work and learn from their mistakes to enhance their work performance in a VUCA environment. Under this circumstance, such employees would make significant contributions to the firm resilience. The same discussion is also true for personal social capital in the Turkish sample. Possession of good connections with coworkers and managers and social influence, as well as having trust in team members, would enhance employee resilience and therefore amplify organizational resilience.

At a time of the changing market environment, the findings discussed above contribute to the pertinent literature and add to the compendium of knowledge on organizational resilience and its predictors. The findings reported above also underscore the importance of resilience at the firm and employee levels and provide valuable implications for *business practice*. First, the management of hospitality and tourism firms should create an environment that promotes the learning culture. To do this, management should invest in continuous learning, inquiry and dialogue, team learning, embedded system, empowerment, system connection, and strategic leadership. With the presence of strategic leadership,

Concluding remarks 187

employees should have the chance to enhance their knowledge, skills, and abilities. However, informal learning and formal learning in training programs would enable them to exchange ideas and provide feedback for better teamwork. In these training programs, it is crucial to make employees think from a global perspective for creating and evaluating multiple alternatives regarding novel problems. Employees having the authority to use resources for the resolution of problems would contribute to organizational resilience. In addition, having an embedded system would enable the management to find out the problematic areas between current and expected performances at the firm and individual levels. Once these are accomplished, it would be possible for firms or organizations to display resilience at high levels.

Second, the presence of organizational culture fosters employees' learning goal orientation. This is critical because employees high on learning goal orientation are more resilient. That is, employees, who are motivated to learn how to develop their knowledge, skills, and abilities, undertake challenging assignments and are ready to take risks as a result of their enhanced ability and talent display heightened resilience. However, the absence of such a hospitality or tourism firm culture that nurtures learning goal orientation is unlikely to stimulate employee resilience. As reported in the Polish, Turkish, and U.S. samples, organizational learning culture positively influences employee resilience via learning goal orientation.

Third, personal social capital and PsyCap amplify employee resilience. With this recognition, the management of hospitality and tourism firms needs to fuel the work environment with good social interaction, camaraderie, and humility. This is especially critical in the U.S. sample because personal social capital did not significantly affect employee resilience. The management also needs to make training interventions to develop employees' PsyCap. Investment in PsyCap via development interventions that would train employees is a critical tool for the enhancement of their resilience (cf. Avey, 2014).

Fourth, the results in the Turkish sample suggest that learning goal orientation and employee resilience are the sequential mediators between organizational learning culture and organizational resilience. Such a unique finding suggests that the management should generate a workplace where employees and managers frequently take advantage of the learning culture to enhance their learning goal orientation. Under this circumstance, employees with high learning goal orientation become more resilient and therefore help the firm to monitor the internal and external environment cautiously and respond to unexpected incidents on time.

Fifth, the management can organize a workshop that is open to employees and their family members. In this workshop, managers can explicate various difficulties associated with the nature of the hospitality job and the industry to employees' family members and ask them to provide social support. Once employees receive social (cognitive and emotional) support from their spouses

188　*Concluding remarks*

and/or children, they will be motivated to focus more on how to develop their knowledge, skills, and abilities needed to be more resilient and amplify the firm resilience. Such employees would also be able to handle conflicts between work and family domains (Karatepe & Bekteshi, 2008).

Lastly, hospitality and tourism managers are supposed to pay utmost attention to the selection of suitable candidates for the vacant posts. That is, they should utilize stringent selective staffing procedures. The ones who do not have the requisite skills and abilities to perform the job in challenging service encounters during turbulent times cannot contribute to the firm resilience. They would not fit the organizational learning culture due to the lack of compatibility with the firm and the work environment. With this realization, managers can take advantage of mini-case studies and/or experiential exercises during the selection process (Karatepe et al., 2023). This would enable the decision makers to ferret out whether the candidates are really willing to use their personal resources, such as learning goal orientation, personal social capital, and PsyCap to help the firm to strengthen its resilience.

The organizational resilience model – where does it lead us?

We proposed and tested a comprehensive conceptual model that examined several direct, single-mediating, and multiple-mediating effects utilizing data gathered from hotel employees in Türkiye and employees in the hospitality and tourism industry in Poland and the United States. As discussed in the preceding parts, there are similarities and differences among the results in the Polish, Turkish, and U.S. samples. In the Polish and U.S. samples, the modified comprehensive conceptual model consisted of a direct link from PsyCap to learning goal orientation and organizational learning culture to employee resilience. It also included the mediating role of employee resilience in the link between organizational learning culture and organizational resilience. The revised comprehensive conceptual model is given in Figure 7.1.

The hypotheses based on the abovementioned model are as follows:

Hypothesis 1: Organizational learning culture positively relates to (a) organizational resilience, (b) learning goal orientation, and (c) employee resilience.
Hypothesis 2: Learning goal orientation (a), personal social capital (b), and PsyCap (c) positively relate to employee resilience.
Hypothesis 3: PsyCap positively relates to learning goal orientation.
Hypothesis 4: Employee resilience positively relates to organizational resilience.
Hypothesis 5: Learning goal orientation mediates the link between organizational learning culture and employee resilience.
Hypothesis 6: Employee resilience mediates the influences of (a) personal social capital and (b) PsyCap on organizational resilience.

Concluding remarks 189

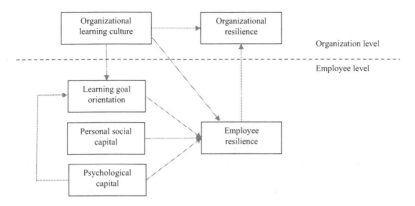

Figure 7.1 The revised comprehensive conceptual model.

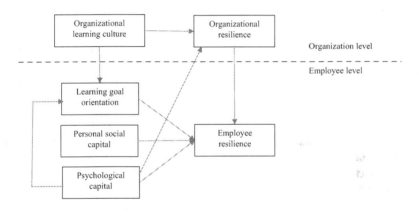

Figure 7.2 The revised alternative comprehensive model.

Hypothesis 7: Employee resilience mediates the link between organizational learning culture and organizational resilience.
Hypothesis 8: Learning goal orientation mediates the association between PsyCap and employee resilience.
Hypothesis 9: Learning goal orientation and employee resilience sequentially mediate the link between organizational learning culture and organizational resilience.

The hypotheses (Figure 7.2) based on the findings in the Turkish and the U.S. samples are as follows:

190   *Concluding remarks*

Hypothesis 1: Organizational learning culture positively relates to (a) organizational resilience and (b) learning goal orientation.

Hypothesis 2: Learning goal orientation (a), personal social capital (b), and PsyCap (c) positively relate to employee resilience.

Hypothesis 3: Organizational resilience positively relates to employee resilience.

Hypothesis 4: PsyCap positively relates to (a) learning goal orientation and (b) organizational resilience.

Hypothesis 5: Learning goal orientation mediates the link between organizational learning culture and employee resilience.

Hypothesis 6: Organizational resilience mediates the influence of organizational learning culture on employee resilience.

Hypothesis 7: Learning goal orientation mediates the link between PsyCap and employee resilience.

Hypothesis 8: Organizational resilience mediates the impact of PsyCap on employee resilience.

Both the revised comprehensive conceptual and alternative comprehensive models *do include significant paths* based on the findings in the Turkish and U.S. samples. Personal social capital was kept in two models since the findings associated with personal social capital in the Turkish sample were significant. In future studies, testing the relationships shown in the aforesaid models using cross-national and cross-cultural data would provide additional support for their viability in a VUCA environment.

As for the limitations of our research, the previously mentioned evaluation of the findings and comparative analysis have been done in light of a limitation that the assessment of the structural models in the Polish and U.S. samples and Turkish sample was performed via covariance-based structural equation modeling and variance-based structural equation modeling, respectively. In future studies, using only covariance-based structural equation modeling or variance-based structural equation modeling for assessing the paths would be helpful. We used cross-sectional data to test the proposed relationships. Since this precludes us from drawing causality among the variables, it would be helpful if future research could gauge the links in the model via longitudinal data collected in Poland, Türkiye, and the United States. We utilized self-report data in this research. Though common method variance was controlled via procedural and statistical remedies, collecting data from multiple sources and/or gathering time-lagged data would be beneficial. In addition, there are significant cultural differences between these three nations. Development of hypotheses based on Hofstede's cultural dimensions, such as uncertainty avoidance and power distance (Hofstede & Bond, 1984), would add to the pertinent literature. Lastly, we invite our colleagues to replicate the findings of this research conducted in

Concluding remarks 191

Poland, Türkiye, and the United States to broaden the database and make further generalizations.

References

Aguiar-Quintana, T., Nguyen, T. H. H., Araujo-Cabrera, Y., & Sanabria-Díaz, J. M. (2021). Do job insecurity, anxiety and depression caused by the COVID-19 pandemic influence hotel employees' self-rated task performance? The moderating role of employee resilience. *International Journal of Hospitality Management, 94*, 102868.

Avey, J. B. (2014). The left side of psychological capital: New evidence on the antecedents pf PsyCap. *Journal of Leadership and Organizational Studies, 21*(2), 141–149.

Cavusgil, S. T., van der Vegt, S., Dakhli, M., De Farias, S., Doria, E., Eroglu, S., & Wang, E. Y. (2021). International business in an accelerated VUCA world: Trends, disruptions, and coping strategies. *Rutgers Business Review, 6*(3), 219–243.

Colmekcioglu, N., Dineva, D., & Lu, X. (2022). "Building back better": The impact of the COVID-19 pandemic on the resilience of the hospitality and tourism industries. *International Journal of Contemporary Hospitality Management, 34*(11), 4103–4122.

Fang, S. (Echo), Prayag, G., Ozanne, L. K., & de Vries, H. (2020). Psychological capital, coping mechanisms and organizational resilience: Insights from the 2016 Kaikoura earthquake, New Zealand. *Tourism Management Perspectives, 34*, 100637.

Ho, G. K. S., Lam, C., & Law, R. (2023). Conceptual framework of strategic leadership and organizational resilience for the hospitality and tourism industry for coping with environmental uncertainty. *Journal of Hospitality and Tourism Insights, 6*(2), 835–852.

Hobfoll, S. E. (2011). Conservation of resource caravans and engaged settings. *Journal of Occupational and Organizational Psychology, 84*(1), 116–122.

Hobfoll, S. E., Halbesleben, J., Neveu, J.-P., & Westman, M. (2018). Conservation of resources in the organizational context: The reality of resources and their consequences. *Annual Review of Organizational Psychology and Organizational Behavior, 5*, 103–128.

Hofstede, G., & Bond, M. H. (1984). Hofstede's culture dimensions: An independent validation using Rokeach's value survey. *Journal of Cross-Cultural Psychology, 15*(4), 417–433.

Karatepe, O. M., & Bekteshi, L. (2008). Antecedents and outcomes of work-family facilitation and family-work facilitation among frontline hotel employees. *International Journal of Hospitality Management, 27*, 517–528.

Karatepe, O. M., Hassannia, R., Karatepe, T., Enea, C., & Rezapouraghdam, H. (2023). The effects of job insecurity, emotional exhaustion, and met expectations on hotel employees' pro-environmental behaviors: Test of a serial mediation model. *International Journal of Mental Health Promotion, 25*(2), 287–307.

Lee, A. V., Vargo, J., & Seville, E. (2013). Developing a tool to measure and compare organizations' resilience. *Natural Hazards Review, 14*(1), 29–41.

Lewin, P., & Baetjer, H. (2011). The capital-based view of the firm. *Review of Austrian Economics, 24*(4), 335–354.

192 *Concluding remarks*

Liu, Y., L. Cooper, C., & Y. Tarba, S. (2019). Resilience, wellbeing and HRM: A multi-disciplinary perspective. *The International Journal of Human Resource Management, 30*(8), 1227–1238.

Luthans, F., & Broad, J. D. (2020). Positive psychological capital to help combat the mental health fallout from the pandemic and VUCA environment. *Organizational Dynamics, 2019*, 100817.

Melián-Alzola, L., Fernández-Monroy, M., & Hidalgo-Peñate, M. (2020). Hotels in contexts of uncertainty: Measuring organizational resilience. *Tourism Management Perspectives, 36*, 100747.

Peng, J., Xie, L., Zhou, L., & Huan, T. C. (TC). (2022). Linking team learning climate to service performance: The role of individual- and team-level adaptive behaviors in travel services. *Tourism Management, 91*(February), 104481.

Rezapouraghdam, H., & Karatepe, O. M. (2020). Applying health belief model to unveil employees' workplace COVID-19 protective behaviors: Insights for the hospitality industry. *International Journal of Mental Health Promotion, 22*(4), 233–247.

Tasic, J., Amir, S., Tan, J., & Khader, M. (2020). A multilevel framework to enhance organizational resilience. *Journal of Risk Research, 23*(6), 713–738.

Index

Note: Page numbers in **bold** indicate tables; those in *italics* indicate figures.

9/11 terrorist attacks 41, 42

adaptive capacity 15, 73
advertising *see* marketing
agility 25–28, **29**, 30
alternative comprehensive model 82–83,
83, 86; comparative analysis 183, 184;
Poland 105, 112–113, 117; revised
189, 189–190; theoretical and practical
contributions 186; Türkiye 147–150,
149; U.S. 171, 185
ambiguous environments 23; *see also*
VUCA concept 23
Argentina 130
Australia 57

bleisure travel 161
bonding social capital 85
bridging social capital 85
business strategy 57–58

Canada 131
capital-based view in management
theory 3, 5, 78–80, 182, 184, 186;
Poland 105
carbon dioxide emissions: Türkiye 131;
U.S. 163
China 22, 57
climate change **27**, 46, 48, 162–163
collectivistic societies **20**, 21, 22; H&T
sector 55–58
competitive advantage 182; agility
30; organizational learning 16;
sustainability 50; Türkiye 136

complex environments 23; *see also*
VUCA concept 23
complexity theory 23
comprehensive conceptual model 81–83,
81, 85–86, 188; comparative analysis
183–185; Poland 105, 112–113, 117;
revised 185, 188–190, *189*; Türkiye
144–147, **148**, 150; U.S. 171, 185
conservation of resources (COR) theory 3,
79–81, 182, 184; employee resilience
12; Poland 112, 118; psychological
capital 84
continuous learning **29**, 84, 183, 186;
Poland **110**; Türkiye 138, **140**; U.S. **172**
corporate social responsibility 47
COVID-19 pandemic 185; cultural
context 56, 57; destination resilience
51, 52, 53; employee resilience 182;
H&T crisis management 41, 42, 43, 45;
H&T sustainability 50; Poland 96–98,
100, 102–105; Türkiye 125–127, 133,
135; U.S. 157–162, 164–167
creativity 55
crisis management 2, 9, 13, 14, 40–45;
cultural context 56–57; destination
resilience 51–52, 54; Poland 92, 97–98
cultural issues *see* national culture;
organizational culture
Cyprus 132

destination management organizations
(DMOs) 52–53
destination resilience 50–54; cultural
context 56

194 *Index*

dialogue *see* inquiry and dialogue
digital nomads 161
digitalization **27**, **29**
Dimensions of Learning Organizations
  Questionnaire (DLOQ) 84, 109, **110**
disabilities, people with 161–162
disaster management 40–45; cultural
  context 56; destination resilience
  51–52, 54; models of organizational
  resilience 78
dynamic capability theory 10

ecological environment, U.S. 162–163
economic environment: Poland 92,
  95–99; Türkiye 125–126, 128–132,
  134; U.S. 158–160, 167
Egypt 16
embedded system 25, 84, 186–187;
  Poland 109; Türkiye 138, **140**; U.S.
  172
employee resilience *2*, 3, 5, 11–12, 14;
  comparative analysis 182–185; lessons
  188–190; models of organizational
  resilience 78–83, 85–86; organizational
  learning 15, 16, 17; Poland 105–106,
  109, **111**, **112**, 112, 114, **115**, 116–118;
  theoretical and practical contributions
  185–188; Türkiye 125, **143**, 144, **146**,
  147, **148–149**, 148–150; U.S. **170**,
  171, **173**, 173–175, **175**, 176–178,
  176, **177**
Employee Resilience Scale 85–86,
  106–7, **110**
employment: Poland 99; Türkiye 130;
  U.S. 166
empowerment 18, 84, 183, 186; cultural
  context **20**, 57; Poland **110**; Türkiye
  138, **140**; U.S. **172**
energy prices, U.S. 157, 159
environmental analysis: Poland 92–98;
  Türkiye 128–136; U.S. 157–163
equality issues, U.S. 161–162
European Union 95, 96, 98, 99
evolutionary theory 11, 16
exchange rates, Türkiye 128–130, 134

feminine societies **20**, 21
Fifth Industrial Revolution **27**
financial disruptions **28**
fourth industrial revolution 1, 22, 25, **27**
France 41

geopolitical disruptions **28**
Germany 130
global economic crisis 41; 96–99
governance **29**; destination resilience
  52–53
Greece 132

health economy **28**
Hofstede's cultural dimensions 19–21,
  20–21, 190; H&T sector 55–58
hope 84–85; Poland **111**; Türkiye 138,
  142; U.S. **172**
hospitality and tourism (H&T)
  organizational resilience: comparative
  analysis 182–185; crisis/disaster
  management versus 40–45; cultural
  context 54–58; destination resilience
  versus 50–54; models 72, 77–86,
  188–191; Poland 92–118; scales 77;
  sustainability versus 45–50; theoretical
  and practical contributions 185–188;
  Türkiye 125–150; U.S. 157–178
human capital: organizational resilience
  model *2*, 2–3, 78–81; Poland 105,
  118; Türkiye 150; *see also* employee
  resilience; learning goal orientation;
  personal resilience; personal social
  capital; psychological capital
Human Centered Management model 25

inclusion and equality issues, U.S.
  161–162
income inequality, Türkiye 130
India 17, 24
individualistic societies **20**, 57, 58
Indonesia 56
indulgent cultures **21**
Industry 4.0 and Industry 5.0 **29**
inflation: Poland 96–97; Türkiye 125,
  128–129, 134; U.S. 157, 159–160, 166
innovation 185; adaptive organizational
  resilience 83; destination resilience 54;
  Poland 109, **110**, 118; sustainability 50
inquiry and dialogue 17, 84, 186; Poland
  110; Türkiye 138, **140**; U.S. **172**
interest rates, Türkiye 129
Israel 57

karmic leadership 25
key vulnerabilities (relative overall
  resilience model) 72–73

labor market: employee resilience 182; Poland 96, 99; Türkiye 125, 130; U.S. 158–159, 165–167
leadership 182; destination resilience 52; karmic 25; and organizational learning 16; transformational 58; VUCA concept 24, 25, 26, **29**, 30; *see also* strategic leadership
Learning and Performance Goal Orientation Scale 86
learning culture 17
learning goal orientation 2, 3, 5, 17; comparative analysis 183–185; lessons 188–190; models of organizational resilience 79, 81–83, 86; Poland 106, 109, **111**, **112**, 112–114, **115**, 116–118; theoretical and practical contributions 185–188; Türkiye **141–142**, 144, 147–150, **148–149**; U.S. **170**, **173**, 173–175, **175**, 176–178
learning mechanisms 16–17
learning organizations *see* organizational learning; organizational learning culture
learning routines 17
legal environment *see* political and legal environment
LGBTQ+ communities 161
linking social capital 85
load capacity factor, Türkiye 131
long-term oriented societies **21**, 21–22, 55

macroeconomic environment *see* economic environment
Malaysia 58, 78
management theory, capital-based view 3, 5, 78–80, 182, 184, 186; Poland 105
marketing 182; cultural context 55; destination resilience 52, 53; Türkiye 126, 128, 135; U.S. 163
masculine societies **20**, 21, 55
mental health: employee resilience 150; social capital 80; VUCA concept 25
mindfulness 25
multi-capital model 81, 118

national culture 18–22; H&T sector 54–58; *see also* Hofstede's cultural dimensions
National Tourism Administration (NTA, Poland) 93

natural disruptions **28**; H&T disaster management 41–42; Türkiye 131–132
Nepal 56
New Zealand 56, 72, **76**, **77**, 78
Nigeria 25

oil prices, U.S. 157
optimism 84–85; Poland **111**; Türkiye 138, **143**; U.S. 171, **172**
organizational citizenship 57
organizational culture 18–19; adaptive organizational resilience 83; crisis/ disaster management 45; learning *see* organizational learning culture; sustainability 47
organizational learning 14–18; capabilities 18; culture *see* organizational learning culture; destination resilience 53, 54; double-loop 16, 17, 54; models of organizational resilience 79; single-loop 16; sustainability 47; theory 16; triple-loop 16; VUCA concept 25
organizational learning culture 2, 3, 5, 17; comparative analysis 183–185; lessons 188–190; models of organizational resilience 79, 81–84, 86; Poland 106, 108–9, **110**, **112**, 112–114, **115**, 116–118; theoretical and practical contributions 185–188; Türkiye 138, **140**, 144, **146**, 147–150, **148–149**; U.S. **170**, 171, **172**, 173–175, **175**, 176, **177**, 178
organizational psychology 3, 5
organizational resilience: adaptation perspective 9–11, 49, **74**, **75**, 78, 83–84; 138, **141**, 186; and agility, intersection between 30; anticipation perspective 9, 11, **74**, **75**; building 11; as a capability 10, **74**, **75**, 78; capital-based view 3, 5, 78–80, 105, 182, 184, 186; cultural context 18–22; defensive approach 8–9, **74**; defined 8, 14–15; developmental perspective 15; ecological perspective 9; as a learning approach 14–18; maturity framework **75**; measurement 83–84; as a meta-capability 11, **74**; models 1–6, 72–86, 188–191; multilevel framework for enhancing 82; as an outcome 10, **74**, **75**; as planned resilience 10, 49, 83, 138, **141**, 186; positive psychology and organizational development perspective 9;

196 *Index*

as a process 10, 72, **74**, **75**, 78; related concepts 11–14; resilience engineering perspective 9; safety and reliability perspective 9; scales 73, **76–77**, 77; strategic perspective 9–10; theoretical studies 10–11; theoretical substantiation of model 78–81; VUCA concept 25, 26; *see also* hospitality and tourism (H&T) organizational resilience
Organizational Resilience Scale 109, **110**
organizational social capital 85
organizational studies 3, 5, 8; resource dependency theory 10; VUCA concept 22–26

particularism 19–21
personal resilience 84–85; Poland **111**; Türkiye 138, **143**; U.S. 171, **173**; *see also* employee resilience; psychological resilience
personal social capital 2, 3; comparative analysis 183–184; cultural context 57; lessons 188, 190; models of organizational resilience 78–82, 84–86; Poland 105–106, 109, **111**, **112**, 112–114, **115**, 116–118; theoretical and practical contributions 185–188; Türkiye 138, **142**, **146**, 147, **148–149**, 148, 150; U.S. **170**, 171, **173**, 174, 176
Poland 3, 5–6; assessment of H&T organizational resilience 109–118, **112–113**, **115–116**; comparative analysis 183–185; crisis shields 98; environmental analysis 92–98; lessons 188, 190–191; local tourist organizations (LTOs) 94; Ministry of Sports and Tourism 93; National Tourism Administration (NTA) 93; Polish Tourist Organization Act 93, 94; regional tourist organizations (RTOs) 94; structure of H&T organizations 98–109, **101–104**, **107–108**, **110–111**; theoretical and practical contributions 185–187; tourism fee 94; Tourism Shield 98; Tourist Events and Related Travel Services Act 94–95; Travel Services Act 95
Polish Classification of Activities (PKD) 99–100, **101–102**
Polish Economic Institute 99

Polish Tourist Organization (POT) 93, 94
Polish Tourist Voucher 97–98
political and legal environment: geopolitical disruptions **28**; Poland 92–95; Türkiye 126, 132–133; U.S. 157–158
positive psychology 12
poverty, Türkiye 130
power distance **20**, 21–22, 55, 57, 190
PsyCap questionnaire 85, 106, **111**
psychological capital 2, 3, 5; *see also* PsyCap questionnaire; comparative analysis 183–185; lessons 188–190; models of organizational resilience 78–81, 81–82, 84–86; Poland 105, 109, **111**, **112**, 112–114, **115**, 116–118; theoretical and practical contributions 185–188; Türkiye 138, 139, **142–143**, **146**, 147, **148–149**, 148, 150; U.S. **170**, 171, **172–173**, 173–175, **175**, 176–178, **177**
psychological resilience 11, 12; cultural context 22; models of organizational resilience 78
public sector debt, Türkiye 125

quality of life, Türkiye 130

racial minorities 160, 161, 167
recruitment 188
regenerative tourism model 25
relational capital 78
relative overall resilience model (ROR) 72–73, 78
remote work **29**; U.S. 161
resource-based theory 10
resource dependence theory 10
resource scarcity **27**
restraint cultures **21**
risk: aversion 50, 157; cultural context 55, 56; destination resilience 51, 52; perception 55, 56; VUCA concept 22, 24
Russia 96, 127, 132, 133, 157
Russian Federal Tourism Agency 133

safety and security: destination resilience 50; Türkiye 133; U.S. 160, 162
self-efficacy 84–85; Poland **111**; Türkiye 138, **142**; U.S. **172**
sequential mediation model 82, 114

service robots, Türkiye 135–136
short-term oriented societies **21**, 21, 56
Singapore 19
situation awareness (relative overall resilience model) 72, 73
small- and medium-sized enterprises (SMEs): agility 28; destination resilience 53–54; Poland 106; sustainability 49
smart tourism 51
social capital *see* organizational social capital; personal social capital
social changes **28**
social environment: Türkiye 133–135; U.S. 160–162, 167
social media **28**, **29**; Turkey 135; U.S. 162
South Africa 24–25, **77**
South Korea 57
spirituality: cultural context 56; sustainability 48
strategic leadership 84, 183, 186–187; Poland **110**; Türkiye 138, **141**; U.S. **172**
strategic management 3
strategic resilience 18
structural alternative modified model, U.S. 176–177, *176*, **177**
structural conceptual modified model, U.S. 173–175, *174*, **175**
structural modified competitive model, Poland 114–117, *116*
structural modified conceptual model, Poland 113–114, *113*, **115**
supply chains: resilience **29**; sustainability 47; U.S. 159, 167
sustainability 13–14, **29**; destination resilience 51; H&T 45–51; Türkiye 128, 131–132; U.S. 163
Sweden 57, **76**
Syrian conflict 132
system connection 84, 186; Poland **110**; Türkiye 138, **140**; U.S. **172**
system theory 23

team learning 15, 17; comparative analysis 183; cultural context 21; Poland 109, **110**, 117; theoretical and practical contributions 186; Türkiye 138, **140**; U.S. **172**
team resilience 11, 13, 14; cultural context 21

technological environment: Türkiye 135–136; U.S. 162
technology leveraging **29**
terrorism: 9/11 attacks 41, 42; Türkiye 132–133
Thailand 58
time orientation **21**, 21–22, 55, 56
tourism crises and disasters 40–45
tourism fees 94
transformational leadership 58
Travel & Tourism Competitiveness Index 99
TripAdvisor 135
triple bottom line 46
Turkey Home Global Image Campaign 126
Türkiye 3, 5–6, 125–128; assessment of organizational resilience 144–150; Central Bank 129; comparative analysis 183–185; earthquakes 129; environmental analysis 128–136; lessons 188–191; measurement model assessment 138–144, **139**, **140–143**, **145–146**; Ministry of Culture and Tourism 126, 131; national culture 58; number of foreign tourists 126, **127**, 133; number of hotels, rooms, and beds 127–128, **128**; organizational resilience scale **76**; research sample 136–138, **137**; theoretical and practical contributions 185–187; tourism receipts 129, **129**, 130

Uganda **76**
Ukraine war 98, 133, 157
uncertain environments 23; *see also* VUCA concept
uncertainty avoidance 19, **20**, 21, 55–58, 190
unemployment: Poland 96; Türkiye 125, 130; U.S. 158, 165, 166
UNESCO heritage sites, Türkiye 126
United States 3, 5–6, 177–178; assessment of organizational resilience 171–177; comparative analysis 183–185; empirical research on organizational resilience 78; environmental analysis 157–163; lessons 188–191; military, and VUCA concept 22; national culture 57, 58; organizational resilience scales **76**,

198 *Index*

77, 77; research sample 167–171, **169–170**, **172–173**; structure of H&T organizations 163–167; theoretical and practical contributions 185–187; trade war with China 22; Türkiye's relations with 132
universalism 19–21
unlearning 17–18

Vietnam 56
virtual teams **29**

volatile environments 22–23; *see also* VUCA concept
VUCA concept 1–2; coping mechanisms and strategies **29**; current challenges, opportunities, and remedies 26–30; H&T sector 182, 184; lessons 190; organizational resilience 9, 22–26, 83; Poland 118; theoretical and practical contributions 185–186; Türkiye 126, 130, 150; U.S. 177; world trends **27–28**

Printed in the United States
by Baker & Taylor Publisher Services